THE PREZELL R. ROBINSON LIBRARY
ST. AUGUSTINE'S COLLEGE
RALEIGH, N. C. 27611

D1401584

Shakespeare: the 'lost years'

Shakespeare: the 'lost years'

E. A. J. HONIGMANN

Barnes & Noble Books
Totowa, New Jersey

822.33
H6
1985
C.1

Copyright © E.A.J. Honigmann 1985

First published in the USA 1985 by
Barnes & Noble Books
81 Adams Drive
Totowa, New Jersey, 07512

Library of Congress cataloging in publication data

Honigmann, E. A. J.
  Shakespeare: the 'lost years'

  Includes index
  1. Shakespeare, William 1564–1616—Biography—Youth
  2. Dramatists, English—Early modern,
  1500–1700—Biography
  I. Title
  PR2903.H6 1985b 822'.3'3 [B] 84-24354
  ISBN 0-389-20549-4

Printed in Great Britain

91-4034

Contents

List of Plates

Plates I, III, IV, VII, VIII by courtesy of Sir Bernard de Hoghton, Bart., photos by Michael Scott; Plates V and IX (*b*) by courtesy of Lancashire Record Office, Preston; Plate IX (*a*) by courtesy of the Shakespeare Centre, Stratford; Plate IX (*c*) by courtesy of The British Library; Plates X–XII by courtesy of the Earl of Derby, photos by J. J. Bagley.

Preface

This book is really a detective-story, and the mystery it grapples with is one that experts have tried to solve for two hundred years. Where was young William Shakespeare in the so-called 'lost years' before 1592, and what was he doing? The correct answer, I believe, was first suggested by Oliver Baker in 1937 and then re-stated by E. K. Chambers in 1944[1] – namely, that the future dramatist served for a while in the household of a wealthy Roman Catholic land-owner in Lancashire. Chambers, our leading authority on Shakespeare in the present century, could not check some of the crucial documents in war-time but developed Baker's surprising theory (it almost certainly implied, among other things, that Shakespeare as a teenager was a practising Catholic), and, dying a few years later, left it to others to prove or disprove. After working on Lancashire archives for many years, in many places, I now publish an interim report on Shakespeare's 'Lancashire connection', a story that centres on the Hoghtons of Hoghton Tower but also throws light on other fascinating problems in the dramatist's later life.

Although I received some training in archive-work at the Shakespeare Institute (where I taught from 1951 to 1954) from our Senior Fellow, the late Professor C. J. Sisson, I have to confess that I felt then, and still feel, a mere dabbler as far as legal records are concerned. From Professor Sisson I learnt how to read almost illegible old manuscripts, and I found his delight in depositions (and demurrers etc.) infectious and irresistible. But, as he often observed, when you discover an interesting bill of complaint you rarely know the outcome or whether the case moved from one court to another: too many indexes for the Elizabethan period are incomplete, or totally chaotic and unhelpful. I mention this because it is perfectly possible that I have missed many opportunities, and that important records bearing on the 'Lancashire connection' still await discovery. I may also have made some mistakes in copying or correcting pedigrees from Baines and other authorities on Lancashire family history. In the sixteenth century husbands and wives often re-married, and the larger family might include twenty or more children, legitimate and illegitimate, with some Christian names repeating several times: it is only too easy, four hundred years later, to confuse two or more individuals with the same name. For these and other sins of omission and commission I apologise in advance.

Everyone who writes about Shakespeare borrows from earlier writers. I am particularly indebted to three studies, which have not had the acclaim they deserved: Oliver Baker's *In Shakespeare's Warwickshire and the Unknown Years* (1937), E. K. Chambers' 'William Shakeshafte' (in *Shakespearean Gleanings*, Oxford, 1944), and *The Annotator* by Alan Keen and Roger Lubbock (1954). I do not share the view, expressed in *The Annotator,* that William Shakespeare is responsible for the marginalia in the Newport copy of Halle's *Chronicle*, but found, when I turned belatedly to Keen's publications, that he had anticipated some of my ideas about Shakespeare and Lancashire. The present book differs from these predecessors in tracing, much more fully, the importance of Shakespeare's early patrons for his plays and poems; and I have burrowed more persistently in both public and private archives, in pursuit of the 'Lancashire connection', and have discovered law-suits, wills and other records, unknown to these earlier writers, that will affect future thinking about Shakespeare's social and intellectual background.

My debts to institutions and individuals have been incurred over several decades. I am grateful for the expert services of librarians and archivists in the British Library; the Public Record Office; the National Trust; the National Library of Wales; the Lancashire Record Office; the Cheshire Record Office; the Borthwick Institute, York; the Shakespeare Institute, Birmingham; the Shakespeare Centre, Stratford; the Bodleian Library; Christ Church Library, Oxford; Queens' College Library, Cambridge; Lambeth Palace Library; the College of Arms; the Goldsmiths Company; the Huntington Library; and, above all, Newcastle University Library. I am also most grateful to these libraries etc. for permission to quote from unpublished manuscripts in their keeping: the British Library, the Public Record Office, the National Library of Wales, the Lancashire Record Office, the Cheshire Record Office, Christ Church Library, the Goldsmiths Company and the Huntington Library. It is likewise a pleasure to record my debts to the following, who gave me advice and help of various kinds: Mr J. Blundell, Dr Susan Brock, Mr Barry Coward, Mrs S. Denyer, Professor D. W. Elliott, Mr P. Fleetwood Hesketh, Mr Levi Fox, the Dowager Lady Hesketh, Mr Roger Lubbock, Professor Brian Morris, Mr and Mrs Ashley Russell, Dr R. L. Smallwood, Mrs Iris Young. As always, I have to thank my wife for checking through my manuscript and proofs, and for correcting errors that I would have missed. I am also indebted to Miss Alison Foster, Miss Kathleen O'Rawe and Mrs Doris Palgrave, who helped me with the typing and took much trouble with a difficult manuscript; and to the University of Newcastle upon Tyne, for ten weeks of study leave, which gave me the time to complete this book. And I am deeply grateful to Professor John A. Cannon, Professor Harold Jenkins and Dr Alan Robinson, who read through my type-script and suggested many improvements.

I owe a special debt to D. L. Thomas and N. E. Evans of the Public Record Office, for permission to refer to their forthcoming paper on John Shakespeare, the dramatist's father; to G. C. G. Thomas of the National Library of Wales, for permission to see his schedule of the *Kinmel Deeds* and for expert advice on Lleweni and Salusbury records; and to J. J. Bagley, who allowed me to see a chapter from his forthcoming book on the Earls of Derby and helped me with 'Derby' problems. I am also indebted to the Earl of Derby, for permission to reproduce the portraits of the fifth and sixth Earls of Derby, and that of Lady Strange; and to Lord Hesketh, who allowed me to quote from the Hesketh archives and to visit the library at Easton Neston.

My greatest debt is to Sir Bernard de Hoghton, Bt., and to his mother (Mrs Richard Adams), for criticism and advice, for their generous hospitality, and for access to unpublished family archives. Also, for permission to include photographs of Hoghton Tower and Lea Hall, and other Hoghton material (Plates I, III–IV, VII–VIII).

Finally, several warnings to the reader. I have almost invariably modernised

Preface

the spelling in quoting sixteenth- and seventeenth-century manuscripts and printed books, and also expanded contractions. Pointed brackets indicate that words or letters in the original are illegible; square brackets are used, in quotations from early texts, for editorial insertions. I have standardised names, as far as possible, even in quotations from early documents: the Stratford schoolmaster as John Cottom (his preferred spelling), though his father and brothers used the form 'Cottam'. The Hoghton family created special problems: in the sixteenth century the name appears as Houghton, Hoghton and de Hoghton. I usually standardise early references as Hoghton, even though de Hoghton is now the official spelling (resumed in the nineteenth century by Sir Henry de Hoghton, the ninth baronet, by royal licence).

Since so many of the men discussed in this book were Members of Parliament, I list below, in alphabetical order, those with biographies in P. W. Hasler's *The House of Commons 1558–1603* (3 vols, H.M.S.O., 1981). Though some of Hasler's contributors are not as reliable as one might have wished (see below, p.15: Sir Richard Hoghton), it is useful to alert the reader to the fact that we have detailed (and, normally, up-to-date) accounts of some of the principals and of some minor figures in our story. These include Sir Robert Cecil, John Fleetwood, Sir Gilbert Gerard, Sir Thomas Gerard, Sir Thomas Heneage, Edward Herbert (Lord Herbert of Cherbury), Robert Hesketh of Rufford, Thomas Hesketh (Alexander Hoghton's brother-in-law), Sir Richard Hoghton, Thomas Langton (baron of Newton), Sir Peter Leigh, Sir Richard Lewkenor, Sir Richard Molyneux, Sir Walter Raleigh, Sir John Salusbury, Sir Robert Salusbury, Simon Thelwall, Sir Edmund Trafford, Sir John Trevor, Sir Richard Trevor, William Waad, Sir Edward Warren.

List of Abbreviations

The following abbreviations have been used for periodicals, the publications of learned societies, works of reference, libraries, etc.

APC—Acts of the Privy Council of England, ed. J. R. Dasent etc., 1890– . (All references are to the reign of Queen Elizabeth I, unless otherwise stated.)

BL—The British Library (formerly British Museum).

CRS—Catholic Record Society.

CS—Chetham Society.

DD (etc.)—Documents in the Lancashire Record Office; thus DDHo refers to the Hoghton archives; DDHe to the Hesketh archives, etc.

DL (etc.)—Duchy of Lancaster records in the Public Record Office.

DNB—Dictionary of National Biography.

EHR—English Historical Review.

HMC—Historical Manuscripts Commission.

HSLC—Transactions of the Historic Society of Lancashire and Cheshire.

LRO—Lancashire Record Office.

MLR—Modern Language Review.

PCC—Prerogative Court of Canterbury (all PCC wills are in the Public Record Office).

PRO—Public Record Office.

Req—Court of Requests.

RES—Review of English Studies.

RSLC—Record Society of Lancashire and Cheshire.

Sh. Survey—Shakespeare Survey.

SPD—State Papers Domestic. (When two numbers follow *SPD*, these indicate the volume and document numbers. All references are to the reign of Queen Elizabeth I, unless otherwise stated.)

S. R.—The Stationers' Registers (cited from *A Transcript of the Registers of the Company of Stationers of London; A. D. 1554–1640.* Edited by Edward Arber. Five vols. London, privately printed, 1875 etc.).

Works frequently referred to are sometimes quoted by short title only: the full titles will be found in the list below. The place of publication is London where not otherwise stated.

Baker, *In Shakespeare's Warwickshire—In Shakespeare's Warwickshire and the Unknown Years.* By Oliver Baker. 1937.

Baldwin, *Small Latine—William Shakspere's Small Latine & Lesse Greeke.* By T. W. Baldwin. 2 vols. Urbana,University of Illinois Press. 1944.

Brown, *Salusbury and Chester—Poems by Sir John Salusbury and Robert Chester.* With an introduction by Carleton Brown. (Early English Text Society. Extra Series, no. CXIII (for 1913.)) 1914.

Chambers, *Gleanings—Shakespearean Gleanings.* By E.K. Chambers. Oxford. 1944.

Chambers, *Shakespeare—William Shakespeare: A Study of Facts and Problems.* By E. K. Chambers. 2 vols. Oxford. 1930.

Chambers, *Stage—The Elizabethan Stage.* By E. K. Chambers. 4 vols. Oxford. 1923.

Coward, *The Stanleys—The Stanleys Lords Stanley and Earls of Derby 1385–1672*. By Barry Coward. (CS, 3rd Series, XXX.) Manchester, 1983.

Fishwick, *Preston—The History of the Parish of Preston*. By Henry Fishwick. 1900.

Gillow, *English Catholics—A Literary and Biographical History, or Bibliographical Dictionary of the English Catholics*. By Joseph Gillow. 5 vols. 1885 etc.; Burt Franklin reprints, New York.

Gillow, *Map—Lord Burghley's Map of Lancashire in 1590*. By Joseph Gillow. London. Privately printed, 1907. Also in *CRS*, 1907, IV, 162 ff.

Hasler — *The House of Commons 1558–1603*. By P. W. Hasler. 3 vols. H.M.S.O. (the History of Parliament Trust). 1981.

Henslowe's Diary—Henslowe's Diary. Edited by R. A. Foakes and R. T. Rickert. Cambridge. 1961.

Hotson, *Shakespeare's Sonnets Dated — Shakespeare's Sonnets Dated and other Essays*. By Leslie Hotson. 1949.

Keen, *The Annotator—The Annotator: The Pursuit of an Elizabethan Reader of Halle's Chronicle Involving some Surmises about the Early Life of William Shakespeare*. By Alan Keen & Roger Lubbock. 1954.

Leatherbarrow, *Elizabethan Recusants — The Lancashire Elizabethan Recusants*. By J. Stanley Leatherbarrow. (CS, New Series, CX.) 1947, reprinted 1968.

Lefranc, *Sous le Masque — Sous le Masque de 'William Shakespeare': William Stanley VIe Comte de Derby*. By Abel Lefranc. 2 vols. Paris. 1918.

Lumby, *Calendar—A Calendar of the Deeds and Papers in the Possession of Sir James de Hoghton, Bart., of Hoghton Tower, Lancashire*. By J. H. Lumby. (RSLC.) 1936.

Miller, *Hoghton Tower—Hoghton Tower: The History of the Manor, the Hereditary Lords and the ancient Manor-house of Hoghton in Lancashire*. By Geo. C. Miller. Preston. 1948.

Nashe—The Works of Thomas Nashe. Edited by R. B. McKerrow (re-edited by F. P. Wilson). 5 vols. Oxford. 1958.

Schoenbaum, *Documentary Life—William Shakespeare: A Documentary Life*. By S. Schoenbaum. Oxford. 1975.

Schoenbaum, *Lives—Shakespeare's Lives*. By S. Schoenbaum. Oxford. 1970.

Sh. Encyclopaedia—A Shakespeare Encyclopaedia. Edited by Oscar James Campbell and E. G. Quinn. 1966.

Smith, *Calendar of Salusbury Correspondence—Calendar of Salusbury Correspondence 1553—circa 1700*. Principally from the Lleweni, Rug and Bagot Collections in the National Library of Wales. Edited by W. J. Smith. (Board of Celtic Studies, University of Wales. History and Law Series, no. XIV.) 1954.

Stanley Papers, The, Part II—The Stanley Papers. Part II. The Derby Household Books; comprising an Account of the Household Regulations and Expenses of Edward and Henry, Third and Fourth Earls of Derby (by W. Farington). Edited by F. R. Raines. (CS, XXXI.) 1853.

Tait, *Quarter Sessions—Lancashire Quarter Sessions Records. Vol. I. Quarter Sessions Rolls 1590–1606*. Edited by James Tait. (CS, New Series, LXXVII.) 1917.

Visitation, 1613—The Visitation of the County Palatine of Lancaster. Made in the Year 1613, by Richard St. George, Esq., Norroy King of Arms. Edited by F. R. Raines. (CS, LXXXII.) 1871.

I

Introduction

Where was William Shakespeare in the 'lost years' before 1592, and how did he make a living? Apart from the records of his baptism (26 April 1564) and licence to marry (27 November 1582), and of the christening of his children, Susanna (26 May 1583) and the twins Hamnet and Judith (2 February 1585), the rest is silence. Then Robert Greene attacked Shakespeare in September 1592, as an upstart crow in the theatrical world, one who 'supposes he is as well able to bombast out a blank verse' as the best contemporary dramatists, and 'being an absolute Johannes factotum, is in his own conceit the only Shake-scene in a country.' Aged 28, Shakespeare is not a complete newcomer on the literary scene, for Robert Greene, one of the most popular writers of the previous decade, regards him as a serious threat; but how long had he been writing plays, and what else had he done?

Shakespeare's lost years are usually said to extend from 1585, when he disappears from the Stratford records, to 1592. I prefer to regard the period from 1564 to 1592 as 'lost'; for, excepting the three dates, 1582, 1583 and 1585, we have no certain knowledge of his activities or whereabouts during these twenty-eight years. About his father, John Shakespeare, we know a good deal; as for William, we assume that he went to Stratford's grammar school, that he did not go to university, and that he had commenced on his theatrical career some time before 1592, perhaps as early as 1586 or 1587. That still leaves many years to be accounted for; if William stayed at school till he was 15 or 16, when boys normally went to university,[1] the 'lost' years would be the period from 1579 to 1592. Did he begin his theatrical career much earlier than has been suspected? How else could he have passed these years? In the pages that follow I suggest that he worked for a while in Lancashire – a possibility explored by E. K. Chambers forty years ago, then rejected in 1970 by Douglas Hamer.

I shall return to Chambers and Hamer in a moment. First,

though, let us note that several early biographers and gatherers of memorabilia tell us about Shakespeare's career before he turned actor or dramatist. Some of their stories inspire little confidence – for example, John Aubrey's that 'his father was a butcher, and I have been told heretofore by some of the neighbours that when he was a boy he exercised his father's trade, but when he killed a calf he would do it in a high style and make a speech'. [2] Shakespeare's father appears several times in the Stratford records as a glover, [3] so we need not take the calf-killing too seriously. Two other stories, however, deserve more attention.

(1) 'His father, who was a considerable dealer in wool, had so large a family, ten children in all, that though he [William] was his eldest son, he could give him no better education than his own employment. He had bred him, 'tis true, for some time at a free-school ... ' (Rowe's *Life of Shakespeare*, 1709). Rowe's *Life* was partly based on hearsay supplied by Thomas Betterton, the actor, who had made a special journey to Stratford to collect whatever gossip he could. Might John Shakespeare have been a dealer in wool as a side-line? It now seems that he was, for three later discoveries have confirmed Rowe's story. (*a*) In the early nineteenth century, when the floors of John Shakespeare's house were taken up, 'the remains of wool, and the refuse of wool-combing, were found under the old flooring, embedded with the earth of the foundation'. (*b*) Leslie Hotson has uncovered a forgotten law-suit of 1599, in which John Shakespeare sued John Walford, a clothier, 'on a debt of £21; alleging that on November 4, 1568, at Stratford-on-Avon, Walford bought twenty-one tods of wool of him for £21'. (*c*) New information about John Shakespeare's illegal wool-dealing has come to light in the Public Record Office, and will be published shortly.[4] Rowe's story has been vindicated, so we have to accept that what Rowe tells us in the same breath – that William went to the 'free-school' (i.e. grammar school)[5] and worked for a while with his father – may be true as well.

(2) 'Though as Ben Jonson says of him, that he had but little Latin and less Greek, he understood Latin pretty well, for he had been in his younger years a schoolmaster in the country' (John Aubrey, *c*. 1681). This story seems to have a different ancestry from the one about calf-killing. Aubrey, an avid collector of biographical gossip, left a memorandum in his papers, 'quaere Mr Beeston who knows most of him from Mr Lacy; he lives in Shore-ditch at Hoglane.' Apparently the actor John Lacy had suggested that Aubrey should consult William Beeston, in Hog Lane; and the 'schoolmaster in the country' story, though written on the same page as 'his father was a

butcher ...', has a note in the margin, 'from Mr ... Beeston'. As others have observed, Aubrey's source is crucially important, for William Beeston (c. 1606–1682) was the son of Shakespeare's former colleague in the Lord Chamberlain's company, Christopher Beeston (died 1638), and was therefore in a position to know the facts.

In the absence of evidence to the contrary, we must be grateful for both of these statements as to Shakespeare's early career. William was the eldest son, and it is likely enough that his father (who owned or leased three houses in Stratford, also owned properties in Snitterfield and Wilmcote, and seems to have had extensive business interests) would want him in 'his own employment'. And the 'schoolmaster in the country' story, coming from William Beeston, is surely the best authenticated of all the early reports of Shakespeare's younger years. Our problem is not whether to believe it, but to know what to make of it. *Where* exactly, 'in the country'? If only we could narrow down this airy generalisation and give it a local habitation and a name – might this not be the key to unlock the mystery of the 'lost years'?

The search for William Shakespeare 'in the country' has yielded one important paper, 'William Shakeshafte', by E. K. Chambers (included in his *Shakespearean Gleanings* (Oxford, 1944)). Chambers here returned to the will of Alexander Hoghton, Esq., of Lea (in Lancashire), which he had already mentioned in *The Elizabethan Stage* and had then inexplicably overlooked while writing his monumental *William Shakespeare: A Study of Facts and Problems* (Oxford, 2 vols, 1930). Hoghton's will, dated 3 August 1581, and proved 12 September 1581, bequeathed his stock of play clothes and all his musical instruments to his brother Thomas, or, if he did not choose to keep players, to Sir Thomas Hesketh, and added 'And I most heartily require the said Sir Thomas to be friendly unto Fulk Gyllome and William Shakeshafte now dwelling with me and either to take them unto his service or else to help them to some good master, as my trust is he will'. The relevant passage (my transcription differs from that printed by Chambers in some details) will be found in Appendix A (p. 136). 'Was then William Shakeshafte a player in 1581?' Chambers wondered in 1923; and in 1944 he returned to this exciting possibility:

> The linking with Sir Thomas Hesketh seems to make it at least highly probable that Foke Gyllome and William Shakeshafte were players. The will goes on, firstly to provide for the payment of a year's wages to every servant of the testator at the time of his death, and secondly to recite a provision in an entail, dated on 20 July 1580, of his landed

property upon his brother Thomas, which reserved an annual rent-charge of £16 13s 4d to be spent in the provision of annuities for some of these servants .... There are eleven of them. One gets £3 6s 8d, four £1, two 13s 4d, and four £2. Among these last are William Shakeshafte and Fowke Gyllom, and also a Thomas Gyllome. There is a further direction that, on the death of any annuitant, his share is to be divided among those still living, so that the last survivor shall get for his life the whole amount of the rent charge (pp. 52–3).

Hoping that Hoghton's 'Shakeshafte' might turn out to be Shakespeare, Chambers listed several points that needed further investigation and hazarded some other suggestions. (1) The poet's grandfather, Richard, 'seems to be both Shakstaff and Shakeschafte, as well as Shakspere ... in the Snitterfield manor records'; 'it is at least conceivable that William might have adopted the variant as a player'. (2) We can learn 'a good deal about the Hoghton and Hesketh families' in *The Derby Household Books* (Chetham Society, xxxi, 1853), the record of weekly expenses of Henry, 4th Earl of Derby. (3) Sir Thomas Hesketh was related to Alexander Hoghton's wife, Elizabeth, she being a daughter of Gabriel Hesketh of Aughton, Lancashire. (4) When Sir Thomas Hesketh visited the Earl of Derby on 30 December 1587, the *Household Books* record 'On Saturday Sᵗ Tho. Hesketh, Players went awaie'. 'I should like to be sure about that comma', Chambers added. 'Could he have written "Hesketh *and*" or "Heskethes"?' (5) Chambers found an abstract of Hesketh's will, which 'contains no clear evidence that he maintained players'. (6) Probably Lord Derby's players, not heard of after 1582, 'passed to his son Ferdinando, Lord Strange'; when unnamed players performed at the Earl's houses, Chambers thought it 'possible that these anonymous players were Strange's own men'. (7) 'If William Shakeshafte passed from the service of Alexander Hoghton into that of either Thomas Hoghton or Sir Thomas Hesketh, he might very easily have gone on into that of Lord Strange, and so later into the London theatrical world.'

Chambers wrote this paper during the war, when some of the documents could not be inspected. In 1970 Douglas Hamer, having re-examined Hoghton's will, demolished several of Chambers's suggestions and concluded that 'it is now clear' that Shakespeare did not begin his dramatic career with the Hoghtons and the Heskeths. Hamer, I think, is right on some points and wrong on others; at the time, though, it was felt that he had effectively answered Chambers, and that the young Shakespeare's whereabouts 'in the country' must be sought elsewhere.

How, then, can we track down the elusive schoolmaster 'in the country'? Where do we start? It may seem a hopeless task, until we put the question differently (and apparently no one has done this) — namely, how does a gifted youth from provincial Stratford, without a university background or degree, find employment as a school-master? The obvious answer is that he must have been recommended as capable of the work of a schoolmaster, or an assistant master, even though he had no degree. Anyone in Stratford could have recom-mended him, but one person in particular would have been an invaluable referee: the schoolmaster at Stratford's grammar school, who would be able to give an expert opinion of young Shakespeare's scholarly attainments.

Although we have no documentary evidence to prove it biogra-phers always assume that John Shakespeare, a well-to-do business-man in Stratford who in 1568 served as high bailiff (equivalent of the modern mayor), would send his son William to the town's grammar school. There is no good reason to suppose anything else — so we know the names of the schoolmasters who almost certainly taught William. In one case we know a good deal more than the name, and when we follow up the clues we are stopped short by a remarkable coincidence, to which I shall return in a moment.

William's first master was probably Walter Roche. In 1571 Simon Hunt succeeded him, but retired in 1575 to attend the Catholic seminary at Douay; he later became a Jesuit. Next in line was Thomas Jenkins, who had previously taught at Warwick grammar school. He was succeeded in 1579 by John Cottom, who remained until 1581 or 1582. 'By that time', says the entry in the *Shakespeare Encyclopaedia* (p. 197), 'Shakespeare had surely left the school. All these four masters were Oxford graduates and by the standards of the day, well-educated men.'

Checking through the information available about these four men, I was startled to learn that John Cottom was a native of Lancashire who returned *c.* 1582 to Tarnacre, where his family owned property, and lived there until his death in 1616. For Tarnacre, I found, is only ten miles from Lea, where the Hoghtons lived at this very time. Why had no one spotted this coincidence? The reason may be that T. W. Baldwin, following a suggestion by E. I. Fripp, demonstrated that Cottom came from Tarnacre in a book published in 1944, the very year of Chambers's essay on 'William Shakshafte'; John Cottom, it turns out, was the brother of the priest Thomas Cottam, who was captured by the authorities in June 1580, was arraigned on 14 November 1581, along with the Jesuit Edmund Campion, and executed as a traitor on 13 May 1582. Baldwin's proof that John Cottom, the Stratford schoolmaster, was the John Cottom of

[5]

Tarnacre, being one small detail embedded in the fact-crammed volumes of *William Shakspere's Small Latine and Lesse Greeke*,[6] was not seen to have importance, and was not connected with the 'Shakeshafte' theory propounded by Chambers in the same year.

Could William Shakeshafte, recommended by Alexander Hoghton in 1581, be William Shakespeare after all? Alerted by the closeness of Tarnacre to Lea, I began to search for further facts about John Cottom in the public archives, and discovered various connections between Alexander Hoghton and his family and John Cottom and *his* family – until it finally dawned on me that one of the many legatees under Alexander Hoghton's will, whose name appears as 'John Cotham' (cf. p. 137), may well be the teacher from Stratford. The 'schoolmaster' theory, it seems, leads straight back to Alexander Hoghton.

And so do many other friends and connections of Shakespeare in his later career. Alexander Hoghton belonged to an immensely wealthy and influential family, closely linked with other Lancashire families that play a part in Shakespeare's later life; the 'Lancashire connection' helps to illuminate people and events hitherto misunderstood or abandoned by biographers who were unable to fit together the jigsaw of Shakespeare's early life when so many pieces were missing. A good example is John Weever, an admirer who referred to Shakespeare in several works, the first being his *Epigrammes* (1599) with their verses *Ad Gulielmum Shakespeare*. The only modern reprint of this book is by one of the outstanding Elizabethan editors of our century, R. B. McKerrow (1911), who unfortunately chose to publish without much preliminary research. Weever had divided the *Epigrammes* into seven parts, or 'weeks', and had dedicated each week to a different man – Sir Richard Hoghton of Hoghton Tower; Robert Dalton of Pilling, Esq.; Sir Richard 'Mullineux'; Sir Edward Warren; Sir Thomas Gerard; Sir Cuthbert Halsey; Sir Peter Leigh. We cannot blame McKerrow for not drawing attention to the fact that Sir Richard Hoghton had inherited the estates of Alexander Hoghton of Lea (through Alexander's half-brother, Thomas Hoghton, Esq., Sir Richard's father), for Chambers had not yet explained the possible significance of Alexander Hoghton's bequest to 'Shakeshafte'; nevertheless, McKerrow should have looked into the family histories of Weever's dedicatees, which would have led to further discoveries about Weever (a neglected minor writer) and about Shakespeare. Dugdale's *The Baronage of England* would have informed him that Sir Richard Hoghton, Sir Richard Molyneux and Sir Peter Leigh had married three sisters, the daughters of Sir Gilbert Gerard, Queen Elizabeth's Master of the Rolls. Further research would have revealed that Weever's four other dedicatees were related to one or more of the three brothers-in-law through other family ties, or were associated with them in other ways; that other contemporaries addressed in Weever's individual epigrams were also related to the Hoghton circle; and that Weever himself was connected with the Hoghtons through his uncle, Henry Butler, Esq., a neighbour of John Cottom. Weever's *Epigrammes*, a collection more or less completed one year before it was published (i.e. in 1598), celebrates the family of its first and principal dedicatee, Sir Richard Hoghton, and, as I shall show, Weever's verses to Shakespeare signal to the informed reader that he is possessed of 'inside' information.

A second example of interconnecting threads that lead back to Lancashire involves the Stanley family and the Earls of Derby, whose *Household Books* so fortunately survive. Henry Stanley, the fourth Earl (*c.* 1531–1593), lived in almost regal style on his Lancashire estates; the Hoghtons and Heskeths and their relations appear frequently in the *Household Books* as visitors, and, as I shall argue, the case for Shakespeare's entering the London theatrical world as one of Derby's or Strange's Men is even stronger than Chambers suggested. In addition, the phoenix of Shakespeare's *The Phoenix and the Turtle* was almost certainly Ursula Halsall or Stanley, an illegitimate daughter of Henry Stanley, the fourth Earl; Ursula's sister, Dorothy, married (Sir) Cuthbert Halsall (or Halsey), one of the dedicatees of Weever's *Epigrammes*; and Sir Cuthbert, the phoenix's brother-in-law, was one of several Halsalls engaged in protracted legal battles with the Duddells of Salwick, one of whom was William Duddell, son-in-law of John Cottom, formerly schoolmaster at Stratford.

I have not attempted, in this introductory chapter, to list all the 'Lancashire' names that will interest future biographers of Shakespeare: many more will be found in the pages that follow. My aim has been to indicate that those who have written about Shakespeare's 'lost years' have missed important clues – which, I hope, will encourage us to look more searchingly at the relevant people and documents. And, first of all, at that fascinating family, the Hoghtons (or Houghtons) of Lea and Hoghton Tower.

II

Hoghton of Hoghton Tower

(a) The early history of the Hoghton family

The Hoghtons are descended directly from Walter, one of the companions of William the Conqueror, and through the female line from the Lady Godiva of Coventry, wife of Leogric, Earl of Mercia. After the third generation from the Norman Conquest, Adam de Hoghton first assumed the family name, holding land in Hoghton in 1203. (*Guide to Hoghton Tower*)

Readers inclined to smile at the Hoghton family's claim to antiquity would quickly mend their ways on opening the catalogues of Hoghton muniments in the Lancashire Record Office, a vast collection of letters and legal documents of every kind, equally rich in the medieval and Elizabethan and later periods.[1] If Shakespeare was indeed a Hoghton retainer we should have little difficulty in reconstructing his employer's family-history.

In the sixteenth century the Hoghtons were indisputably one of the premier families in Lancashire. Sir Richard de Hoghton (1498–1559), however, was succeeded by a son who became a recusant (i.e. a Roman Catholic who refused to attend the services of the Church of England) and left England in 1569, never to return: the Right Worshipful Thomas Hoghton (1518–80) died in exile at Liège, and could do little after 1569 to promote his family's fortune. Before that, though, he had re-built Hoghton Tower (1562–8) on a ridge about six miles south-east of Preston – a magnificent baronial residence, with upper and base courts, so large, it has been said, that it 'appears at a distance almost like a fortified town'. The tower itself was blown up during the civil war, but was described by Richard Kuerden in the seventeenth century as 'a most princely tower ... a very tall strong tower or gate-house', 'a stately fabric ... environed with a most spacious park'.[2] Thomas's son, a priest, was debarred from the succession, so the next head of the family was Thomas's brother, Alexander, who died next year (1581) and recommended William Shakeshafte in his will to his half-brother, another Thomas, who now succeeded him. This Thomas died in a night-skirmish in 1589, and was followed by his son, Richard (1570–1630), who was knighted in 1599 and became the first baronet in 1611. A family tree will be found in Appendix B, p. 000.

Seekers of the 'schoolmaster in the country' will be particularly interested in Alexander and Thomas Hoghton, but we must begin with Thomas the exile, whom I shall call Thomas I. The whole family appears to have remained ardently Catholic until Richard Hoghton turned Protestant, probably in the 1580s. (According to Dugdale, Richard Hoghton and his brothers-in-law, who married the daughters of Sir Gilbert Gerard, the Master of the Rolls (cf. p. 000), had all 'formerly been in Ward to him [Sir Gilbert], as I have credibly heard': it is believed that Sir Gilbert saw to it that his future sons-in-law turned Protestant.[3] Thomas I, being a recusant, took elaborate precautions to safeguard the family's inheritance, which can be traced in various deeds and conveyances from near the beginning of Elizabeth's reign; he listed his father's sons and illegitimate sons as his heirs,[4] and conveyed some properties to faithful family retainers, one of whom (George Beseley) reappears later as one of the executors of Alexander Hoghton's will in 1581. Having made over messuages etc. to 'Georgio Besely de Gosenarghe generoso' (i.e. George Besely of Goosnargh, gentleman) and another, he explained that 'the intent of this deed is that the said George and Roger shall stand seized of the premises ... unto the use of the said Thomas Hoghton and his heirs male'.[5] Two of Alexander Hoghton's executors in 1581, George Beseley and James Helme, were involved in a similar legal manoeuvre in 1585: a damaged seventeenth-century copy of an indenture dated 27 Elizabeth (i.e. 1585) records an agreement between Thomas Hoghton of Hoghton (Alexander's heir) and George Beasley and James Belme, but *Bretton v. Adam Hoghton* (2 James I) referred back to this indenture and correctly named the two men as Besely and 'James Helme'.[6] Other recusant families protected their interests in similar ways; in the case of the Hoghtons, the resulting legal documents help us to disentangle some of the mysteries of Alexander's will of 1581.

The Catholic sympathies of the older Hoghtons (including Alexander) are important for us, since it is highly unlikely that such a family would employ, at a time so dangerous for recusants, a servant who was not a practising Catholic. The phrasing of Shakespeare's will suggests that he died a Protestant, but there are reasons for believing that his father and daughter, Susanna, may have been Catholics (cf. p. 000) If the dramatist changed his religion in his teens or later — as did John Donne, Ben Jonson and many more — this would certainly interest readers of *King John* and *Hamlet* (to name only two of the plays concerned with anti-papal propaganda and/or Catholic ideas). I return to the Shakespeares later (p. 114 ff.), and, at this stage, merely outline some of the basic facts about the Hoghtons and *their* religion. As good a starting-point as any is the ballad, 'The Blessed Conscience', celebrating Thomas I and his honourable decision that religion comes before worldly profit. It is popularly ascribed to Roger Anderton, Thomas's butler, who went into exile with his master, and it seems to be based on detailed knowledge of Thomas's affairs. Much of the ballad (it consists of twenty-three eight-line stanzas) purports to give Thomas's own dying words.[7]

> At Hoghton, where I used to rest
> Of men I had great store,
> Full twenty gentlemen at least,
> Of yeomen good three score!
> And of them all, I brought but two
> With me, when I came thence.
> I left them all ye world knows how
> To keep my conscience!

It was clearly a difficult time, for 'I durst not trust my dearest friend, / But secretly stole hence'. And even Thomas's brothers, he thought, let him down.

> When to my brethren I had sent
> Ye welcome that they made
> Was false reports me to present,
> Which made my conscience sad.
> My brethren all did thus me cross
> And little regard my fall,
> Save only one, that rued my loss,
> That is Richard, of Park Hall.

> He was ye comfort that I had;
> I proved his diligence;
> He was as just as they were bad,
> Which cheered my conscience. ...

Richard Hoghton of Park Hall, in Charnock Richard, 'was the son of Sir Richard Hoghton by his fourth wife, Anne, daughter of Roger Browne, though he was born out of wedlock'.[8] By great good fortune, the letters sent by Thomas I to his brother Richard survive in the John Rylands Library, Manchester (English MSS. 213). They begin on 22 September 1576, and continue at regular (sometimes weekly) intervals, with many references to Hoghton retainers who travelled to and from the continent carrying money and messages. Richard Hoghton clearly acted as 'business manager' for his exiled brother, and may have been the most committed Catholic of the 'brethren' who remained in England: when Edmund Campion was captured by the authorities in 1581 it was reported that the Jesuit had stayed with leading Catholics in Lancashire, whose houses were searched by order of the Privy Council – 'and especially the house of Richard Hoghton, where it is said the said Campion left his books'.[9] Examined upon his oath 'whether the said Campion had ever to his knowledge been in his house', Richard Hoghton 'deposed the contrary', and witnesses deposed that Hoghton was 'conformable in religion' i.e. attended the Anglican church; however, many Catholics 'conformed outwardly', and deposed falsely about their religion; Richard's role as 'manager' for Thomas I, and other contemporary evidence (cf. p. 20), make it likely that he was a Catholic.

Let us return to Thomas I, the head of the family until 1580. His importance (and consequently Alexander's, when he succeeded as head of the family) can be illustrated from many sources. Thomas's unlicensed departure from the country was reported to the Privy Council (29 September 1571), and shortly afterwards a Special Commission was ordered to report on his possessions and tenants.[10] In 1576 the Queen signed a licence permitting Richard Hoghton to travel to Antwerp 'to the intent to advise, persuade and counsel Thomas Hoghton, late of Hoghton, ... to return unto this our realm', two sureties being 'bound' with Richard to lose £200 if Richard failed to come back within two months.[11] The government looked upon Thomas I as a person of considerable importance. So did the Catholic church, for the future Cardinal Allen attended the opening of Hoghton Tower when Thomas I had re-built and extended the family's old home, and shortly after Thomas's death the Cardinal wrote that he had received £100 from Thomas's executors for the benefit 'of the church at Preston, when the time should serve'. And a handsome monument was erected for Thomas I in the church of Gervais, Liège, where he was buried, with the following inscription: 'Hic e regione sepultus est vir Illustris D. Thomas Hoghton, Anglus, qui post decem an. exilium spontaneum variasque patrimonii et rerum omnium direptiones propter Cath. fidei confessionem a sectariis illatas, obijt 4 Non. Jun. 1580. Ætat. 63'.[12]

Precisely how the 'bad' brethren of Thomas I managed to 'cross' him may never be fully known. The ballad alleges that his brothers offered a thousand marks (i.e. £666 13s 4d) 'to hinder my licence / That I should not come home again'; my own guess is that they felt they had to protect themselves, and perhaps refused to surrender legal documents that were needed by Thomas I – a common dilemma in recusant families, whose properties might be confiscated by the crown. Something of the sort may lie behind the complaint of Brian Jackson (the principal messenger between Thomas I and Richard Hoghton in the 1570s) and others to the Privy Council (1 March 1581) 'against Alexander Hoghton of Hoghton, Esq., and others his brethren, for the detaining of sundry leases and annuities given heretofore unto the plaintiffs by Thomas Hoghton, their oldest brother deceased, in consideration of eighteen years' service'.[13] The Hoghtons had to contend with many problems in the 1570s and 1580s, which we need to know about to understand Alexander's will of 1581 and the flurry of legal activity that preceded and followed it; and it may be that they were a divided family, which would increase their anxieties. Catholic families were not necessarily held together by their fear of Queen Elizabeth's Protestant government. Alexander's widow, to give one more example, thought that two men whom he had asked in his will to be his executor and supervisor behaved disgracefully towards her; they happened to be her own brothers – but that is another family and another story, and must wait till later.

Alexander survived as head of the family for just over a year (1580–1). I shall look more closely at his will, and his household and circle of friends, in the next two sections, and continue here with a brief account of Alexander's brother and heir, Thomas II (died 1589), and his son and heir, Richard. Many records survive about both men, from which I select a few of the more interesting ones. Thomas II, in the lifetime of Thomas I and Alexander Hoghton, 'did occupy ... one messuage or tenement called the Brynscowes' and received the rents of divers other lands in 'Whelton [i.e. Wheelton] and Withnell' (DL4.29.39: deposition of Richard Hoghton of Park Hall, 29 Eliz.). On 19 August 1581, Thomas II made an agreement with 'Elizabeth Hoghton, widow, late wife of Alexander Hoghton, Esq.', conveying to her 'Alston Hall and all lands late the inheritance of Thomas Hoghton, Esq.' (BL: Add. MS. 32, 106, fo. 165b).[14] In 27 Elizabeth (1585), Thomas II made an indenture 'for the preferment of William, Thomas and Adam Hoghton, his younger sons' (ibid., fo. 223), leaving them lands in Hoghton, Lea, Withnell, etc. In 1588 he paid the Crown £100 for the defence of the realm (DDF 2440, fo. 20b). On 16 September 1589, he signed a receipt for £300 to Sir Gilbert Gerard 'due unto me the said Thomas Hoghton this present day, being the day of the marriage of Richard Hoghton my son unto Katherine Gerard, daughter of the said Sir Gilbert Gerard' (DDHo 345). Throughout this decade Thomas II also battled with Ann Halsall, the grandmother of Sir Cuthbert Halsall (cf. p. 53), over rights of pasturage, turbary, etc., in Lea and in adjacent lands; witness a bill of complaint of 1582, a decree of 1584, interrogatories of 1585, etc.[15] These disputes are probably connected with Thomas's death on 20 November 1589, when Thomas Langton, baron of Newton, with about eighty armed men, attacked Thomas Hoghton's house at midnight, ostensibly in a dispute about cattle; Hoghton had thirty men to defend him, but was killed in the melee. It was, it seems, a dark night; the Langton party used the watch-word 'The crow is white!', and Hoghton's men cried 'Black, black!'

The Earl of Derby reported to the Privy Council on 10 December that he had taken great pains to investigate this riot, in which several leading Lancashire families were involved,[16] and the Queen herself sent a most unusual letter to the justices at Lancaster. (The manuscript contains so many deletions and insertions that I quote from the *Calendar* summary of State Papers Domestic.)

> The Queen to Justices Clinch and Walmsley. Understands that Justice Walmsley, contrary to her express commands, signified by a letter from the late Lord Chancellor, has bailed sundry persons indicted of the murder of Thos. Houghton, of Lancashire; wonders how he dared to presume so far, showing both contempt of her commandment, and little regard for the due administration of justice. ... Commands him to cause the said parties to be immediately returned to prison, and to proceed ... to a speedy trial without further bail, and not to fail at his peril.[17]

In the much-corrected original we find the Queen's personal concern even more strongly expressed: the Lord Chancellor's letter was 'written by our order' (interlined); and the letter ends 'as you will avoid our furder indignation, and answer for the contrary at your peril'. Lord Strange, the Earl of Derby's heir (and probably Shakespeare's patron at this time), attended the spring assizes in Lancaster in April 1590, and stayed a whole week on account of the baron of Newton's trial.[18] In the end the baron made his peace with the Hoghtons by ceding to them the manor of Walton le Dale.

According to the 'valor and extent of the estate inherited by Richard Hoghton', dated 1590, the manors of Hoghton and Lea descended from Thomas II to his son Richard. These encompassed 800 messuages, 400 cottages, 20 water mills, 10 wind mills, 1000 gardens, 1000 orchards, 2000 acres of meadow, 3000 acres of pasture, 2000 acres of woodlands, 6000 acres of land, 6000 acres of moor, 1000 acres of turbary and 1000 acres of heath.[19] Round numbers, it will be noticed, and they need to be compared with the inquisition post mortem in the Public Record Office (DL7. 15.39), where the names of Hoghton tenants are listed, and the rents they paid. Without going into detail we can see that the family was immensely wealthy, and that Mrs Anne Hoghton (the widow of Thomas II) might indeed have been able to live at the rate of £1,000 a year, as rumour reported.[20]

The most eventful year in Richard Hoghton's life was 1598–9, when he became High Sheriff of Lancashire. It was perhaps because he served as Sheriff that, as John Chamberlain wrote on 28 June 1599, he was knighted on Sunday at court.[21] Sometime in the next five months John Weever dedicated his *Epigrammes* to 'Sir Richard Hoghton of Hoghton Tower, Justice of Peace, and Quorum; High Sheriff of Lancashire, etc.', and mentioned 'the experience which many scholars have had of your kindness, never to be forgotten'. Sir Richard, particularly in his year as Sheriff, proved a notable hunter of recusants, and reported his catches to the Bishop of Chester and to Sir Robert Cecil;[22] the Bishop wrote to Cecil in October 1600 that Sir Richard and his successor as Sheriff 'have done great service in apprehending of sundry priests, pestilent persuaders to rebellion, and are the ablest and fittest persons ... to hunt out the seditious priests'.[23] A few days earlier Sir Richard informed Cecil that he had caught a seminary prist, one who 'seems a very mean scholar' (*SPD*, 1 Oct. 1600), which may mean that Sir Richard was something of a scholar (cf. Weever, above). What would the older Hoghtons have thought of these activities?

Sir Richard, of course, appears in the official records of the period as Sheriff or J.P., and also in many legal documents. In 1593, when Sir Richard Molyneux made out a deed of gift for his wife (since she 'hath no jointure'), his brothers-in-law figure as sureties – Sir Thomas Gerard, and Peter Legh and Richard Hoghton, Esquires (DDCl.910); as his friend Sir Cuthbert Halsall sank more and more into debt, Sir Richard Hoghton helped him as security:[24] all these men, it will be recalled, receive dedications in Weever's *Epigrammes*. Richard's widowed mother continued to live at Lea Hall, where Alexander and Thomas II had died, even after she married Richard Sherburne, Esq.; in her will (9 James I) she asked to be buried near her former husband, Thomas Hoghton.

Weever referred to the splendour of Sir Richard's principal residence, the 'gold-gilded tower' (sig. F6). In August 1617 James I and his court visited Hoghton Tower, and stayed three days. Harrison Ainsworth gave a detailed account of this visit in Book III ('Hoghton Tower') of *The Lancashire Witches* (1848), a romance partly based on contemporary records. The king inspected Sir Richard's alum mines, and later asked the Lord Chancellor and Lord Treasurer to advise him whether or not to take over these mines, as

Sir Richard requested. (Sir Richard had mortgaged the manor of Walton to finance the mines, which seem to have been a bad speculation; 'towards the end of his life', said G. C. Miller, 'Sir Richard was for some years imprisoned for debt in the Fleet'[25].) Sir Richard's son, Gilbert (born 1591) had been knighted in 1606, at an unusually early age, and Sir Richard himself was elevated to the Baronetage in 1611.

Hasler's account of Sir Richard Hoghton in *The House of Commons 1558–1603* differs from mine in several respects. It states that Thomas I was the father of Thomas II and grandfather of Sir Richard; and that Richard Hoghton was married *c.* 1590 and knighted in 1598.

(b) Alexander Hoghton's will (1581) and 'Shakeshafte'

We are now ready to go back to Alexander Hoghton of Lea, and to ask whether he was eliminated prematurely from our search for the 'schoolmaster in the country'. Since John Cottom, a Stratford schoolmaster in 1579 when Shakespeare was 15, belonged to a family with property so close to Alexander Hoghton's house, and since John Cottom actually lived at Tarnacre from *c.* 1582, we must re-open the case of 'William Shakeshafte'. What, in the first place, made Douglas Hamer so certain in 1970 that Shakespeare did not work for the Hoghtons and Heskeths? I begin with a summary of Hamer's argument.[26]

(1) 'If he actually were employed in far-off Lancashire under an alias in and before 1581, it is strange that, reverting to his paternal and baptismal name of Shakespeare, he should ... marry Anne Hathaway in 1582, live continuously in Stratford until after the birth of his twins in 1585, and then ... reappear in 1587 as a "player" ... in the service of Sir Thomas Hesketh in Lancashire'. (2) Hamer also showed 'Shakeshafte' to be a not uncommon name in the Preston Burgess Rolls (Preston was close to Alexander Hoghton's house at Lea), and published, among others, an entry for 1582: 'Johannes Shakeshafte Glover Juratus / Willelmus Shakeshafte frater eius Juratus / Willelmus Shakeshafte filius eius'. (3) He contended that Hoghton's bequest of annuities to eleven servants, including Fulke Gyllom and William Shakeshafte, amounts to 'an early non-subscription form of the Tontine system – survivor takes all'.

> [Since] the annuitants draw annuities which increase with the death of each annuitant until the last draws the whole income for life, the annuitants are initially graded according to their actual ages at the time when the capital sum or capital income is established. The basic

idea is that over the years all the annuitants shall, in the normal way of living and dying, receive approximately the same amount. The oldest annuitant thus receives the highest initial annuity.

William Shakeshafte was one of four legatees who received £2 each; only one of the thirty named legatees (cf. p. 137) received more; therefore, said Hamer, the inescapable deduction is that Shakeshafte 'may have been as old as thirty to forty'. William Shakespeare of Stratford, on the other hand, was only seventeen in 1581. (4) Chambers assumed that the players referred to in Hoghton's will must be actors. The straightforward interpretation of this passage in the will (see p. 136), thought Hamer, 'is that the musical instruments, play-clothes, and players all go together, and that here we have to do, not with musical instruments and actors, but with musical instruments and musicians'. The term *player* had been current since 1463 to signify 'One who plays an instrument of music' (*OED*); *play-clothes* 'are not recorded in *OED*'. (5) Two years after publishing 'William Shakeshafte', Chambers announced that 'Sir Thomas Hesketh had in fact players in 1587';[27] this was partly because he now knew that in the printed version of *The Derby Household Books*, the entry 'Sir Thomas Hesketh, Players went awaie' has a comma added by the editor. Hamer, however, observed that the *Household Books* 'invariably used the terminal -s of the possessive' (i.e. 'Hesketh' is not a possessive); and that, comparing this Hesketh entry with others recording comings and goings at the earl's houses, it most probably means 'Sir Thomas Hesketh came, and the players went away'.

As already indicated, I disagree with several of Hamer's arguments. I shall comment first on (3), which, if correct, would put an end to all further discussion. A legal colleague, Professor D. W. Elliott, advised me some years ago that Alexander Hoghton's provisions in his will should not be seen as an early non-subscription tontine.

I guess that each annuitant enjoyed his annuity for life, it then went to the survivors, who enjoyed augmented annuities for their lives, and then to the last survivor, who enjoyed a large annuity but only for the remainder of his life. The capital then reverted to the testator's estate. A tontine was quite different; it was an early form of life insurance, very crude and with a strong element of gambling. No participant enjoyed anything unless and until he became the last survivor, when he took the whole capital absolutely. In other words, annuities played no part in the scheme at all ...

Nor do I think it at all credible to deduce the age of the annuitants from the comparative size of the annuities given to them. I take it the argument is that an old servant has not long to live, and will not enjoy accretions by survival, so must be given more than a young servant. Perhaps, but other deductions from a large gift are: satisfaction with the servant, long service by the servant, status of the servant ... other resources of the servant ... It is the way of the world to reward long and faithful service, but there has never been any 'practice' to do so. I would be most unconvinced by any reconstruction of servants' comparative ages from their comparative bequests.[28]

Professor Elliott pretty well disposes of Hamer's tontine argument. And, in case any doubts remain, I can now give some additional information: several of Hoghton's annuitants appeared as deponents in later law-suits, identifying themselves and stating their age. We can therefore work out how old they were in 1581: and the figures do not bear out Hamer's argument.

(a) *Thomas Barton* was Alexander Hoghton's steward. Lawrence Fydler of Lea deposed in 1605 that he was 'three several times sent unto the now complainant by Mr Alexander Hoghton and Thomas Barton, gent., then steward to the said Mr Alexander Hoghton for to come to agree with Mr Hoghton for a lease' (*Bretton v. Adam Hoghton*, DL4.48.49). Barton described himself in 1587 as 'Thomas Barton, gentleman and servant to Thomas Hoghton, Esq.', aged about fifty, and referred to Alexander Hoghton as 'his late master' (*Mary Lyvesey v. Thomas Hoghton*, DL4.29.39). Barton, therefore, was 44 or so in 1581.

(b), (c) *Thomas Coston* and *Henry 'Bonnde'* are deponents in *Singleton v. R. Hoghton*, 1586 (DL4.28.25). Coston gives his age as 34, Bond his as 60. Coston states that Thomas Hoghton I used to send him 'into England divers and sundry times yearly to the said Richard Hoghton to receive money of him to his use'. Richard Hoghton, of Park Hall in Charnock Richard, Thomas's 'base brother', managed his estates for him in his absence (cf. p. 10) and, as we learn from Henry Bond in the same suit, delivered the rents to George Hoghton or Brian Jackson or Thomas Coston. No doubt the Thomas 'Costin' named as one of Thomas Hoghton's defenders in the Earl of Derby's report on the 'affray' of 1589[29] was the same faithful family retainer. Coston would have been 29 and Bond 55 in 1581.

For our immediate purposes these three names suffice. Thomas Barton, aged 44 in 1581, would have to be one of the younger annuitants according to Hamer's theory, since he was left no specified sum; Bond, aged 55, would also have to be one of the younger annuitants, for the same reason; and Coston would have to be older than either Barton or Bond, since he was left an annuity of £1 a year; yet Coston was in fact younger. Hamer's argument (3) collapses.

We have still to consider Hamer's other arguments. Let us begin with (1) and (2): it seems to me misleading to think of Shakespeare's switching to 'Shakeshafte', if this happened, as going 'under an alias'. Names simply were not thought of as fixed and unalterable in the sixteenth century: Marlowe is also Marley, Morley and Marlin in contemporary records; Philip Henslowe is also Hinslye, Hinshow, Henshlowe, Henseslowe; Shakespeare, even when famous, appears in the Revels accounts as Shaxberd,[30] and his grandfather, Richard, figures in the Snitterfield records as 'Shakstaff' (but not as 'Shakeshafte', as Chambers thought);[31] and the only other Snitterfield Shakespeare, Thomas, is also 'Shakesmore' in 1578.[32] In Lancashire the familiar name was Shakeshafte, and so it would not be surprising if a name as unusual (in this area) as Shakespeare were assimilated, or perhaps merely confused by the scrivener in 1581.

As for Hamer's (4) and (5), a weakness in his case is that he can cite no example of *play-clothes* meaning 'the official costumes of musicians'. I believe, as he does, that Hoghton's *instruments, play-clothes* and *players* go together, but not that instruments point exclusively to a band of musicians. Richard Jones's deed of sale of 1589, making over to Edward Alleyn his share 'of playing apparel, play-books, instruments and other commodities'[33] helps to explain: actors at this time had to be all-purpose entertainers, acrobats and musicians as well as *histriones*. Quite a number of Shakespeare's colleagues were definitely singers or instrumentalists; Henslowe's players spent large sums to buy apparel and instruments – these being the indispensable tools of their trade. In the very year of Hoghton's will, 1581, 'certain companies of players' petitioned the Privy Council for a licence to perform publicly, since they 'were only brought up from their youth in the practice of music and playing', and this was granted because the plague had abated and 'they are to present certain plays before the Queen's Majesty'.[34] Unless an example turns up of *play-clothes* meaning musicians' clothes, the natural interpretation of Hoghton's bequest must be that he kept a group of 'players' who produced plays, or who made music and sometimes produced plays. (At least some of the boy-actors in Shakespeare's company were trained singers; his colleague Augustine Phillips, who bequeathed musical instruments to his 'apprentices', had clearly taken an interest in their musical skills; another colleague, R. Cowley, took a musician's part in *Seven Deadly Sins*, and another, R. Armin, was called on to sing in several plays. See also *Henslowe's Diary,* pp. 102, 122 etc, for the purchase of instruments.)

The actual phrasing of Alexander Hoghton's will contradicts

Hamer's interpretation of *play-clothes*. Why would Alexander describe them as 'all my instruments belonging to musics *and all manner of play-clothes*' except to imply the diversity of these garments? If Alexander had in mind some sort of uniform worn by the musicians, or his own livery, as Hamer suggested, why *all manner of*? This phrase surely points to a stock of costumes kept for theatrical entertainments by Alexander's players. And, though Hamer is probably right in claiming that *The Derby Household Books* do not prove the existence of 'Sir Thomas Hesketh's players',[35] the really important point is that Alexander Hoghton, though uncertain whether or not his brother would want to keep players, ordained that if Thomas II declined then Sir Thomas Hesketh 'shall have' the instruments and play-clothes; that is, he knew that Hesketh would take them, presumably because Hesketh kept players. Moreover, as Chambers saw, although Gyllom and Shakeshafte are not positively identified as players in Hoghton's will, 'the linking with Sir Thomas Hesketh seems to make it at least highly probable'.

This last point is placed in a new perspective when one compares the printed version of Alexander Hoghton's will with the manuscript in the Lancashire Record Office. The nineteenth-century editor omitted some of the meaningless phrases of the will, and also the word 'Itm' (Item), which is used to introduce the testator's different bequests. For our purposes it is crucial that a single 'Itm' covers three related matters: (1) the instruments and play-clothes are left to Thomas II, if he will keep players; (2) they go to Sir Thomas Hesketh, if Thomas II declines; (3) Sir Thomas is asked to employ Gyllom and Shakeshafte, or 'to help them to some good master'. In this three-part bequest Alexander Hoghton is concerned with his players and their future, and it follows that Gyllom and Shakeshafte are mentioned after (1) and (2) because they are connected in his mind with his players.

How does all this help us in our search for the 'schoolmaster in the country'? As already stated, I believe that William Shakespeare could have been recommended to Alexander Hoghton by John Cottom, the master of Stratford's grammar school. Schoolmasters, of course, had to be officially licensed at this time, but Catholic families, as well as illegally harbouring priests, frequently maintained unlicensed schoolmasters; and this was particularly common in Lancashire. Indeed, a report to the Privy Council 'on the condition of Lancashire and Cheshire' of *c.* 1591 complained that even licensed school-masters were 'unsound': 'small reformation has been made there by the Ecclesiastical Commission, as may appear by the emptiness of churches on Sundays ... The youth are for the most part trained up by such as profess papistry; no examination is had of schools and schoolmasters'.[36] Young William Shakespeare could have gone to Lancashire as an assistant teacher in 1579 or 1580, when he was fifteen or sixteen, and, like the master of the Children of Paul's and of the Children of the Chapel, could have been drawn into 'theatricals' in the course of his normal duties.

Apart from Alexander Hoghton's concern for William Shakeshafte in 1581, and other Hoghton–Shakespeare links that will emerge presently, there are good reasons for pursuing what may at first seem a far-fetched hypothesis. (1) John Shakespeare, William's father, began to experience financial difficulties from about 1577. He mortgaged a house and land, and at the same time stopped attending regularly at the Stratford council's meetings. Whatever his problems, his financial future must have looked less secure than formerly; if William was reluctant to help his father 'in his own employment' (cf. p. 2), this would have been his opportunity to break away. (2) Other precocious boys of sixteen or so have worked as teachers. Richard Mather (1596–1669), later one of the most celebrated New England Puritans, began to teach at a grammar school in Lancashire at the age of fifteen; Simon Forman, still in his teens, taught as an unqualified usher from 1572; and, in a later period, Mrs Gaskell records that Patrick Bronte, the father of the Bronte sisters, 'opened a public school at the early age of sixteen', and taught for five or six years.[37] Others have done it, so why not Shakespeare? (3) Other members of the Hoghton family, and other Catholics closely connected with the family, reputedly maintained unlicensed schoolmasters at this very time. An apostate priest informed Lord Burghley in 1592 that Richard Hoghton of Park Hall (cf. p. 10) 'hath kept a recusant schoolmaster I think this twenty years. He hath had one after another; the name of one was Scholes, of the other Fawcett, as I remember, but I stand in doubt of the names'. The same informer claimed that Mrs Anne Hoghton, the widow of Thomas II, kept at her house in Lea 'Richard Blundell, brother to William Blundell, of Crosbie, gent., an obstinate papist', to teach her children to sing and play on the virginals; and that Mr Bartholomew Hesketh (the brother of Alexander Hoghton's widow) 'had kept for sundry years a certain Gabriel Shaw to be his schoolmaster'; and that William Hulton of Hulton, Esq., a close friend of the Hoghtons, had kept a recusant school-master 'many years.[38] (Hulton is named in an indenture, 30 Elizabeth, with Thomas Hoghton, Esq., and Sir Richard Molyneux, as surety for the jointure of Anne Hoghton, Thomas's wife; and Hulton and his two sons aided Thomas Hoghton at Lea on the fatal night when Thomas was killed.)[39]

Accepting, then, that an excellent witness like William Beeston (cf. p. 3), who was in a position to know the truth and had no conceivable motive for lying, must be trusted when he asserts that Shakespeare was in his younger years a schoolmaster in the country – we can now add that 'William Shakeshafte' fits the picture quite remarkably. I suggest the following reconstruction of events: John Cottom, recently arrived in Stratford as the new schoolmaster, hears that a Lancashire magnate, landlord to Cottom's own father (cf. p. 42) and a near neighbour of his, needs a master to teach the children in his large household. Cottom recommends William Shakespeare, a brilliant boy of sixteen or so whose father is going through hard times. On his arrival the new schoolmaster, an admirer of Terence and Plautus, quickly teams up with Hoghton's players, and so impresses Hoghton that a career in 'playing', rather than as an unqualified schoolmaster, seems the obvious way forward. I partly base this last suggestion on the fact, unknown to Chambers and Hamer, that Thomas II not only took over Alexander's house at Lea but also his servants, in so far as they can be traced, except for Fulk Gyllom, who surfaces again ten years later as a witness for Sir Thomas Hesketh's son Robert, and appears to have become attached to the Heskeths, together with Alexander's musical instruments (cf. p. 32); that is, as already stated, I assume that Gyllom and Shakeshafte moved to Sir Thomas Hesketh's (perhaps after a short interval with Thomas Hoghton II), and that Alexander wanted them to go to Hesketh instead of staying in the Hoghton establishment because Thomas Hoghton's interest in players was uncertain, whereas Hesketh was a committed patron. (Had Sir Thomas Hesketh been wealthier than plain Thomas Hoghton, Esq., or better connected, one might have inferred that Hesketh would be better able to advance Gyllom's and Shakeshafte's general (rather than specifically theatrical) prospects. Not so: many contemporary records, including the *inquisition post mortem* of Sir Thomas Hesketh and of Thomas Hoghton II,[40] establish that the Hoghtons were at least as rich as the Heskeths, and probably much more so. An angry letter from Sir Richard Hoghton, son of Thomas and nephew of Alexander, claimed that 'my father (being captain of Amounderness) had the first place in the field and the last off, when this county was first charged with the trained band';[41] after the Earl of Derby and his family, the Hoghtons were second to none in Lancashire. Consequently, Gyllom and Shakeshafte must have been recommended to Hesketh because he had a special interest in which Thomas Hoghton could not rival him: an interest in players.)

Had Alexander Hoghton's will been our only reason for connecting the 'schoolmaster in the country' with Lancashire, we would have to give up at this point. The existence of other Shakeshaftes in Lancashire would make it unlikely that Alexander's servant was *not* a local man. Even though, in the hundreds of Hoghton and Hesketh documents that I have examined, from the 1560s to the 1620s, I have come across no other trace of a 'servant' called William Shakeshafte, to argue that Shakeshafte was Shakespeare simply because the names are similar and both men were players, would be irresponsible. Establish a link between Stratford and the Hoghtons, however, in the person of John Cottom – an obvious 'referee' for Shakespeare if he was indeed 'in his younger years a schoolmaster in the country' – and the situation changes entirely. Not one of Hamer's arguments rules out the possibility that Shakeshafte was Shakespeare; on the other hand, Shakespeare's later connections with the Hoghtons and their associates make Alexander Hoghton's mention of William Shakeshafte – in a section of his will concerned with 'players' – a clue that it would be irresponsible to ignore.

(c) Alexander Hoghton's will (1581), continued

Shortly before Alexander Hoghton made his will, on 3 August 1581, the situation of English Catholics had worsened dramatically. The government decided to tighten procedures against recusants, and issued a new Ecclesiastical Commission in June 1580; new anti-Catholic legislation 'to retain the Queen's Majesty's subjects in due obedience' received the royal assent on 18 March 1581, at the very time when many captured priests (including John Cottom's brother, Thomas) were being interrogated.[42] Lancashire was known to be a hotbed of Catholicism, and, since many Catholics 'conformed' publicly and harboured priests privately, was seen as a serious problem by the government. 'Even the magistrates and law officers of the county were repeatedly reported to the Council as being mostly temporizers in religion or otherwise recusants.'[43] Catholics were heavily fined if they did not conform; many were imprisoned and tortured, and, in the Queen's last years, many dozens were executed. There were informers everywhere.

As will be seen from Appendix A (p. 139 ff.), several of Alexander Hoghton's closest friends were Catholics. In 1580, according to *The de Hoghton Estate*,'[44] the Jesuit Campion had visited and preached in 'the house' (at Lea?), and the following year it was raided on that account. The phrasing of Alexander's will ('the communion of saints and fellowship of all the company of heaven') confirms that he was a practising Catholic – which helps to explain why he took special pains at this time to protect his family and servants, all of whom were presumably Catholics as well. 'I have already, by sufficient conveyance in the law ... disposed [of] all my manors [etc.]' he says, near the beginning of his will, and this turns out to be no idle statement. The will refers to a deed of 20 July 1580 that established all of Alexander's manors, lands etc. upon his brother Thomas. In addition we learn from a bill of complaint (DL1.127 W7) by George Warburton, gent., and Elizabeth his wife, 'late wife of Alexander Hoghton, Esq.', not only that Alexander's widow married again soon after his death – the bill is dated 26 May 1582 – but also that Alexander had bestirred himself on 2 and 3 August, 1581. The bill mentions several indentures made by Alexander on these two days (and of course his will dates from 3 August as well): in these he made over various properties to Bartholomew Hesketh, Esq., and Thomas Hesketh of Gray's Inn, gent., the brothers of his wife Elizabeth, 'upon special confidence and trust' that when Elizabeth would request her brothers to convey these properties to her, they would do so. But no, they refused; and when brother Thomas asked Elizabeth to let him see one of the indentures and she unwisely delivered it to him, he refused to return it.

Exactly what lay behind these legal manoeuvres is not clear. Alexander may have wished to protect his widow against fortune-hunters, or against Thomas II, the next head of the family if she produced no heir. The family's Catholicism must have been another factor; like Thomas I, Alexander may simply have wished to disperse the family's properties among reliable friends or retainers, to forestall possible confiscations by the government.

Several other points in Alexander's will require some additional comment. First, his 'servants'. He uses the word loosely, as did others at this time, to include (i) those 'hired with me for yearly wages', (ii) tenants, and other feudal retainers. Some of his servants might be 'gentlemen', as was Thomas Barton, his steward, the younger son of a wealthy neighbour (cf. p. 17), not household servants; we are not even entitled to assume that all of his 'servants' lived in his house. Nevertheless it is interesting that twenty-nine male servants are named just before Alexander lists his proposed annuities, and that when Thomas II died in 1589 about thirty men issued from Lea Hall and helped to defend him. Not too much should be read into these figures (the thirty included some visitors, and the twenty-nine may well have excluded very junior servants), except that they help to indicate that Alexander Hoghton kept a considerable establishment. If most of his household servants were married, and if we add to them Hoghton tenants who lived in or near Lea or Hoghton, Alexander might well have employed one or more schoolmasters to teach their children.

We are chiefly concerned with one servant, William Shakeshafte, and with the possibility that he worked for Alexander as school-master, or as a teaching assistant. I have suggested that John Shake-speare's difficulties in Stratford may partly explain his son's departure, at the age of fifteen or sixteen (cf. pp. 20, 115); it remains to ask whether Alexander Hoghton had a special reason for engaging a schoolmaster at about this time. And one is not hard to find: he succeeded his brother, Thomas I, as head of the family in June 1580, and this will have brought new responsibilities. It may be that he made Lea Hall and Hoghton Tower his residences before 1580, since Thomas I, 'the fugitive', was apparently declared an out-law, and Thomas's only son, a priest, was not eligible to succeed;[45] at any rate, Alexander took over in June 1580, if not before, and, like other Catholic squires in Lancashire, would look for a Catholic school-master to preserve the children in his domains from the taint of Protestantism. (The informer who wrote to Burghley about Catholic squires in Lancashire with unlicensed schoolmasters stated or implied that these teachers – like priests – lived with the squires (cf. p. 20); one wonders why Alexander Hoghton, who names so many servants in his will, asked Sir Thomas Hesketh 'to be friendly unto Fulk Gillam and William Shakeshafte *now dwelling with me*'. Does this not suggest that the two men dwelt with him in a special capacity, unlike some of his other servants? Were the two bracketed, perhaps, because they plied the same trade, as schoolmaster and assistant?) Here it is worth repeating that Alexander Hoghton's family and friends seem to have had an active interest in education; in addition to their unlicensed schoolmasters in Lancashire, they even played their part abroad. Thomas I greatly assisted his friend, the later Cardinal Allen, in founding Douay College.[46] It is almost inconceivable that Thomas's brother, Alexander, did not maintain a schoolmaster when he became head of the family, considering that his less affluent relatives thought it their duty to do so.

Those who have previously discussed Alexander Hoghton's will appear not to have known that a deed of 20 July 1580, in which he made preliminary arrangements for the annuities to his servants (as he explained in his will: cf. p. 135), still survives. I have transcribed this deed – an essential document in the Shakeshafte story – and some readers may prefer to examine it now (p. 141 ff.), before I attempt to explain Alexander Hoghton's quixotic instructions when he lay on his death-bed.

It will be recalled that Thomas Hoghton I died abroad in June 1580. The news quickly reached England, and Alexander Hoghton (the heir to the family's vast estates) and Thomas Hoghton II (Alexander's half-brother, and the next heir, since Alexander was childless) met on 20 July 1580 together with their legal advisers to make provisions for the future. Alexander and Thomas II reaffirmed the family's earlier arrangements (cf. p. 9), and, said Alexander (p. 136), agreed to 'the establishing of all my manors lands & tenements after divers remainders upon the said Thomas & the heirs male of his body lawfully begotten'. The 'remainders' included the sum of £16 13s 4d, to be paid annually from the family's Withnell rents into a special fund; and the deed that set up this fund, also executed on 20 July 1580, is the document that helps – a little – to explain Alexander's thinking in his will. The fund was set up 'for divers good & reasonable causes & considerations', with Thomas Fleetwood and Robert Talbot as administrators, or trustees; yet whereas the deed of 1580 is quite specific in detailing the sources of the annual income of £16 13s 4d, viz. twenty-five tenancies in Withnell, it remains silent as to its ultimate destination. For whose benefit has this income been set aside? We are not told. More than that: Alexander Hoghton declares that unless he indicates in his last will and testament how long the fund is to continue, it will not come into being at all.

What are we to make of these arrangements, so specific in some respects and so unspecific in others? Read together with Alexander's will of 1581, the deed of 1580 appears to have earmarked an annual income of £16 13s 4d for annuities to be paid to Alexander's servants after his decease. Wealthy masters not uncommonly left annuities to their servants (cf. pp. 36, 47), and the normal procedure would be to name beneficiaries in one's will. Alexander, it seems, wished to have a fund available to reward faithful service; if he chose not to make use of it when he came to make his will, the fund reverted to the Hoghton estate.

It is important for our purposes that Alexander Hoghton's plans were so undefined in July 1580 that he contemplated the possibility of not leaving any annuities whatever. He had not decided that certain servants *must* be rewarded with an annuity – which, of course, might imply that William Shakeshafte, if already seen by Alexander as a future annuitant, entered his service some time before July 1580. On taking over as head of the family, Alexander simply reserved an annual sum, to be used if and when he chose to reward his servants in a particular way. Alexander, we may assume, did not intend to die a mere thirteen months later; and if, like most human beings, he hoped to live on for many more years, he left himself the option of giving annuities to servants not yet employed by him in 1580.

As far as we can follow it, the deed of July 1580 makes sense. A year later, however, when Alexander dictated his will, the arrangements laid down for his annuities are unusual and, I think, perplexing. Why should the fund continue for the duration of thirty lives, when only eleven of the thirty named individuals are to receive payments? One might suppose that when the eleven have died, the two trustees or their estates will receive the £16 13s 4d per annum until all thirty 'servants' are dead – except that Alexander carefully states that it is 'not intended nor meant that any profit or commodity should grow thereby unto the said Thomas and Robert [the trustees] or their heirs' (cf. p. 137). It could be that when one of the eleven dies, the remaining twenty-nine will benefit, and so on; if that was what he meant, Alexander could have said it more clearly. This, indeed, seems the likeliest explanation to me, even though some of the 'annuitants' might then die before the eleven who are to benefit first. There is a trace of what George Eliot called 'the dead hand' here: Alexander, on his death-bed, so arranges things that some of his servants only benefit on certain conditions – from one another's deaths. Even if I am wrong in thinking that all thirty servants could ultimately benefit, the hypothesis that just eleven servants will receive annuities introduces the same ghoulish touch, that legatees in a sense have to look forward to one another's deaths: how much any single servant receives is to be a gamble, and the survivor takes all. In the hundreds of Elizabethan wills that I have seen I have not come across any other in which annuities grow in this way. (The Queen and others granted some posts 'in reversion', which also involved a benefit resulting from someone else's death, and an element of gambling; Alexander's annuities could have been inspired by this practice.) Alexander himself recognised that his annuities were most unusual: he foresaw that his provisions might be challenged 'in the Chancery' (cf. p. 137), and he concluded this section of his will with a solemn adjuration. 'And it is my especial desire, and I straitly charge [the two trustees] as they will answer me before God that they see my will in this point duly and truly executed' (p. 137). As I see it, the will is unclear and eccentric where the annuities are concerned, and could have caused all kinds of trouble. To give one more example: had Sir Thomas Hesketh helped Fulk Gillam and William Shakeshafte to some other 'good master', as Alexander Hoghton requested, Fulk and William might have moved away from Lancashire, and the trustees would then have found it difficult to pay them their annual dues.

The next point in Alexander Hoghton's will that needs some attention is the implicit claim that he kept 'players'. The Banqueting Hall at Hoghton Tower would have been an ideal place for theatrical performances, both in size and shape. One can easily imagine the minstrels' gallery at one end as an upper stage, with a main stage or acting area below it; equally, the gallery might have been reserved for some of the spectators, and a stage could have been fitted up at the other end of the hall. (There are detailed descriptions of this hall, and of other major rooms at Hoghton Tower, in *The Victoria History of the County of Lancaster*, 1911, VI, 43 ff.). Being 52 ft 6 in long and 26 ft wide, this imposing hall could accommodate an audience of 150 or so – but how often would Alexander Hoghton wish to throw open his home and put up with so much inconvenience? I have already stated my belief that the players would have had a dual function: Alexander bequeathed 'play clothes', or a stock of apparel for theatrical performances, and, like other actors at this time, his men seem to have been musicians as well. Yet one wonders inevitably about the economics and professionalism of the Hoghton players – and I am driven to the conclusion that, since no records survive indicating that they travelled to act elsewhere, music-making will have been their first duty at home and acting a side-line. Music-lovers like to hear music whenever possible, whereas theatre-lovers cannot expect new plays every few days, and will soon weary of the old ones. The lifestyle at Hoghton Tower, I believe, will have resembled that of Sir Peter Leigh of Lyme, who died in 1590 (he was the grand-father of Sir Richard Hoghton's brother-in-law): 'Living at Lyme *en prince,* Sir Peter was not satisfied with distributing his game and venison bountifully to gratify his friends' palates, but he aspired to please their ears also by maintaining a party of musicians, who, while they generally exercised their quality at home, occasionally visited his neighbours' houses and enlivened them with the strains of their minstrelsy.' Sir Peter's men were paid for making music, and also now and then for performing plays, and it is reasonable to assume that the same men did both.[47] I would guess that in such a household as Alexander Hoghton's the 'players' would also be very competent musicians who occasionally produced interludes or other shows; and that where the environment was already so favourable, the arrival of a genuine enthusiast, an instinctive Shake-scene – let us call him William Shakeshafte – would act like thunder on a bed of eels. If simple Mr Yates could carry all before him at Mansfield Park, what might not a brilliant young schoolmaster have achieved at Hoghton Tower?

Alexander Hoghton could not have lived on the same scale at Lea Hall, his other residence. (In his will he described himself as 'of the Lea,[48] in the county of Lancaster', either because he had lived at Lea for most of his life, until he succeeded Thomas I in 1580, or because he actually made his will at Lea; but Lea Hall does not compare with Hoghton Tower in size or splendour.) This second home is still part of the Hoghton estate; it was modernised in the eighteenth century, however, and extensively rebuilt. Oliver Baker described it as follows in in 1937:

> As seen from the highway it promises no sign of antiquity, but rather resembles a large farm-house of the last century, but on the other side towards the Ribble its tall elevation is much more interesting. There it is easy to recognize that the ornamental timbers of an oak-framed manor-house such as are more perfectly preserved at Samlesbury ... [and] especially at Rufford, have here at Lea been almost entirely replaced by Queen Anne or Georgian brickwork.
>
> At the eaves the medieval coving of plaster and oak ribs is still in position undisturbed, and has below it a very massive wall-plate beam carved with the billet moulding.[49]

Baker added that there 'must have been originally a very noble great chamber', which is 'now divided into various bedrooms and passages'. Players could therefore have entertained Alexander Hoghton at Lea Hall, even though there was less accommodation here for servants than at Hoghton Tower.

How old was Alexander Hoghton when he died? *A Short Guide to Hoghton Tower* states that he was born in 1500 – if so, he was older than Thomas Hoghton I, who succeeded to the estate before him and was 'born 1518'. I think that Alexander must have been born later. The covenant for Alexander's first marriage (to Dorothy, daughter of Richard Ashton, Esq., of Middleton) is dated 1 February 1565, and men do not often marry for the first time at the age of 65.[50] At any rate Alexander's second wife, Elizabeth, must have been quite young when he died, for according to Ormerod's *Cheshire*,[51] she was the mother of many children by her next husband, George Warburton of the Lodge in Crowley. She appears to have died in 1599: a release by Richard Hoghton of Hoghton Tower, Esq., to William Hilton (i.e. Hulton) of Hilton, Esq. refers to the death 'of Mrs Warburton, who had been wife of Mr Alexander Hoghton', and is dated 16 June 1599 (DDPt.4).

This chapter on the Hoghtons of Hoghton Tower must not close without mentioning a long-standing tradition that William Shakespeare worked for the family for two years in his youth. Sir Bernard de Hoghton, the 14th Baronet, and his mother (Mrs Richard Adams, formerly the wife of Sir Cuthbert), both assure me that, as they understand it, this tradition was handed down within the family from father to son, and, though undocumented, goes back 'for generations'. Could this be a tradition of the genus 'Queen Elizabeth slept here'? I think not, for several reasons. (1) Sir Cuthbert de Hoghton, the 12th Baronet (who died in 1958) succeeded Sir James, who lived from 1851 to 1938, and Sir James's father, Sir Henry Bold Hoghton, was born in 1799. Going back only two generations from Sir Cuthbert we reach a point in time preceding the first publication of Alexander Hoghton's will (in 1860). (2) Alexander's references in his will to William Shakeshafte were not connected with Shakespeare until 1937, when Oliver Baker first suggested this possibility.[52] In other words, going back just one generation from Sir Cuthbert we reach a point when the world at large did not connect Shakespeare and the Hoghtons: the family tradition antedates what we may call 'scholarly interest'. (3) Indeed, the family seems not to have been aware that 'William Shakeshafte' might be Shakespeare, until very recent times. Neither J. H. Lumby's *A Calendar of the Deeds and Papers in the Possession of Sir James de Hoghton, Bart.* (1936) nor George C. Miller's *Hoghton Tower* (1948) mentions William Shakeshafte. Miller actually quoted the passage from Alexander Hoghton's will concerning 'my instruments belonging to musics and all manner of play clothes', yet stopped there, omitting Fulk Gillam and William Shakeshafte.[53] This proves, I think, that the family tradition and 'scholarly interest' in William Shakeshafte are entirely independent of one another. (4) Mrs Adams, formerly the wife of Sir Cuthbert de Hoghton, remembers that when she married Sir Cuthbert, in 1944, the tradition that Shakespeare served the Hoghtons in his youth was already talked about in the family, before Alan Keen appeared on the scene. This again confirms that the family tradition and 'scholarly interest' in Shakeshafte are independent of one another. (5) Although Chambers, and some earlier biographers, believed that Shakespeare could have started his theatrical career as one of Lord Strange's Men, no one seems to have thought of Shakespeare as resident in rural Lancashire before he joined Lord Strange's men, until Alexander Hoghton's will came to notice; that is, no one apart from the Hoghtons and the Heskeths (cf. p. 34). And how would the Hoghtons have dreamed up something so inherently improbable, unsupported by any recorded evidence of Shakespeare in Lancashire – unless, perchance, it was true?

[29]

Family traditions must always be treated with caution. When the other available evidence appears to connect Shakespeare and Alexander Hoghton, however, and one hears subsequently – as happened to me – that a family tradition going back 'for generations' links Shakespeare in his youth with the Hoghtons, I find this encouraging. While I do not claim that the connection is proved beyond all possible doubt several quite distinct kinds of evidence now point in the same direction.

I. Alexander Hoghton. This portrait, said to be of Alexander Hoghton, is in the
Banqueting Hall, Hoghton Tower

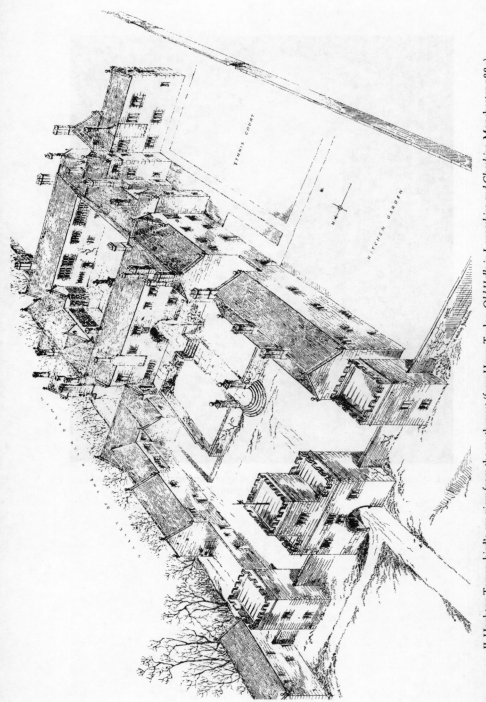

II. Hoghton Tower: bird's-eye view from the south-west (from Henry Taylor, *Old Halls in Lancashire and Cheshire*, Manchester 1884)

Hoghton Tower today: III. (*above*) the outer courtyard,
and IV. (*below*) the Banqueting Hall

Rufford Old Hall V. (*above*) sketch of the exterior in 1823,
and VI. (*below*) the great hall (from Taylor, *Old Halls*)

The great hall looking towards the dais

The great hall looking towards screen

F Hanson

VII. (*above*) Lea Hall, near Preston, from the south;
VIII. (*below*) the de Hoghton crest

MALGRE · LA · TORT

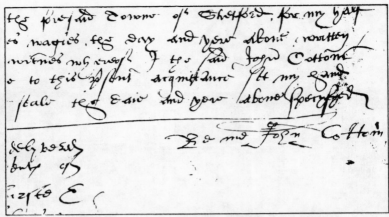

IX. John Cottom's signatures: (*a*) 1579 (from the Minutes and Accounts of the
Corporation of Stratford-upon-Avon, 21 December 1579)

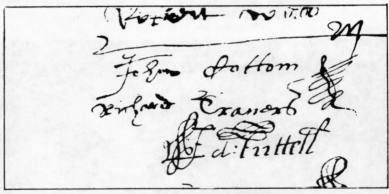

(*b, above*) 1606 (from an indenture, LRO, DDH 710),
and (*c, below*) 1613 (from BL, Harleian MS. 1437, fo. 100)

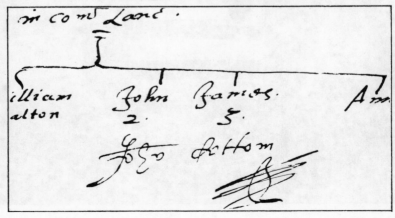

X. (*left*) Ferdinando Stanley, Lord Strange (fifth Earl of Derby), and XI. (*right*) Alice, Lady Strange, his wife

XII. William Stanley (sixth Earl of Derby)

III

━━━━◍◍◍◍◍◍◍◍━━━━

Sir Thomas Hesketh of Rufford

Thomas Hesketh of Rufford succeeded to the family estates on his father's death in 1539, and was knighted at Queen Mary's coronation in 1553. In 1557 he raised a hundred men to serve in the Scottish wars, was badly wounded at the siege of Leith, and later became High Sheriff of Lancashire, in 1563, under Queen Elizabeth. It is recorded at Rufford that 'in his latter days [he was] a notable good house-keeper, and benefactor to all men singular in any science, and [he] greatly repaired the houses at Martholme and Holmes Wood [Martholme Tower, near Great Harwood, and Holmes Wood Hall], and the Chapel at Rufford'.[1]

Anyone interested in Shakespeare and the Hoghton family will want to know more about Sir Thomas Hesketh of Rufford, a friend whose good-will Alexander Hoghton took for granted when disposing of his wordly possessions in 1581: if Thomas Hoghton II prefers not to maintain players then Hesketh 'shall have' Alexander's instruments and play-clothes; and, said Alexander, 'I most heartily require the said Sir Thomas to be friendly unto Fulk Gyllom and William Shakeshafte now dwelling with me, and either to take them unto his service or else to help them to some good master, as my trust is he will'. There must have been a special reason for recommending these two servants to Hesketh, whilst other servants remained with the Hoghtons. I have suggested that Alexander's will implies that he knew Hesketh to be a patron of players; that apart, five facts unknown to E. K. Chambers make it even more important to investigate the Heskeths of Rufford.

(1) The very unusual name 'Fulk Gyllom' appears in the Hesketh archives in 1591 and 1608. The typewritten index of the Hesketh collection in the Lancashire Record Office describes a feoffment of 1591 (T. Nelson to Robert Hesketh, Esq.; DDHe 11.93) that was witnessed, amongst others, by 'Foulke Gillard' (altered in the typescript to 'Gilland'). Reference to the original reveals that it reads 'ffoulke gillame'. A conveyance of 1608 (J. Haughton to Robert

Hesketh, Esq.; DDHe 28.44) was witnessed by 'ffoulke Gillam' ('Gillan' in the typewritten index). The 1608 signature is in a shaky hand, and does not resemble the earlier one: we may deduce that Gillam (as I shall call him henceforth) changed his handwriting over a period of eighteen years, or that the second signature belongs to another man, presumably the son of Fulk the first. Either way, Fulk Gillam seems to have become a servant of Sir Thomas Hesketh, as Alexander Hoghton requested, if only for a while – so it is likely that William Shakeshafte moved to Rufford as well. (Shakeshafte was named immediately after Gillam three times in Alexander's will, which confirms that the two men were somehow connected; compare also p. 24, 'now dwelling with me'. Robert Hesketh was the son and heir of Sir Thomas, who died in 1588.)

(2) Alan Keen cited in the *Times Literary Supplement*, 1955 (18 November, p. 689), an extract 'from the records of the Chester Midsomerday pageant' printed in the Record Society's *The Rolls of the Freemen of the City of Chester* (ed. J. H. E. Bennett, 1906): 'Oct. 15 [1595–96], Foulk Gillam s. of Thomas Gillam of Chester embroiderer [Broderer]'. From this it is clear, said Keen, that the two Gillams 'were both guild-players'. (I owe this reference to Mr J. J. Bagley). Mark Eccles added that 'a Fulk Gillam became a freeman in 1596' in Chester (*Shakespeare in Warwickshire*, 1961, p. 74).

(3) The inference that Gillam and Shakeshafte moved to Rufford for a while is borne out by the fate of the musical instruments. Sir Bernard de Hoghton said to me 'You must go to Rufford Old Hall and see the instruments.' The first time he said it I was preoccupied with other things and failed to grasp the significance of his remark. A year later, when we met again, he repeated it, and I thought I saw what he was driving at. 'What instruments?' I said. '*Our* instruments', was his reply. I knew that Sir Bernard knew that Alexander Hoghton bequeathed his instruments to his brother Thomas or to Sir Thomas Hesketh, but could it be proved, after four hundred years, that these were the Hoghton instruments? 'How do you *know* that they were your instruments?' The answer was stunningly simple. 'Because when my father saw them, many years ago, they were still marked with the de Hoghton crest.' He added that he had heard that the instruments were no longer on display at Rufford, and that he would like to know what had become of them – because 'we want our instruments back.' I replied that, yes, one would like to know what had become of them, but Alexander Hoghton did bequeath them to Sir Thomas Hesketh in 1581 and Sir Thomas's descendants might well dispute their ownership. The next day I drove to Rufford, where the Old Hall is now a National Trust

property. (Lord Hesketh presented it to the National Trust in 1936.) The officials here were most helpful; unhappily, though, they knew nothing about Sir Thomas's instruments.

It looked as if the evidence had survived intact at Rufford for almost four hundred years, and that I arrived just thirty or forty years too late to see it with my own eyes – most frustrating. Yet I was not the first 'Shakeshafte' sleuth to follow this trail. Alan Keen had written in 1954 that

> a fortuitous discovery was brought to my attention, one that suggested that at any rate the 'instrumentes belonging to mewsyckes' found their way from Lea Hall to Rufford. Shortly after I reached this stage in my quest, Lord Hesketh found at his home, Easton Neston, some old musical instruments which were among household effects moved some years previously from Rufford. These may well be some of those catalogued in an inventory, now in the County Records at Preston, of the goods of 'Robert Hesketh late of Rufforth' at 16 November 1620. The list of instruments includes 'vyolls, vyolentes, virginalls, sagbutts, howboies and cornetts, cithron, flute and taber pypes'. An assortment that would have well suited a small stage orchestra.[2]

So the instruments that Sir Cuthbert de Hoghton had seen before 1958, and on which he recognised the de Hoghton crest, might still be traced! The dowager Lady Hesketh (mother of the present Lord Hesketh) kindly wrote, in answer to my enquiry, that 'the musical instruments are in my son's house at Easton Neston, and have been there ever since my father-in-law brought them south from Rufford in the 20's.' Lord Hesketh later invited me to examine his instruments, most of which are now housed in the library at Easton Neston; several of them could be two or more centuries old (they have not been dated by experts). Not one, however, carried the de Hoghton crest. When I asked whether other instruments had survived, Lord Hesketh explained that when he was a boy, in the 1950s or early 1960s, a lot of old 'junk' had been put on sale locally, without a sale catalogue, and that it was not impossible that old instruments were accidentally sold off at the same time. Musical instruments aged four hundred years or so might well begin to come apart (some of the older ones at Easton Neston showed signs of this), and could all too easily be thought mere 'junk'.

That is as far as I have got with the musical instruments. Perhaps they were sold, or thrown out as rubbish. It is quite possible that they no longer exist. Yet just in case they do, I reproduce the de Hoghton crest (Plate VIII): if any reader finds this crest on an old musical instrument, I should be glad to hear from him. While we may never learn what song the sirens sang, I have not given up hope that we may yet recover an instrument to which William Shakeshafte sang.

(4) Before I visited Easton Neston the dowager Lady Hesketh had mentioned, in a letter, an 'odd fact about the Hesketh–Shakespeare connection', that 'there is a folk tradition of long standing at Rufford which links Shakespeare with the Hall'. I now asked about this tradition – how far back could it be traced? I was told that the late Mr Philip Ashcroft, a Rufford man, had been so intrigued by this local tradition that he had written a research paper about it. Alan Keen, I recalled, long ago met Philip Ashcroft, 'the founder of the Folk Museum' at Rufford, heard that there had been Ashcrofts at Rufford for centuries and was told of 'the oral tradition that William Shakespeare had been at the Hall as a young man' (*The Annotator*, p. 49 ff.). Ashcroft claimed 'that his mother had the tale from her father, Lawrence Alty; and that Alty, who can have had no special motive or inclination for fabricating such a tale, was born in Rufford in 1837. In Alty's day, no link between Shakespeare and Rufford had been recorded'.

(5) When Shakespeare and four colleagues acquired a half-interest in the Globe theatre in 1599, one of the two London merchants who assisted in the legal arrangements was a wealthy goldsmith, Thomas Savage. Leslie Hotson, having located Savage's will, announced in 1949 that Savage was a native of Rufford in Lancashire.

> When we find the player William Shakespeare in 1599 in London choosing as a trustee a man not only from Sir Thomas Hesketh's Lancashire village of Rufford – a speck on the map more than two hundred road-miles from London – but also related to the Rufford Heskeths by marriage, it clearly does not make [E. K. Chambers's 'William Shakeshafte' and his] conjectural identification look less interesting. To be sure, we may have here an astonishing coincidence and nothing more.... Perhaps means may be found to follow the clue.[3]

Had Hotson known about (1), (2), (3) and (4) he would have been all the more eager to 'follow the clue'. An excellent starting-point (I return later to Thomas Savage and his will) is a paper by W. G. Procter, 'The Manor of Rufford and the Ancient Family of the Heskeths'.[4] From this we learn that Sir Thomas was a Catholic, and – more unexpectedly – that he was 'put under arrest in A.D. 1581 as a "disaffected Papist"'; also, that his wife Alice and all her family connections were Catholics as well.

The information that Sir Thomas Hesketh was 'put under arrest' in 1581 – the very year of Alexander Hoghton's will – may explain

why William Shakeshafte soon moved on to other employment if, as
I believe, he accompanied Fulk Gillam to Rufford after Alexander's
death. How long Sir Thomas remained under arrest is not known; a
petition from him to be released is tentatively dated '1584?' in the
Calendar of State Papers Domestic (175.92), but this may refer to
another term of imprisonment. It is addressed to the Earl of
Leicester.

> Most humbly beseecheth your Honour Sir Thomas Hesketh, Knight.
> That whereas he is committed to the custody of Sir Edmond Trafford,
> Knight, Sheriff of the County of Lancaster, upon complaint made by
> one Thomas Hesketh his kinsman unto your Honour and others the
> Lords of Her Majesty's most honourable Privy Council. That for so
> much as he trusteth it hath appeared unto your Honour and their said
> lordships by the certificate of the said sheriff and others appointed for
> the examination of the said cause, that he is innocent in the most
> material matters of the said complaint, and only hath offended (as he
> thinketh) in that he hath been over-negligent to see the reformation of
> some in his family, for which he is right heartily sorry.... Sir Thomas
> protesteth both before God and your Honour to reform the same
> offence, in such sort, that those which are under his government,
> and will not from henceforth use themselves dutifully and obediently
> unto Her Majesty and her most godly laws in every respect, shall
> neither abide in his house nor have any favour at his hands, but all
> extremity.

Quite clearly, Sir Thomas had not suppressed Catholic worship in
his house, and now promised to do so. Sir Edmund Trafford was
sheriff of Lancashire in the regnal year 1579–80 and again in
1583–4, and therefore 1584 is a likely date for Sir Thomas's petition.
I should add immediately, though, that it seems improbable that he
remained in custody from 1581 to 1584: he acted as a witness to at
least one legal document in these years, and transacted other normal
business, authorising leases (8 December 1582; 16 April 1583) and
making indentures (1582).[5] His petition, indeed, suggests that he
may have been committed to Trafford during Trafford's term as
sheriff; if so, Sir Thomas was imprisoned twice, in 1581 and 1584.

Procter also quoted extracts from Sir Thomas Hesketh's will. No
bequests to Fulk Gillam or William Shakeshafte! However, those
who prepare abstracts of wills are not always interested in minor
bequests to servants, so it was necessary to find the original or an
early copy. I came across a copy of Sir Thomas's will quite by chance,
in Add. MS. 32,104, a huge collection of transcripts and abstracts of
Lancashire wills. This copy (of an original dated 20 June 1588)
transmits the names of several servants to whom Sir Thomas left
bequests and annuities, and states (near the end): 'Item I give to

Thurstan Knowles and other eight persons 40s. yearly during their lives'. Most unfortunately the copyist saved himself trouble and condensed the names of eight minor legatees, probably servants, as 'other eight persons', a short cut that would have been impossible in the original. The near-certainty that 'Thurstan Knowles' was actually Tristram Knowles (a Hesketh retainer who witnessed the 1591 feoffment together with Gillam, as well as many other Hesketh documents) confirmed that the copyist had worked in haste.

I knew that there was one other copy of Sir Thomas's will, in the Cheshire Record Office. About a year later, when I visited Chester, it was a relief to find that this copy is the fullest that survives, that it correctly identifies Sir Thomas's servant as Tristram Knowles, and that it names the 'eight persons' omitted from Add. MS. 32,104. There is no bequest to Fulk Gillam or William Shakeshafte.

It was disappointing, but not too surprising. Sir Thomas was under no obligation to leave bequests to all of his servants; Fulk Gillam would be seen as a comparative newcomer in the household, and he already enjoyed an annuity of 40s from his former master, Alexander Hoghton; as for Shakeshafte, in all probability Sir Thomas had already helped him to some other 'good master', as Hoghton had requested. The will nevertheless gives us other valuable information, about Sir Thomas's life and character, and about the style in which he lived. A typical Lancashire gentleman, Sir Thomas had fathered bastards and made provision for them in his will (like the Earl of Derby and Alexander Hoghton: cf. pp. 91, 136). To one, Thomas Hesketh, 'my bastard son, whom I acknowledge to be my real son, whatsoever the laws of this land do adjudge or deem to the contrary', he left land called 'the Carres' together with the Carr Moss, close to Rufford. Sir Thomas's second son was another Thomas – so here are two Thomas Heskeths of Rufford, either of whom could have been the husband of Thomas Savage's 'cousin Hesketh, widow, late wife of Thomas Hesketh of Rufforth' (cf. p. 144). I fancy that we hear Sir Thomas's *ipsissima verba* when he speaks of 'my bastard son', and again when he gives orders for his tomb in the chapel of Rufford.

> My will is that a tomb of stone shall be raised and made to stand one yard in height above the ground in the middle of the said chancel, of the length of two yards and in breadth four foot. And in the midst of it a slender wall, either of brick or stone. ... And my body to lie on the north side thereof, and the body of Alice my wife to lie on the south side of the same, when it shall please God to take us from this life. And upon the top of the said tomb both our bodies to be

wrought in proportion, of alabaster stone in such full manner and good sort as may every way answer our callings.

E. K. Chambers observed in 1944 that if William Shakeshafte passed from the service of Alexander Hoghton into that of Thomas Hoghton or Sir Thomas Hesketh 'he might very easily have gone on into that of Lord Strange'. Procter had previously noted that the *Derby Household Book* 'shows there was a considerable intimacy between the Derby and Hesketh families at this time'. He quoted several extracts: 'On Sunday [11 Oct. 1587], Mr Robert Hesketh at dinner'; 'On Thursday, My Lord and Lady Strange went to dinner at Rufford', etc. It should be added that the first wife of Sir Thomas Hesketh's son and heir, Robert, was Mary Stanley, daughter of Sir George Stanley of Cross Hall, a cousin of the Earl of Derby. She died in July 1586; Robert then married Blanche, daughter of Henry Twiford and 'relict of [blank] Stopforth [William Stopford], secretary to the Earl of Derby'.[6] The Heskeths of Rufford were indeed in close touch with the Earl of Derby's family. And they were also closely associated with the Hoghton family over a period of many years. Alexander Hoghton's wife, Elizabeth, was the daughter of Gabriel Hesketh of Aughton, and related to Sir Thomas Hesketh; her brother, Thomas Hesketh, was one of the executors of Alexander Hoghton's will in 1581 and of Sir Thomas Hesketh's in 1588. After the death of Robert Hesketh of Rufford, in 1620, his third wife and widow (Jane, daughter of Thomas Spencer of Rufford) married Sir Richard Hoghton of Hoghton Tower.

'Robert Hesketh', wrote Procter, 'appears, outwardly at any rate, to have conformed to the Church as by law established, but his mother and two brothers were strong Roman Catholics.' Thomas, Sir Thomas's second son, was known to be a recusant, and Richard, the third son (according to Procter: but see below) served with the Spanish army in Flanders (i.e. fighting against the English forces and their allies), and took part in a notorious conspiracy. On the death of Henry Stanley, the fourth Earl of Derby (in 1593), Richard Hesketh returned to England, urged on by a Jesuit priest

to encourage the earl's son and heir, Ferdinando, Lord Strange, to lay claim to the succession to the crown of England on the death of Elizabeth, on the ground that he was closely related to the Royal Family. Hesketh was commissioned to promise Spanish aid. The new earl, although at first probably inclined to entertain the proposal, as is thought by some, took fright when he found the Government spies had discovered the plot, and in order to save his own neck, threw Hesketh to the wolves. He was condemned, and executed at St. Albans on the 29th November A.D. 1593.[7]

This tragic story again shows how close the Heskeths were to the Earls of Derby – though the conspirator was actually Richard Hesketh of Aughton, and not Sir Thomas's son. A few months after Richard's execution, Ferdinando (the fifth Earl of Derby) died unexpectedly, and it was widely believed that he had been poisoned.

When Sir Thomas Hesketh's widow died in 1605 her principal heirs were Thomas and Richard Hesketh, 'my two younger sons'. She never alludes to Robert, the eldest son, in her will (nor does she mention Fulk Gillam or William Shakeshafte).[8] This may have been because Robert, unlike his parents, made his peace with the government and actively supported it. He was a J.P., he committed recusants, and he served as High Sheriff in 1600, the year after Sir Richard Hoghton, and again under James I.

Sir Thomas's religious sympathies, about which there can be little or no doubt, were again confirmed in 1949, when the Great Hall at Rufford had to be repaired. A secret chamber or 'priest's hole' was discovered during the rebuilding of the west gable; while the date of its construction is not known, other Lancashire families had such secret rooms built in the sixteenth century, and Sir Thomas is the owner of Rufford most likely to have ordered it.

The Great Hall will particularly interest students of 'Shakeshafte', since Sir Thomas Hesketh's 'players' must have performed in it. While not as large as the great Banqueting Hall at Hoghton Tower, which is lengthened by its minstrels' gallery, its magnificently-carved screen and other woodwork make it a most beautiful and impressive room.

> Forty-six feet six inches long, twenty-two feet six inches wide, and eighteen feet high to the wallplate, it has undergone scarcely any alteration since it was first built approximately five hundred years ago. While it follows the usual medieval plan for such a room, with the high table at one end, near the private wing, and the entrance and screen at the lower, or kitchen end, it possesses the unusual feature of a movable screen between 'speres', in place of the more customary fixed screen. Other examples of this arrangement were to be found at Ordsall Hall, Smithills Hall and Samlesbury Hall in Lancashire, and at Adlington Hall in Cheshire, but all these have been subsequently altered in one way or another and only at Rufford is the massive movable screen still in position. This screen is seven feet wide and is panelled on each side, the panels being elaborately carved with quatrefoils in circles and other late Gothic ornaments.[9]

Exactly how 'movable' the screen really was I cannot say, as it must weigh many hundredweights, perhaps tons. It is immediately clear, however, that actors would find it useful, either in its present position, or (if more spectators had to be crammed in) across a corner of the Hall: it could serve as the rear of a stage, and actors could retire behind it when they went 'off'.

Assuming that William Shakeshafte, together with Fulk Gillam and Alexander Hoghton's musical instruments, took the road to Rufford (some twelve miles from Hoghton Tower), how long did he stay? A few months at most, if Shakeshafte was Shakespeare. This could have been because Sir Thomas Hesketh's household needed no additional schoolmaster or player while he was in custody, or because Sir Thomas's players, like Alexander Hoghton's would be musicians first and actors only now and then – whereas Shakeshafte, we may assume, wished to specialise in drama. Alexander Hoghton had asked Sir Thomas 'to be friendly' to Shakeshafte and, if necessary, to help him to 'some good master'. The obvious patron for Shakeshafte, in Sir Thomas's eyes, would be the Earl of Derby or Lord Strange, whose professional players were not home-based but toured the land; and, as I explain in chapters VI and IX, there are good reasons for believing that William Shakespeare served in the 1580s as a retainer of Lord Strange. If Shakeshafte was Shakespeare, he visited or lived in Stratford in 1582 – he married Anne Hathaway in November, and their daughter Susanna (born in May 1583) will have been conceived in August 1582, with or without a previous troth-plighting ceremony. The Shakespeare twins followed in 1585 – so we may infer that their father either worked in Stratford from 1582 to c. 1585 (in John Shakespeare's business?) or belonged to a travelling company and returned home for occasional visits, as he did later from London. Sir Thomas Hesketh could have recommended his talented player to Lord Strange in 1582 or some years later, in 1585 or 1586.

IV

John Cottom of Tarnacre

> a pure pedantic schoolmaster, sweeping his living from the posteriors
> of little children, and hath no thing good in him.
>
> (Ben Jonson of John Owen)

According to T. W. Baldwin, John Cottom the Stratford school-master was the brother of the priest Thomas Cottam, and therefore the son of Lawrence Cottam of Dilworth and Tarnacre.[1] The brothers, John and Thomas, both graduated from Brasenose College, Oxford, and, said Baldwin, 'in view of the Brasenose records for the two, this identification becomes certain.' As John Cottom is an essential link in the chain that connects William Shakespeare of Stratford and Alexander Hoghton's 'William Shake-shafte', we had better make sure that Baldwin's identification can be relied on. I shall try to summarise a complicated argument as briefly as possible.

(1) John Cottom, 'late of London', succeeded Thomas Jenkins as Stratford's school-master in 1579. Cottom had taken his B.A. on 19 June 1566 (the same year as Jenkins, another Oxford graduate); and he stayed in Stratford till 1581 or 1582. An unnamed Stratford teacher was licensed on 31 January 1582, so it was probably at this time that Cottom was succeeded by Alexander Aspinall, another Lancashire man, who had matriculated at Brasenose in 1566 (the year Cottom left).

(2) Thomas Cottam was born in 1549, graduated B.A. from Brasenose in 1569, M.A. in 1572, and had gone abroad to become a Catholic priest by May 1575. He returned to England and was captured in June 1580, and arraigned together with Campion in November 1581. 'The trials of Campion and these companions were notorious; and equally notorious was the execution of Thomas Cottam, on May 30, 1582.' 'The brevity of John Cottom's career at Stratford is now easily explained ... Since John Cottom was a brother of Thomas Cottam, the city fathers of Stratford had very good reason for dismissing him shortly before January 31, 1582.'

[40]

(3) Thomas Cottam was a close friend of Robert Debdale, who on 4 June 1580 'commended Cottom to his parents at Shottery, and was sending by him certain tokens, etc. Though Cottam and the note were captured, he had intended to visit the Stratford neighbourhood. . . . Since John Cottom, then schoolmaster at Stratford, was the elder brother of Thomas Cottam, we see one of the prime motivations for the visit.'

(4) At Thomas Cottam's trial, he was urged to confess 'a certain sin committed in the [London] fish or meat market some four years ago'. Thomas protested that he, 'not having for these seven years past been in London', could not have sinned as was alleged. The accusers then affirmed 'that it was not Father Cottam but a brother of his who had committed the offence in question'. And, Baldwin reminds us, John Cottom was described as 'late of London' in 1579. This again helps to identify the Stratford schoolmaster as Thomas Cottam's brother.

(5) Baldwin also copied a useful (but slightly misleading) entry from Joseph Gillow's *Biographical Dictionary*. John and Thomas Cottam were the sons of

> Lawrence Cottam of Dilworth and Tarnaker, gent., [son of William Cottom of Dilworth,] and his wife Ann, daughter of Mr Brewer, or Brewerth, of Brindle, Co. Lancaster, who after her husband's death married William Ambrose, of Ambrose Hall, in Woodplumpton, gent.
>
> This ancient family had been seated at Dilworth for many generations, and returned a pedigree at St George's Visitation of Lancashire in 1613. The martyr's brother, John Cottom, succeeded to the estates, and resided at Tarnaker. Both he and his wife Catherine, daughter of Mr Dove, of Birtwood, in Essex, frequently appear in the Recusant Rolls with their only child, Priscilla. . . . Though other members of the family appear in the Recusant Rolls, Fr Cottam's parents were Protestants.

'About John Cottom', Baldwin concluded prophetically, 'considerable [sic] could and should be learned.'

It will not have escaped the lynx-eyed reader that Baldwin's evidence for identifying the Stratford schoolmaster and John Cottom of Tarnacre is circumstantial, and not 'proof absolute'. The identification being so important for my argument, can we build on Baldwin's brilliant suggestion (which was made, it should be remembered, before he could have read E. K. Chambers on 'William Shakeshafte'), and prove it beyond all reasonable doubt? Yes, we can: the Stratford schoolmaster's signature survives in the town's archives, and I have found two documents signed by John Cottom of

Tarnacre (Plate IX). We must keep in mind, of course, that (a), the Stratford signature, dates from 1579, whereas (b), from an indenture in the Lancashire Record Office, was written twenty-seven years later, and (c), from Harleian MS. 1437, thirty-four years later. After so many years Cottom switched to a capital 'C' in secretary hand, but several distinctive features remain as in (a): Cottom never joins an 'o' to the following letter; the final minim stroke in 'm' goes a fraction lower than the preceding one ((a) and (b)); and there is a characteristic horizontal line through the 'J'. Separated by such a span of years, Cottom's signatures are very much alike (as much so as Shakespeare's three signatures of 1612 and 1613, or the three in his will), and support Baldwin's argument that the Stratford schoolmaster and John Cottom of Tarnacre are one and the same man — which I have queried only because so much depends upon it.

We must now see what more can be learned about John Cottom of Tarnacre. Baldwin mentions that his will, 'made in 1616, appears to survive'. I have located and transcribed the will (Appendix A, p. 144), which is disappointingly short. Very much the same information about Cottom's daughter, and her husband and children, appears in Harleian MS. 1437, fo. 100, the pedigree prepared in 1613 by Richard St George, the Norroy King of Arms (Appendix B, p. 148). For further information about his parents, we are indebted to Tom C. Smith's *History of the Parish of Ribchester* (1890).

> Lawrence Cottam, of The High House [Dilworth, Ribchester], gent., married Anne Brewer, of Brindle, and by her had issue, sons, John, who apparently died in his father's life-time; Thomas; and Richard. He was buried at Ribchester, Jan. 17, 1619. His widow afterwards married William Ambrose, of Woodplumpton, gent. At the *inq.p.m.*, held in 1619, Lawrence Cottam was declared to be seized of a messuage and sixteen acres of land in Dilworth, held of Sir R. Hoghton, in free and common socage. (p. 242)

Sixteen acres may not sound a lot, but Lawrence Cottam is thought to have made over some Tarnacre property to John much earlier, probably when John left Stratford in 1581 or 1582. More significant than this (I think) misleading glimpse of Lawrence Cottam's financial position (cf. p. 44 for John Cottom's finances) is the link established here with the Hoghton family.

Neither John Cottom's will nor the 1613 pedigree reveals that he actually had three daughters. I learned this from litigation, between John Cottom and William Walton, gent. (father-in-law of John Cottom's daughter Priscilla), concerning the will of James Cottam (John's brother, not mentioned in Smith's *Ribchester*, who died in 1594):

And this deponent further saith that the said complainant [John Cottom] had three daughters at the time of the death of the said James Cottam, as namely Priscilla, Mary and Martha. And also saith that the said Priscilla is now wife to Thomas Walton, son to the defendant [William Walton] as the thinketh, and that Mary is now wife to Mr William Duddell, and also that Martha was married to one James Ellis and is now deceased. And further saith that the said complainant, after the death of the said James, entered as executor upon the goods and chattels of the said James Cottam. . . .[2]

The 'deponent' is Thomas Parkinson of Tarnacre, husbandman, aged three score and three years or thereabouts, who had been present at the making of James Cottam's will. I assume that Mary, the wife of William Duddell, died without issue before John Cottom made his will in 1616, and therefore received no bequest. As we shall see, though, William Duddell had interesting connections with the Hoghtons and their circle (as had the Waltons) – and helps to give us a clearer picture of John Cottom's social position.

From *Cottom v. Walton*, referred to above, we learn that John Cottom impressed those who knew him as a man of considerable wealth. William Walton alleged that when his son Thomas and Priscilla Cottom were to be married, John Cottom promised a portion of £200 (£40 remained unpaid); also that when James Cottam (John's brother) died in 1594, he left very considerable bequests to Priscilla, which her father (James' executor) had withheld; and further, that when Priscilla's marriage articles were drawn up, John Cottom had fraudulently inserted a clause that her £200 was in full satisfaction of all bequests to her (i.e. included James Cottam's bequests), whereas the Waltons thought that Priscilla's £200 was her marriage portion. John Cottom's original bill of complaint no longer survives, but we can reconstruct his very different version of these financial transactions from the interrogatories drawn up on his behalf. He claimed that he offered a marriage portion for Priscilla consisting of one third of his land at his death, or alternatively a sum of money at the time of the marriage. James Ellis, Cottom's son-in-law, aged 50 or thereabouts (5 James I), deposed that he wrote the articles of agreement when Priscilla was married, and that Walton 'did then desire rather to have a portion of money in hand than to stay and expect the complainant's [Cottom's] death'. So the Waltons 'did then receive the same sum in full satisfaction of her the said Priscilla her filial or child's portion and portion of lands, other than such as it shall please the complainant upon his fatherly goodness to bestow upon her, as it is set down in the th' articles of agreement'. That Walton took the money is clear because he 'at that time acknowledged a statute for money borrowed', which had to be repaid. Ellis remembered this 'because he was with the complainant [Cottom] when he did discharge the statute in the Office of Statutes in Holborn for the defendant [i.e. for Walton, by paying Priscilla's portion]'. John Cottom's interrogatories also claimed that Priscilla's portion was to be £160, and that William Walton entreated him, 'upon a vainglorious mind ... to set down in the said articles the sum of two hundreth pounds, and did plainly agree that £160 thereof only should be paid [i.e. as the marriage portion], and to that intent acknowledged the receipt of £40'; and Ellis explained that when he wrote the articles of agreement Walton asked to have £160 'blotted out', so that 'it might be reported both for his credit and his son's that his son [here the MS. is mutilated, but presumably it read "received two"] hundred pounds with a wife'.

A seventeenth-century abstract of James Cottam's will, in Add. MS. 32,115, states that 'he gives one half of all his goods, chattels, leases and debts unto Jane his wife, and the other half he gives to his brother John Cottam and his children. And he makes Jane his wife and John Cottam his said brother his executors.'[3] Jane Brown, wife of George Brown of Tarnacre, gent., subsequently deposed that she knew James Cottam, deceased, 'who was her late husband', but 'she knoweth not what part or portion ... was given, bequeathed or devised unto Priscilla'.[4] We shall probably never know whether Priscilla's portion included her share of James Cottam's estate, but what is clear is that Walton thought John Cottom capable of giving each of his daughters £200 without paying out what they had inherited from their uncle; Walton, in short, believed Cottom to be an affluent man. And even if we accept Cottom's own account of these transactions, we cannot escape the inference that he was living very comfortably: supposing that Priscilla's £160 included her share of James Cottam's estate, this sum was only her 'child's portion' and might be added to when John Cottom made his will, 'upon his fatherly goodness'. Since John Cottom treated his three daughters as equals, he could not have been worth much less than £1,000 at the time of Priscilla's marriage. And at the time of his death, the bequests in his will (cf. p. 144) suggest a similar or larger sum. William Walton, his oldest grandson, is to inherit his lands and leases in Tarnacre and Sowerby, but has to give £400 to his sister and two younger brothers. It is not clear whether William will become the owner after his mother, as her heir, or whether Priscilla is to inherit all lands, leases etc. other than those in Tarnacre and Sowerby, which will go immediately to William; it is a fair inference, though, that John Cottom's estate was worth more than £1,000 in 1616 (when, as we learn from his inventory, a horse cost about £3 and a chair one shilling). And Cottom had probably paid the dowries for his three daughters long before this – another considerable sum.

The discovery of James Cottam, a brother of John and Thomas hitherto unknown to students of the family, helps to solve a problem that long puzzled me. Why should John, if he was the eldest son of a well-to-do family that returned a pedigree, choose to become a schoolmaster? I suspect that James was really the eldest son, and that John and Thomas were sent to university because they would have to earn their own living. James's widow deposed in 1608 that she was 'three score years or thereabouts'; ladies rarely make themselves out to be older than they really are, so I deduce that she was born in 1548 or earlier. Edward Gregson also deposed that he had been James Cottam's servant for twenty-six years; assuming that he served till James died in 1594, he must have begun in 1568, and we may reasonably guess that by 1568, or earlier, James had set up house on his own. Gregson also supplied a list of the many leases held by James Cottam at the time of his death, which shows that James was wealthier then one would expect of a mere gentleman's younger son, in his father's lifetime.[5] The evidence is only circumstantial, but suggests that James was the eldest son and that John (who took his B.A. in 1566, and must have been born around 1547) turned to schoolmastering because he expected James to succeed his father. In 1594, however, John and his daughters inherited half of James's estate, and John became his father's heir presumptive. That probably explains how a schoolmaster, who had earned £20 a year at Stratford, could give such considerable 'portions' to each of his three daughters.

Cottom v. Walton provides many fascinating insights into the schoolmaster's later life. William Walton alleged that, for seven years after Priscilla's marriage, John Cottom and James Ellis, his son-in-law, had had free lodging, food and drink, for themselves and their horses, at Walton's expense. Mrs Walton thought Priscilla's father an expensive nuisance, who visited too often (Thomas and Priscilla lived with Thomas's parents); but Katherine Walmisley, widow, deposed that Cottom and Ellis lay divers times at Walton's house, and had meat, drink and lodging there, 'sometimes for a night, but never a week together at one time'. On Cottom's side it was alleged that William Walton beat Priscilla, pulled her hair, and threatened to tie her up with ropes. We hear that Walton ordered his son Thomas to quit his house, with Priscilla and all her family; Thomas answered that 'he would kill him that put them out'. Asked whether he would kill his own father, Thomas remained silent. One wonders whether one of Cottom's former pupils ever heard of these domestic battles. For by far the most intriguing fact that emerges from *Cottom v. Walton* is that the former schoolmaster did not live out his life in rural seclusion, as the inventory prepared at the time of his death might suggest to the unwary. He continued to visit London (cf. p. 44).

Before we leave the Waltons I should add that two inventories were made out in June and July 1618 of the goods and chattels of Thomas Walton of Walton le Dale, gent., deceased, relating to his houses in Walton and Tarnacre. This was Priscilla's husband, John Cottom's son-in-law; and since John Cottom's will (cf. p. 144) referred to no books, it is interesting to note, in the inventory for Thomas's principal residence at Walton, the following items: in the 'porch chamber' two trunks, one chest, etc., 'twelve little books, one desk, and other little shelves'; and in 'the chamber over the parlour', one 'evidence chest' and three other chests. The shorter inventory for the Tarnacre house (formerly, we must assume, John Cottom's home) was prepared by George Brown (cf. p. 44) and others, and describes the house as 'in Tarnacre, near St Michael's church upon Wyre'. These inventories are in the Lancashire Record Office.

To resume: John Cottom also battled, over a period of years, with Brian Jackson, gent., of Tarnacre, each accusing the other of making riots against him. They quarrelled about property once owned by James Cottam, and John Cottom was supported by George Brown, gent., who married James's widow.[6] It could be that Brian Jackson was related to the Hoghton retainer mentioned on an earlier page (p. 12), but that cannot be proved.

More important for our purposes, John Cottom turns up as a witness in a Hoghton document dated 11 April 1606 – an indenture between Sir Richard Hoghton, Felix Gerrard and Leonard Hoghton, gent.[7] And the families of two of Cottom's sons-in-law also associated with the Hoghtons. Richard Hoghton of Grimsargh, gent., who in his will (1614) mentions Adam Hoghton, 'his half-brother', and was therefore presumably a half-brother of Sir Richard Hoghton, left 40s to Sir Richard, another 40s to Lady Hoghton and 10s each to William Walton, gent., and to his wife.[8]

William Duddell of Salwick, gent., the husband of Mary Cottom, is the son-in-law who comes to life most completely. In *Bretton v. Adam Hoghton* (2 James I) Duddell described himself as 47 years old or thereabouts, and deposed that he was present when Adam Hoghton of Lea (son of Thomas Hoghton II and brother of Sir Richard) made an agreement with Bretton.

He this deponent and Gabriel Cross, gent., were by and present at the sealing, signing and delivering of the said note, whereunto they have subscribed their names as witnesses ... and saith that he saw money paid, but how much he took no notice, more than the acknowledging of the receipt of £20.[9]

William Duddell was the son of George and Jane Duddell; and George, Jane, William and other Duddells were at law with the Halsalls of Halsall (including Sir Cuthbert Halsall: cf. p. 53), off and on, over several decades. George Duddell, possibly a money-lender,[10] participated in a Settlement and Final Concord in 1572, when Henry Halsall, Esq., and his wife Ann adopted Cuthbert Halsall, the bastard son of their deceased son Richard.[11] From Jane Duddell's will (1604) we learn that she had four sons – William, John, Richard, Cuthbert – and two daughters, one of whom had married Edward Halsall.[12] Richard Duddell claimed in 1591 that the Old Hall, Salwick, had been devised to him and his wife by Henry and Ann Halsall, and then by Edward Halsall after the decease of Henry and Ann – a claim disputed by Cuthbert Halsall.[13] At about the same time William Duddell pleaded against Ann Halsall, widow, and Cuthbert Halsall about enclosures.[14] In 1606 and 1607 Sir Cuthbert Halsall lodged bills of complaint against William Duddell but relations between the Halsalls and Duddells were not always hostile, for W. Duddell witnessed a lease for Cuthbert Halsall in 1598, and William and Richard Duddell witnessed another for Sir Cuthbert Halsall, High Sheriff, in 1601.[15] Some of the relevant documents are damaged or lost; there can be no doubt, though, that the Duddells of Salwick were a family to be reckoned with.

Three other points about William Duddell deserve to be mentioned. (1) A schedule at the end of the will of Henry, Earl of Derby (21 Sept. 1593) lists 'servants' of the earl who received annuities from him 'for term of their several lives'. William Duddell received £5 a year.[16] (2) According to John Watson's *Memorials of the Ancient Earls of Warren and Surrey* (2 vols, 1782), Frances Warren, a younger sister of Sir Edward Warren of Poynton (cf. p. 53 below), married 'William Dedall of Salwick in L'ancashire, whose arms were *gules a goose argent*' (II, 136): William Duddell, one wonders? He could have been married twice. (3) William Duddell's will (12 Sept. 1614) mentions James Ellis, his brother-in-law, but no wife and no other member of John Cottom's family.[17]

Since John Cottom's family had long-standing connections with the Hoghtons, and the Waltons and Duddells also knew the Hoghtons in the early seventeeth century and no doubt earlier, it seems not unreasonable to suggest that the John Cotham mentioned in Alexander Hoghton's will might be the Stratford schoolmaster (cf. p. 6), even though John Cottom was still at Stratford when Alexander made his will. At any rate, I know of no other John Cotham similarly connected with the Hoghtons at this time.

I must not conclude this chapter without a caveat: it is all too easy, especially when working with secondary sources four hundred years after the event, to confuse different men or women with the same name, and even experts in local history (I do not claim to be one) can get into tangles. Take John Cottom's mother, for example: as my friend J. A. Cannon has pointed out to me, it is a problem that Gillow and Smith (cf. pp. 41,44) claim that she married William Ambrose after Lawrence Cottam's death. For John Cottom took his B.A. in 1566, therefore must have been born about twenty years earlier, when his mother must have been at least fifteen years old; if we date Mrs Cottam's birth just thirty-five years before John took his B.A., in 1531, she would still have been eighty-eight when John's father died in 1619 – a goodly age for a second marriage, and she could well have been older. This, however, is not so much a reason against identifying the Stratford schoolmaster with John Cottom of Tarnacre as an unresolved problem within the Lancashire family. Leaving aside the Stratford schoolmaster, we still have an antique bride on our hands if we accept Gillow's account of Thomas Cottam, the priest: he was born in 1549, so his mother could scarcely have been born later than 1535, and would have to be at least eighty-four when she married again in or after 1619. I think that the likeliest explanation is either that Ann Brewer married William Ambrose *before* she married Lawrence Cottam, or that a different Mrs Cottam, widow of Lawrence, married Ambrose in or after 1619. Such confusions are not uncommon in early pedigrees, especially where comparatively unimportant families are concerned. To pursue the second possibility: John Cottom's father was Lawrence Cottam of High House, Dilworth, but there was a second Lawrence Cottam of Dilworth; the two men were carefully distinguished in the will of James Helme (5 June, 44 Elizabeth) a wealthy Preston draper.[18] Helme, probably *not* the man who was Alexander Hoghton's servant and executor in 1581, named three executors – Richard Sowerbutts, 'Lawrence Cottom of the High House in Dilworth ... yeoman, and Lawrence Cottom of Dilworth aforesaid ... yeoman, son and heir of Edmund Cottam deceased'. The two Lawrences create havoc in *The Victoria County History* (*Lancashire*, VIII, 53).

John Cottom of Tarnacre also had a namesake who lived not far away from him but was a considerably younger man. This second John was examined in 1600 by Robert Hesketh (High Sheriff), Sir

Richard Hoghton and others after an attack by masked men on the vicarage at Garstang, and described himself as 'of Garstang Kirk-houses, of the age of 25 or thereabouts'.[19] John of Garstang Kirk-houses, being still a child in 1581, is unlikely to have been the John Cotham mentioned in his will by Alexander Hoghton and described as his 'servant'.

V

John Weever and the Hoghtons

'My dear boy', major Pendennis would say, with a mournful earnestness and veracity, 'you cannot begin your genealogical studies too early; I wish to Heavens you would read in Debrett every day. Not so much the historical part (for the pedigrees, between ourselves, are many of them very fabulous ...) as the account of family alliances, and who is related to whom. I have known a man's career in life blasted, by ignorance on this all-important subject.' (*The History of Pendennis*, IX)

John Weever is a figure of some importance in our story, as I have already hinted (p. 6). But who was John Weever, and how is he connected with Hoghtons? In his last publication, *Ancient Funeral Monuments* (1631), he described himself as a Lancastrian –

> Lancashire gave him breath,
> And Cambridge education.
> His studies are of death,
> Of Heaven his meditation.

These verses are placed beneath a portrait of Weever, engraved by Thomas Cecil, with the legend 'Vera Effigies Iohannis Weever Ætatis Suae 55. Anno 1631'. So he was born in 1575 or 1576, and went to Cambridge. That helps to identify him as the John Weever who is recorded as a student at Queens' College, Cambridge (from 1594 till about 1598). We also know him to have published several books of verse: *Epigrammes in the oldest cut, and newest fashion* (1599), *Faunus and Melliflora* (1600), *An Agnus Dei* (1601), *The Mirror of Martyrs* (1601) – all printed by Valentine Simmes – followed, thirty years later, by *Funeral Monuments*, a masterly antiquarian work in prose.

Weever's *Epigrammes*, with their verses *Ad Gulielmum Shakespeare*, were dedicated to Sir Richard Hoghton and other landowners in Lancashire and Cheshire. The only modern editor of this book, R. B. McKerrow, failed to notice the connections between Sir Richard Hoghton and the rest of Weever's dedicatees (cf. p. 6), and, more surprisingly, also failed to follow up the single clue as to Weever's own family connections. Weever's first epigram in 'the fourth week' (or section) is addressed *Ad auunculum suum Henricum Butler Armig.*, and begins –

> If from the conquest thy antiquity
> I would derive, when William gave thy mot,
> Or boast the Butlers' true gentility,
> My praises yet augment thy praise would not.

Henry Butler, Weever's maternal uncle, called himself *armiger* or esquire, and came from an ancient family. McKerrow commented that 'there are two pedigrees of Lancashire families of the name Butler in Harl. MS. 6159, fo. 14, but neither contains a Henry'. Had he glanced at Dugdale's *Visitation of Lancashire* (1664–5) he would have found a Henry Butler of Rawcliffe, Esq., husband of Anne, daughter of Henry Bannister of Bank, Esq. Since Rawcliffe is in the parish of St Michaels-on-Wyre, I turned to Henry Fishwick's *History of the Parish of St Michaels-on-Wyre* (Chetham Society, 1891), which contains, amongst other invaluable information about the Butlers, a pedigree with two promising entries. (1) Henry Butler's elder brother, Richard Butler, married 'Agnes, dau. of Sir Richard Hoghton of Hoghton' (that is, Sir Richard the father of Thomas I, Alexander and Thomas II (cf. p. 146); in short, Agnes was the aunt of the Sir Richard Hoghton to whom Weever dedicated his *Epigrammes*). (2) Henry Butler's uncle, John Butler, was grandfather of Ann Radcliffe, who married Gilbert Gerard, Queen Elizbeth's later Master of the Rolls; and of course (Sir) Gilbert and Ann Gerard were the parents of the three sisters who married Sir Richard Hoghton, Sir Richard Molyneux and Sir Peter Leigh, three of the dedicatees of Weever's *Epigrammes*, and of Sir Thomas Gerard, almost certainly a fourth dedicatee (cf. p. 53). Henry Butler, if I have identified the correct man, was not only John Weever's maternal uncle but also 'grand-uncle' to three or four of Weever's dedicatees.

As exciting as the strong probability that John Weever, a very early admirer of Shakespeare, was connected with the Hoghtons through his uncle, Henry Butler, is the fact that Rawcliffe is in the same parish as Tarnacre, where lived John Cottom, the former Stratford schoolmaster. Alexander Hoghton's house at Lea and Henry Butler's and John Cottom's were just a few miles apart. Another thread connecting Henry Butler and the 'Shakeshafte' circle, not so immediately obvious, came to my notice when I began to sift through the abundant Hesketh papers that still survive: Henry Butler's father-in-law, Henry Bannister 'of Bank in Bretherton' was a near neighbour of

Sir Thomas Hesketh of Rufford (to whom Alexander Hoghton particularly recommended Fulk Gillam and W. Shakeshafte), and a close business associate of Sir Thomas's in the 1570s and 1580s.[1]

The many other 'Hoghton' verses in Weever's *Epigrammes* make me confident that we have now tracked down the correct Henry Butler. However, I have found no certain documentary evidence linking Henry Butler of Rawcliffe and the poet John Weever. At first this seems strange, since pedigrees of armorial families are readily available; the explanation must be that a sister of Henry Butler married a man of lower rank, or perhaps that, at a time when just about every gentleman sired bastards, John Weever's mother was an illegitimate child of Nicholas Butler, the father of Henry. Seventeenth-century pedigrees waste little space on younger daughters, sometimes simply stating 'and three daughters' without indicating names or spouses; whilst illegitimate children were not normally mentioned at all, and have to be traced through wills or legal disputes. John Weever's determination to attach himself to as many influential members of the Hoghton circle as possible, viz. his insertion of so many respectful dedications and complimentary verses in the *Epigrammes*, makes it hard to resist the inference that he was a poor relation; and his other publications in 1600 and 1601 support this guess – like other poor scholars at this time he had to scramble for a living, and hoped to make a name for himself as a poet.

A new edition of Weever's *Epigrammes* will soon be published. Much of the detailed information about Weever's friends that can be gathered from Lancashire records must wait for the edition, but several points missed by McKerrow require our immediate attention. First, that Weever's complimentary epigrams can be arranged in three groups connected with (*a*) Cambridge, (*b*) Lancashire and the north, (*c*) London. The Lancashire link is not immediately obvious in every case, unless one knows the family connections of the Hoghton circle; being particularly interested in Weever as a fringe member of the circle, I list below the 'Lancashire' dedicatees, and indicate very briefly some of the ways in which they were related. (Roman numbers refer to the seven 'weeks' or sections of the *Epigrammes*; arabic, to the epigrams in each week).

(i) Sir Richard Hoghton of Hoghton Tower. Son of Thomas Hoghton II, and nephew of Alexander Hoghton, the master of 'William Shakeshafte'. Brother-in-law of Sir Richard Molyneux, Sir Thomas Gerard and Sir Peter Leigh (iii, v, vii).

(ii) Robert Dalton of Pilling, Esq.[2] Son of Ann Molyneux of Sefton, and cousin of Sir Richard Molyneux (iii).

(iii) Sir Richard Molyneux (of Sefton). (See i, ii, iv.)

(iv) Sir Edward Warren (of Poynton, Cheshire, and Woodplumpton, Lancs.). Son of Margaret Molyneux of Sefton, and cousin of Robert Dalton and Sir Richard Molyneux. (See ii, iii.)

(v) Sir Thomas Gerard, Knight Marshal.[3] Son of Sir Gilbert Gerard, brother-in-law of Hoghton, Molyneux and Leigh (i, iii, vii).

(vi) Sir Cuthbert Halsey (i.e. Halsall). Friend of Sir Richard Hoghton and Sir Richard Molyneux (i, iii); brother-in-law of Sir John Salusbury (cf. p. 92).

(vii) Sir Peter Leigh of 'Underline' (i.e. Lyme, Cheshire; and of Winwick, Lancs.). Brother-in-law of Hoghton, Molyneux, Gerard (i, iii, v).

One might suppose, from this list, that Sir Richard Molyneux and not Sir Richard Hoghton is the central dedicatee. Look beyond the dedications, however, and you find that Sir Richard Molyneux then vanishes, whereas Sir Richard Hoghton opens and also closes the book. Apart from a concluding epigram 'Ad Lectorem', the author self-consciously addresses Hoghton 'in the end':

> O chide me not, for that I do enroll
> Thy worthy name here (Hoghton) in the end, ...

In addition, Weever includes three more specific 'Hoghton' epigrams: vi,1, *Ad Richardum Houghton Militem*; vi,3, *In tumulum Thomae Houghton Armig.*; and vi,4, *In Gulielmum Houghton*. The first of these three must be Richard Hoghton, Esq., before he was knighted in June, 1599, for Weever alludes to 'thy gold-gilded tower'; the second, Thomas Hoghton II (cf. p. 12); and the third, William Hoghton, Thomas's second son. Weever's awareness of Thomas Hoghton's tragic death, a remote event of little public interest in 1599, and of Sir Richard Hoghton's links with so many Lancashire worthies, shows that the poet was an 'insider', and clinches the case that Henry Butler of Rawcliffe must have been the *avunculus* of iv,1. Weever, I believe, similarly makes an implicit claim to 'inside' information in his verses to Shakespeare. (Some of the verses are so obscure that it will help to quote them in old spelling, misprints and all. The original layout is reproduced to show how exigences of spacing may have influenced the printer's spelling etc.)

Epig. 22. Ad Gulielmum Shakespeare.
Honie-tong'd *Shakespeare* when I saw thine issue
I swore *Apollo* got them and none other,
Their rosie-tainted features cloth'd in tissue,
Some heauen born goddesse said to be their mo-
Rose-checkt *Adonis* with his amber tresses, (ther:

Faire fire-hot *Venus* charming him to loue her,
Chaste *Lucretia* virgine-like her dresses, (her:
Prowd lust-stung *Tarquine* seeking still to proue
Romea Richard; more whose names I know not,
Their sugred tongues, and power attractiue beuty
Say they are Saints althogh that Sts they shew not
For thousands vowes to them subiectiue dutie:
They burn in loue thy children *Shakespear* het them,
Go, wo thy Muse more Nymphish brood beget
(them.[4]

The important point here, missed by McKerrow, is that Weever's book consists of about 150 epigrams, most of them between four and twenty lines in length. One, and only one, is fourteen lines long, and takes the form of a Shakespearian sonnet – the 'epigram' addressed to Shakespeare. Adopting the form of Shakespeare's still unpublished sonnets, Weever signals to those in the know that he is one of the privileged few who have read them. (Compare Francis Meres's *Palladis Tamia* (1598): 'the sweet witty soul of Ovid lives in mellifluous and honey-tongued Shakespeare, witness his *Venus and Adonis*, his *Lucrece*, his sugared sonnets among his private friends, etc.')

We must not forget, of course, that *The Passionate Pilgrim* ('By W. Shakespeare') also came out in 1599, and could have preceded Weever's *Epigrammes* of the same year (the precise date of publication of the two books is uncertain.)[5] Only eight of the twenty poems in this surreptitious collection are fourteen-line sonnets, however, and only four of the eight are actually by Shakespeare. Those familiar with the London literary scene would soon have heard that other poems in *The Passionate Pilgrim* were reprinted from works by Barnfield, Weelkes, Griffin and Marlowe, and would have been suspicious about the attribution of the volume as a whole. (We know that Shakespeare was 'much offended' with the publisher who 'presumed to make so bold with his name' when *Passionate Pilgrim* was later reissued, and may assume that he repudiated this book as soon as he was told of it.) In 1599, before the sonnets as a whole had appeared in print, there was no good reason to consider the 'Shakespearian' sonnet Shakespeare's characteristic form, and Weever's choice of this particular sonnet form, for just one epigram out of 150, almost certainly implies that he had seen a manuscript of the 'sugared sonnets among his private friends'.

The hint contained in the epigram on Shakespeare becomes even more intriguing once we realise that this poem was probably written by 1598. In an epistle 'To the generous Readers' Weever explains that although 'epigrams are much like unto almanacs, serving especially for the year for the which they are made', his own, 'being for one year penned, and in another printed, are past date before they come from the press'. Printers, we learn from i, 7, are in no hurry to oblige an unknown poet:

> My epigrams were all new ready made,
> And only on the printer's leisure stayed.
> One of my friends on Sheep's Green I did meet
> Which told me one was printing in Bridge Street ...

A false alarm, as it turned out:

> I thanked him. My book to press now goes!
> But I am gulled: he printeth only hose.

We are not entitled to assume, though, that *all* of Weever's epigrams were 'penned' a year before they were published. Two or three refer to events that occurred in 1599: the death of Edmund Spenser (vi.23; January 1599), and the death of Thomas Egerton (vii.11; almost certainly the son of Sir Thomas Egerton, Baron Ellesmere, who died in August 1599). Nevertheless, a closer examination suggests that the epigrams were written over a period of years, and that the one on Shakespeare dates from 1598 or earlier, not from 1599. What is the evidence? The number of epigrams in each 'week', which is as follows: i, 23; ii, 25; iii, 23; iv, 23; v, 24; vi, 25; vii, 17. Taking into account that two epigrams in week ii are blanks ('*Epig.* 3 *In Titum* / When hare-brain'd *Titus.* / *Desunt nonnulla*'; '*Epig.* 10. / – *Nihil hic nisi carmina desunt.*') we find the totals to be 23, 23, 23, 23, 24, 25, 17. (The fourth week in fact includes an unnumbered epigram, after iv.3, but the numbered sequence runs to 23; I shall return to this in a moment.) It looks as if Weever at one stage aimed at twenty-three epigrams per week, sorted out the first four weeks by deleting ii.3 and ii.10 to get the numbers right, and later added, or added to, weeks v–vii. There are other signs that this is what actually happened. (1) The first four weeks all end with the word '*Finis*', whereas v and vi omit it. (It reappears at the end of vii because this is the end of the whole book.) This confirms that weeks i–iv and v–vii probably had different textual origins. (2) Thomas Bastard's *Chrestoleros* was published in 1598 (S.R., 3 April), comprising 'seven books of epigrams', and was closely followed by William Rankins's *Seven Satires* ('applied to the week' (S.R., 3 May)). From all of which I deduce that Weever, inspired by Bastard and Rankins, decided to rearrange his epigrams in seven 'weeks' in 1598, having already suffered from the printer's delays

('My epigrams *were all new ready made*': cf. p. 55, above), and subsequently found that there were more delays and wrote a few more epigrams. If we now add to week vii the two deleted epigrams from week ii, the unnumbered one from week iv, and the three from weeks v and vi in excess of twenty-three, we discover that the result is seven weeks each containing exactly twenty-three poems – and this, I take it, was Weever's final intention. In short, the interval between 1598 (when the epigrams were 'ready made' for the second last time) and the autumn of 1599 (when the final copy was prepared) gave Weever the opportunity to add a few new epigrams to weeks v–vii, and then to transfer others to week vii, thus achieving a symmetry (seven weeks, twenty-three poems in each) that he had not originally contemplated. The printer[6] unfortunately misread Weever's directions and partly bungled his job, but left enough clues to make it a very strong probability that the epigram to Shakespeare belonged to the collection 'penned' and pretty well completed in the year 1598. (It is no. 22 in week iv; if my reconstruction proves correct, Weever meant to transfer some epigrams *from* weeks i–iv, but placed late additions in weeks v–vii).

This has been a digression. It seemed worthwhile because Weever's epigram could have been the very first written of all the 'allusions' to Shakespeare's sonnets, even though Francis Meres's thoughts about those 'sugared sonnets' reached print a year earlier;[7] and if so, Weever would have known about the sonnets at a very early stage, perhaps before they were completed. But that remains a matter of conjecture. The really important point for us is the fact – I hope that I have established it as a fact – that Weever, connected as he was with the Hoghtons of Hoghton Tower, celebrated the dramatist in a 'Shakespearian sonnet' at a time (1598 or 1599, no matter which) when only 'private friends' could understand the significance of this particular sonnet-form.

It now remains to trace, very briefly, Weever's career after 1599. Apart from the poems of 1600 and 1601 already mentioned (p. 50), Weever almost certainly wrote *The Whipping of the Satyre* (1601),[8] an attack on the 'vainglorious' satirist, epigrammatist and humorist. The first target was John Marston and the third Ben Jonson – two writers praised by Weever in the *Epigrammes* (vi.11). Yet there can be no doubt that Weever's loyalties had changed, for Jonson repaid him in kind. Unless a man had studied begging all his lifetime, Jonson wrote in *Every Man In His Humour* (III.2), 'and been a weaver of phrases from his infancy ... the world cannot produce his rival'. And, more explicitly,

John Weever and the Hoghtons

To my mere English censurer.
To thee, my way in Epigrams seems new,
When both it is the old way, and the true.
Thou saist, that cannot be, for thou hast seen
Davies and Weever, and the best have been,
And mine come nothing like. I hope so ...⁹

Weever, however, continued to admire Shakespeare. His *Faunus and Melliflora* repeatedly echoes *Venus and Adonis* and *Love's Labour's Lost*. *The Mirror of Martyrs, or The Life and Death of Sir John Oldcastle* contains a very early reference to *Julius Caesar*:

> The many-headed multitude were drawn
> By Brutus' speech, that Caesar was ambitious;
> When eloquent Mark Antony had shown
> His virtues, who but Brutus then was vicious?

If it is true, as Weever alleged, that this poem 'some two years ago was made fit for the print', it could have been the very first allusion to Shakespeare's play. (Compare, incidentally, Weever's similar claim that *Epigrammes* appeared in print a year late.) And while there may be an implied criticism of Shakespeare in Weever's praise of Oldcastle as 'that thrice valiant captain, and most godly martyr', *The Whipping of the Satyre* certainly takes for granted that Falstaff needs no introduction:

> I dare here speak it, and my speech maintain,
> That Sir John Falstaff was not any way
> More gross in body, than you are in brain ...¹⁰

In Weever's last work, *Funeral Monuments*, he still echoes Shakespeare. Describing the killing of Lord Say and his son-in-law during the 'Cade rebellion', he recalls a sensational scene from *2 Henry VI* (IV.7), where the two heads are brought in on two poles and Cade cries 'let them kiss one another', 'ride through the streets, and at every corner have them kiss!' Weever asks for the reader's indulgence ('give me leave to go a little further'), and amplifies: the heads, 'upon high poles, were carried by the villains through the city of London, who caused their trunkless faces (in spite and mockery) *to kiss one another at every street-corner*'.¹¹ He also quotes an impressive poem, *A Memento for Mortality*, ascribed to 'one lately having taken view of the sepulchres of so many kings ... in this Abbey of Westminster' (*Funeral Monuments*, pp. 492–3). It ends:

[57]

Then bid the wanton lady tread
Amid these mazes of the dead.
And these, truly understood,
More shall cool and quench the blood
Than her many sports a day
And her nightly wanton play.
Bid her paint till day of doom,
To this favour she must come.

(Compare *Hamlet*, V.1: 'get you to my lady's chamber, and tell her, let her *paint* an inch thick, *to this favour she must come*'). I believe Weever himself may be the author of *A Memento* (his epigram on the death of Robert Shute (iv.15) is in exactly the same vein), even though it seems more carefully written than most of his signed verses. After all, if his, it would be the work of a more mature poet, and the subject – and *Hamlet* – would have appealed to the connoisseur of funeral monuments.

We may take it that Weever continued to admire Shakespeare. Though we know little about his later years, except that he had forced his way into London's literary world by 1601 and died possessed of the leases of two London houses in 1632 (cf. p. 145), it seems that he also continued on good terms with the Hoghtons and their circle. He praised Sir William Molyneux, 'whose epitaph I have out of the pedigree of that honourable worthy gentleman, Sir Richard Molyneux of Sefton ... now living';[12] and, apropos of Harrow on the Hill, he dragged in that it is 'now the habitation of a worthy gentleman, Sir Gilbert Gerard, knight and baronet' (p. 531). He returned to his native parts at least once, as we learn from an aside (p. 405): 'They call this *Corpus Christi Play* in my country, which I have seen acted at Preston, and Lancaster, and last of all at Kendal, in the beginning of the reign of King James'. More tantalisingly, in his account of Sir John Mandeville he mentions (p. 568) that 'within these few years, I saw his tomb in the city of Liège'. Did he go to Liège, one wonders, to see the tomb of Thomas Hoghton I (cf. p. 11)? Weever's will, however, is silent about his former patrons; and Henry Butler, of Rawcliffe, Esq., left no bequest to Weever when he died in 1619.[13]

[58]

VI

Shakespeare and Lord Strange's Men

'If William Shakeshafte passed from the service of Alexander Hoghton into that of either Thomas Hoghton or Sir Thomas Hesketh,' wrote Chambers in 1944, 'he might very easily have gone on into that of Lord Strange, and so later into the London theatrical world'.[1] It is time to return to this possibility, Shakespeare's 'Lancashire connections' being so much more intricate than Chambers suspected. I shall begin with two points that have been much discussed already.

(1) The Chamberlain's Men, the first London company with which we definitely know Shakespeare to have been associated, was formed in 1594 around a nucleus of actors who were previously Lord Strange's Men. Of the eleven men thought to have formed the new company, five (Will Kempe, Thomas Pope, John Heminges, Augustine Phillips and George Bryan) were named as Lord Strange's Men in a Privy Council Licence, dated 6 May 1593, permitting them to 'exercise their quality of playing comedies, tragedies and such like ... so it be not within seven miles of London or the court'.[2] (Performances in London were stopped on 28 January 1593 because of the plague.) Three of the five (Pope, Phillips, Bryan) were also named in the plot of *Seven Deadly Sins*, Part 2, performed *c.* 1590 by Strange's and Admiral's Men, or by Strange's Men alone,[3] and three more members of the later Chamberlain's Men (Richard Burbage, William Sly, John Duke) had parts in the same plot. That adds up to eight of the eleven Chamberlain's men, the remainder being Christopher Beeston, Henry Condell, and Shakespeare. If 'Kitt' and 'Harry' in the plot are Beeston and Condell, as others have conjectured, Shakespeare is the only member of the later Chamberlain's Men unaccounted for, and may well be another actor in the plot called 'Will', who played one of the women's roles. (Women were sometimes acted by fairly mature 'boys' in their late teens;[4] Shakespeare would have been 26 in 1590.)

(2) The title-page of *Titus Andronicus* (1594) states that the

[59]

tragedy 'was played by the Right Honourable the Earl of Derby, Earl of Pembroke and Earl of Sussex their Servants'. We happen to know from Henslowe's *Diary* that Sussex's Men performed *Titus* in January and February 1594; the play was entered in the Stationers' Register on 6 February 1594, so Sussex's Men are likely to have been the last company that acted it before it was published. 'I suppose it to have pased ... from Pembroke's to Sussex's, when the former were bankrupt in the summer of 1593' Chambers explained, alluding to a letter of 28 September 1593 in which Henslowe reports that Pembroke's Men 'are all at home ... for they cannot save their charges with travel, as I hear, and were fain to pawn their [ap]parel'. At about this time several of Pembroke's Men's plays came into the booksellers' hands;[5] it is therefore a fair inference that they sold *Titus* to Sussex's Men. We are driven to conclude that the *Titus* title-page names the companies that acted the play in the correct order – that is, that Shakespeare wrote it for Derby's Men.

The Earl of Derby's Men disappear from the records in 1582–3, whereas Strange's Men received payments at court and in the provinces throughout the 1580s. Consequently it is as good as certain that the *Titus* title-page refers to the *former* Lord Strange, now – in 1594 – Earl of Derby. (Ferdinando, Lord Strange, succeeded his father as fifth Earl of Derby on 25 September 1593.) Since at least five and probably ten of the Lord Chamberlain's Men of 1594 were previously Strange's Men, and Shakespeare, also one of the Lord Chamberlain's Men in 1594, was connected with (Derby's, i.e.) Strange's Men when *Titus* was first produced, it seems highly probable that he, too, was one of Strange's Men before 1594.

Having leaned on E. K. Chambers at several points in the last three paragraphs, I must now attempt to walk on my own. As I have explained elsewhere,[6] Chambers inherited the 'late start' Shakespeare chronology, according to which Shakespeare wrote his first plays no earlier than 1590 or 1591; he also believed that the dramatist began his career as a play-patcher, regarding many of Shakespeare's early plays as revisions of other men's work – *Titus Andronicus, The Taming of the Shrew*, the three parts of *Henry VI*, to name but a few. Both the 'late start' chronology and the play-patcher theory are now discredited, largely because Peter Alexander[7] established that Parts 2 and 3 of *Henry VI* were not, as others had thought for more than a century, revisions of two anonymous plays with very similar plots and dialogue, *The First Part of the Contention betwixt the two famous Houses of York and Lancaster* (1594) and *The True Tragedy of Richard Duke of York* (1595); quite the contrary, said Alexander – *The Contention* and *True Tragedy* were really unauthorised reconstructions of Shakespeare's two plays. Chambers conceded that he had been wrong about Parts 2 and 3 of *Henry VI*, and tinkered with his 'late start' chronology to fit in with the new facts. In *The Elizabethan Stage* (1923) he had written 'Shakespeare's first dramatic job, which earned him the ill will of Greene, was the writing or re-writing of *1 Henry VI* for Strange's, in the early spring of 1592. During the winter of 1592–3 he revised *The Contention ...*'.[8] Converted by Alexander, Chambers pushed back 'Shakespeare's first dramatic job' to 1590–1 when he came to publish his *William Shakespeare* in 1930. He could do no less, but should have done much more – for Alexander's work had far-reaching implications for the dating of Shakespeare's early plays, and of other contemporary plays, that Chambers could not bring himself to admit. Had Chambers conceded on this larger front, however, he would have had to re-write many chapters of *The Elizabethan Stage*, and also much of *William Shakespeare* (two volumes that must have been pretty well advanced when Alexander published the book that re-stated and clinched his case, in 1929).

It has been necessary to return to 'old, unhappy, far-off things and battles long ago' because Chambers remains an indispensable authority for anyone concerned with Shakespeare and Elizabethan acting companies. And Chambers, trapped by the 'late start' chronology and the play-patcher theory, made two decisions about *Titus Andronicus* that have to be placed in this larger context. (1) He chose to disregard one of the few really specific statements by an informed contemporary about the dating of one of Shakespeare's plays, and (2) so convinced was he of Shakespeare's 'play-patching' that he persuaded himself, for the flimsiest of reasons, that 'it is not so clear ... that some form of *Titus Andronicus* did not exist before 1594, and if so, that it was not *Titus and Vespasian*'. (The negatives tell all, I think. – A lost play, *Titus and Vespasian*, marked 'ne' (which Chambers thought meant 'new') by Henslowe on 11 April 1592, was performed by Strange's Men until 25 January 1593.)

(1) In *Bartholomew Fair* (1614) Jonson mocked admirers of *The Spanish Tragedy* and *Titus Andronicus* as men whose judgment has stood still 'these five and twenty, or thirty years', thus dating the two plays between 1584 and 1589. 'Twenty-five or thirty' is more carefully precise than a single round number would be; and Jonson also spoke of *The Spanish Tragedy* as 'departed a dozen years since' in *Cynthia's Revels* (1600), implying that *The Spanish Tragedy* had ended its 'run' by 1588, and so presumably first appeared in 1587 or earlier. Jonson's two statements corroborate one another, and

his dating of *The Spanish Tragedy* is now widely accepted. Chambers, however, dated *Titus Andronicus* 1593–4.

(2) Now that Hereward T. Price and Emrys Jones have shown that 'construction' and 'scenic form' in *Titus Andronicus* are typically Shakespearian, of a complexity quite beyond any of his predecessors, the once fashionable view that this is a play merely revised by Shakespeare, and originally written by someone else, has few if any backers.

When we try to trace Shakespeare's company connections before 1594, the date and authorship of *Titus Andronicus* are crucial evidence. Without Jonson's specific statement, dating the play between 1584 and 1589, one might suppose that it was written in 1591 or 1592, and passed in quick succession from Strange's to Pembroke's to Sussex's Men. This would be to cling to the 'late start' chronology at all costs, in defiance of a contemporary witness whose dating of *The Spanish Tragedy* fits in best with all the other known facts. (For example, Jonson ridiculed *The Spanish Tragedy* and *Titus Andronicus* as two long-admired 'Senecan' tragedies; the vogue for such tragedies of blood had already continued for a while when Nashe, in 1589, attacked those who write 'Senecan' tragedies and 'imitate the Kid in Aesop' (i.e. imitate Thomas Kyd, whose one important play in this genre was *The Spanish Tragedy*): it follows that *The Spanish Tragedy* must have been written some time before 1589). What is the alternative? To give up the 'late start' in favour of the 'early start' chronology – as more and more biographers have now realised.

I have laboured this point because I shall turn, in a moment, to other plays with interesting 'Derby' connections, *Richard III* and *Love's Labour's Lost*, *Henry VI* and *A Midsummer Night's Dream*. First, though, let us ask whether Shakespeare necessarily remained with one company (Strange's Men), if *Titus Andronicus* was indeed performed by it as early as 1586 or so. He was not named as a member of Strange's Men in their licence to travel of 6 May 1593, which can be explained in several ways. Either (1) he did not join the former Strange's Men until they re-grouped in 1594, as the Lord Chamberlain's Men: as I have suggested, this is unlikely. Or (2), though one of Strange's Men in 1593, he preferred not to 'travel'. We must keep in mind that when the plague raged in London, touring players associated with London would not draw good audiences, and might well go bankrupt (as happened to Pembroke's Men in or before September 1593); also, that the travelling player had to endure discomforts, about which there were many complaints. It is relevant, therefore, that *Venus and Adonis* was entered in the

Stationers' Register on 18 April 1593, and was published soon after with a dedication to the Earl of Southampton. Let us place this, Shakespeare's first publication, in a larger context. After ominous signs in the last months of 1592, 1593 'was a year of continuous plague',[9] which meant that the London theatres were closed: an ambitious dramatist, with a wife and three young children to support, would inevitably have to consider making his living in other ways. I deduce that Shakespeare belonged to Strange's Men some time before 1593 – exactly as Jonson's dating of *Titus Andronicus* would lead us to believe. Or (3), Shakespeare may have moved, with *Titus Andronicus*, from Strange's to Pembroke's Men. The origin of Pembroke's Men, according to Chambers, 'is to be explained by the special conditions of the plague-years 1592–3, and was due to a division for travelling-purposes of the large London company formed by the amalgamation of Strange's and the Admiral's'.[10] When Pembroke's Men 'broke', in September 1593, they raised cash by selling plays: Marlowe's *Edward II*, and the anonymous *Taming of a Shrew* and *True Tragedy of Richard Duke of York*, went to publishers, *Titus Andronicus* to Sussex's Men. Chambers, holding that three of these four plays involved Shakespeare as 'play-patcher' (i.e. that Shakespeare re-wrote *A Shrew* as *The Taming of the Shrew*, *True Tragedy* as Part 3 of *Henry VI*, *Titus and Vespasian* as *Titus Andronicus*), thought it quite possible that Shakespeare 'is to be looked for during these years in Pembroke's company until its collapse and then in Sussex's'.[11] I do not rule out this possibility, even though Chambers argued from an assumption that can no longer be sustained, namely Shakespeare's 'revision' of the three plays. Pembroke's Men may well have been an 'overflow' company, and the title-page assertion that *A Shrew* and *True Tragedy* were acted by Pembroke's may just mean that the two plays they impersonate, *The Shrew* and Part 3 of *Henry VI*, were acted by Pembroke's. If so, however, we would still have to look for Shakespeare's first company before 1592–3, and that again leads us back to Strange's Men.[12]

Although Shakespeare's company affiliations from 1592 to 1594 are uncertain, he appears to have been with Strange's Men until at any rate the autumn of 1592, when Pembroke's Men are named in provincial records;[13] and that prompts us to look more closely at references to Lord Strange and the Stanley family in some early plays. Thomas Stanley, the first Earl of Derby, who established the family's fortune, figures in *Richard III* (dated 1591 by the New Arden editor): and Shakespeare rearranged history so as to make Stanley's services to the incoming Tudor dynasty seem more momentous than they really were. As stepfather of Henry of Richmond, the later Henry VII, the historical Thomas Stanley might have been expected to side with him against Richard III; in fact, though, he was much more cautious than Shakespeare's 'Derby' in the play. (1) Before Bosworth Richmond deferred to his step-father by going to a secret meeting with him; in the play, Stanley takes the risk of going to Richmond. (2) Just before the battle, Richmond sent to Stanley, requiring him 'to approach near to his army, and to help to set the soldiers in array'; Stanley refused, saying 'he would come to him in time convenient'. The play omits this rebuff. (3) The play clearly implies that Derby fought for his stepson, and that this ensured Richmond's victory. Again, a clever re-touching of the facts: Stanley left it to his brother, William, to lead the Stanley forces. By omitting William Stanley, Shakespeare manages to suggest that the direct ancestor of his patron, Lord Strange, decisively aided Queen Elizabeth's grandfather when he became king. (4) According to the chronicles, Stanley 'took the crown of King Richard, which was found amongst the spoil in the field', and set it on Richmond's head. There is no suggestion that Stanley himself found the crown; in the play Derby claims not merely to have found it but to have plucked it 'from the dead temples of this bloody wretch' (V.5.4. ff.), which depicts him more flatteringly and symbolically as 'king-maker'. Shakespeare, it seems, went to some trouble to magnify Derby's commitment to the future Henry VII. Furthermore, Shakespeare makes Derby the only nobleman of the Yorkist faction not deceived by Richard, indeed builds him up as the one politician who out-manoeuvres Richard until and during the Battle of Bosworth; and, though some of Derby's political perceptiveness comes straight from the sources (e.g. his dream of the boar, and his distrust of the 'two councils, III.2.9 ff.), the play adds other instances: (5) Derby advises Dorset to flee to Richmond (IV.1.48 ff.), and skilfully fences with a suspicious and dangerous tyrant (IV.4 etc.). (6) Derby, again, is the only bystander of note *not* cursed by Queen Margaret in Act I, scene 3. While I would not pretend that all the earls and dukes of the history plays reflect upon their Elizabethan namesakes, the drama-tist's careful remodelling of Derby becomes understandable when we recall that the play is now assigned to the year 1591 when, in all probability, he was one of Strange's Men; and we may add, con-versely, that the play's treatment of Derby supports the theory that Shakespeare was one of Strange's Men at this time.[14]

The treatment of Ferdinand, King of Navarre in *Love's Labour's Lost*, is equally revealing. Others have noticed that this name points at Ferdinando, Lord Strange, the most illustrious Ferdinand in the land, and that the play's repetition of *strange* and *stranger* has the same effect.

> In the afternoon
> We will with some strange pastime solace them ....
>
> What would these strangers? Know their minds, Boyet.
>
> Since you are strangers, and come here by chance
> We'll not be nice. Take hands. We will not dance.
>
> (IV.3.372, V.2.174, 218 ff.)

These are little local jokes; the very structure of the play, however, could have been devised to 'send up' Lord Strange's mottos, *'Dieu et ma Foy'* and *'Sans changer ma vérité'* .[15] Ferdinand and his friends are caught out repeatedly 'breaking faith' (I.1.147 ff., V.2.471), persuade themselves that 'it is religion to be thus forsworn' (IV.3.357 ff.), and prove 'men of inconstancy' (IV.3.176) who change 'Even to the opposed end of our intents' (V.2.746): at the close they all have to agree to a year's delay, 'remote from all the pleasures of the world', to see whether such a life 'change not your offer made in heat of blood'. The changeableness and untruthfulness of men – of Ferdinand and his 'strangers' – is a basic theme of the play, a comic idea that shapes its plot. And it expresses itself in many puns, as when Ferdinand asks Rosaline to dance.

> Then in our measure do but vouchsafe *one change*.
> Thou bid'st me beg; this begging is *not strange*.
>
> (V.2.209–10)

Precisely the same puns are found in the 'Verses penned upon the etymology of the name of the Right Honourable, Ferdinando, Lord Strange' in Richard Robinson's *A Golden Mirror* (1589). In this poem every stanza ends with four lines rhyming *change* and *strange*, alluding to Ferdinando's motto, *'Sans changer ma vérité'*, as transparently as *Love's Labour's Lost*.

> Arise (quoth she) write after me,
> My sentence do not *change:*
> Here shalt thou view a creature *true*
> Who may be callèd *Strange*.
>
> ... A man so fixed and firm of faith
> That never yet did *change*,
> And stands to *truth* for life or death:
> This man is very *Strange*.

Strange and *change* may seem innocuous words in *Love's Labour's Lost* – until one sees that here, in Shakespeare's most allusive comedy, there are so many other teasingly topical puns. Let us pause briefly to savour one set of 'in' jokes that illustrates the play's technique. The many quibbles on pierce, purse, person, penny etc. refer, it is generally agreed, to Nashe's *Pierce Penilesse* (July 1592); and Moth, the 'tender Juvenal' and 'acute juvenal' (I.2.8, III.1.60), partly represents young Thomas Nashe, the satirist who was beginning to lay about him in London, and who was believed to have attacked Shakespeare as author or part-author of Greene's *Groat's Worth of Wit* (September 1592);[16] in addition, Shakespeare either invented or adapted a joke about 'Pierce' (Nashe's nickname, which he himself used in his later pamphlets). According to Gabriel Harvey, 'she knew what she said, that entitled Pierce the hogshead of wit, Penniless the toss-pot of eloquence. ... She it is that must broach the barrel of thy frisking conceit.' Compare *Love's Labour's Lost*, IV.2.79 ff.: '*Holofernes*. Master Person, quasi pers-one. And if one should be pierced, which is the one? *Costard*. Marry, Master Schoolmaster, he that is likest to a hogshead. *Holofernes*. Piercing a hogshead! A good lustre of conceit. ...' Nashe, it should be added, courted Lord Strange's favour at this very time, and so would be known to his literary circle.[17]

The *Shakespeare Encyclopaedia* speaks for all the commentators in claiming that '*Love's Labour's Lost* is, above all, a topical play'. The fact that 'many of the references to contemporary jokes, events and men have become unintelligible to modern audiences' in no way diminishes one's sense that the author aims his shafts at many contemporary targets – and Ferdinando, Lord Strange, has been identified as one. This was because of the play's alleged allusion to a group of scholars who met to study mathematics and astronomy, and who were also interested in poetry and theology. Sir Walter Raleigh was a leading spirit of the group, and Chapman named other members in *The Shadow of Night* (1594): 'most ingenious Derby, deep-searching Northumberland, and [the] skill-embracing heir of Hunsdon'. Chapman wrote about the three from hearsay, but clearly regarded them as examples of the very intellectual dedication that he advocated in his poem. And what did Chapman propose? He wanted men to cultivate their minds, which was only possible if they would 'subdue their monstrous affections.' 'Passion-driven men', he explained, will achieve nothing 'in the deep search of knowledge', for what is required is 'invocation, fasting, watching'.[18] It sounds remarkably like Ferdinand's opening speech, exhorting his friends to 'war against your own affections', to study for three years and abjure the 'world's delights' – a programme that is later renounced.

Have at you then, affection's men-at-arms.
Consider what you first did swear unto:
To fast, to study, and to see no woman –
Flat treason 'gainst the kingly state of youth.
(IV.3.286 ff.)

As Chapman's poem was entered in the Stationers' Register on 31 December 1593, the 'ingenious Derby' who so exactly fulfilled his requirements, and so curiously resembled King Ferdinand in his simple-minded plans, must be Ferdinando, the fifth Earl and former Lord Strange.

Once we are alerted by the play's apparent allusions to Lord Strange, a related question demands some attention. Why Ferdinand King of *Navarre*? There never was a Ferdinand King of Navarre; the gifted Ferdinando, Lord Strange, resembled the brilliant Henry of Navarre, however, in his relationship with his sovereign. Henry, King of Navarre, a remote cousin of Henry III of France (who died childless), was thought heir to the French throne by Protestants; he united the two kingdoms and ruled as Henry IV of France from 1589. Lord Strange, likewise, was a distant cousin of a childless sovereign, Queen Elizabeth, and, as we have observed (p. 37), he was seen as a possible successor to the throne. In addition, the Earls of Derby kept an establishment little inferior to the Queen's, with a similarly constituted household.[19]

Henry Earl of Derby had his Council, which embraced some of the nobility, the Bishop, and a large body of the superior Clergy of the Diocese, besides the principal gentlemen of the two palatinate counties. The powers vested in this Council were not dissimilar to those of the Privy Council of the sovereign. ... Like the Queen, the Earl of Derby had his Comptroller and Steward of the Household, his Grooms of the Bedchamber, and Clerks of the Kitchen. ...[20]

The Court of Navarre, in *Love's Labour's Lost*, ingeniously suggests something very similar – a royal household in the provinces, overshadowed by the King of France, as the Earl of Derby's was by Queen Elizabeth. A dramatist who wished to put Lord Strange into a topical comedy, but preferred not to do it too openly, could copy the Derby household in his play and call it by a different name – a technique employed by Lyly and many others who wished to flatter a patron.

Those who believe that *Love's Labour's Lost*, with its young lords dedicated to the pursuit of knowledge, laughs at Raleigh and his associates have, in general, thought of Shakespeare as belonging to a rival group. That would be a fair inference if Ferdinand and his friends were treated unkindly. But is the dramatist really so hostile? He speaks of Ferdinand as

> the sole inheritor
> Of all perfections that a man may owe,
> Matchless Navarre!
>
> (II.1.5–7)

If those are the words of an enemy, who needs friends? I suggest that we consider an alternative hypothesis – that *Love's Labour's Lost* may be seen as a bantering comedy written for Lord Strange's own entertainment by a privileged 'servant' who had observed Ferdinando over a period of years, and who knew what he could get away with. The New Arden editor dates the play late in 1593;[21] I think that late 1592 is more likely, but, for present purposes, it makes little difference, since the plague visibly worsened in 1592 and raged in 1593, and a lengthy closing of the London theatres was inevitable. Either in late 1592 or in 1593 Shakespeare might well have been tempted to write an 'allusive' comedy with many 'in' jokes for a largely private audience, deprived as he was of his public audience in London. I do not mean that *Love's Labour's Lost* was intended solely for Lord Strange and his immediate circle, for that would not make economic sense, but merely that the play's excessive freight of private jokes unintelligible to a modern reader is best accounted for in some such way.

Love's Labour's Lost has been described as a satire on 'the school of night', the Raleigh group. I think that we must distinguish between the treatment of (1) the lords and ladies, and (2) their social inferiors. The portraits of Don Armado and Moth, Sir Nathaniel and Holofernes are by general consent partly or largely satirical – that is, we are invited to laugh at them, and to enjoy their discomfiture. Those of the lords and ladies, on the other hand, are so very flattering that they could be seen as a celebration rather than as satirical. Ferdinand himself and his friends are presented as perfect gentlemen, a little confused in their thinking, perhaps, as any gentleman may be when ladies appear on the scene, yet otherwise beyond reproach. Shakespeare leaves us in no doubt that he admires these courtiers, and, in so far as the play as a whole adopts Berowne's 'point of view', that he is or would like to be one of them; one could even say that the writing of the play seeks to prove that he *is* one of them, displaying as it does his 'inside' awareness of every kind of courtly formality and informality, and his astonishing ease in this world.

The fact that *Love's Labour's Lost* also smiles at Ferdinand and his lords need not mean that the play was written to amuse opponents of 'the school of night'. It smiles indulgently, almost lovingly, and at the same time idealises 'matchless Navarre' – a combination that is best explained as a tribute from a privileged follower, rather than as satire from political opponents. If I am correct, Shakespeare must have been very sure of himself, and of the goodwill of his patron. And would that be so surprising? Many contemporary witnesses agree that he had an irresistible way with him, and the sonnets – whatever their date, and whoever the 'young man' – prove that he knew how to charm his social superiors. All the same, there were limits: it seems to have occurred to Shakespeare in the course of writing that to call his hero Ferdinand was to go too far, if the comedy was to be performed before Ferdinando, Lord Strange, or publicly by Lord Strange's Men. Although there were other Ferdi-nands in England, particularly in Lancashire (so called after Lord Strange?), it would give the game away, it might be construed as impudence. Shakespeare, I think, wanted Lord Strange and his friends to recognise themselves in the courtiers – not as straight portraits, however, but as general likenesses that now and then turn disconcertingly into known individuals. It is a technique of hints and half-light. 'What's your dark meaning? ... We need more light to find your meaning out' (V.2.19–21). The name Ferdinand was therefore dropped, although it survives in stage directions and speech prefixes in the quarto (which is thought to have been printed from Shakespeare's autograph papers); the King of Navarre is never called Ferdinand in the dialogue. It is a clue as to the author's thinking, invaluable for us but not needed by the contemporary audience – for in a topical play so much could be conveyed through dress, gesture, make-up and the like.

Apart from these apparent allusions to Lord Strange and his family in *Richard III* and *Love's Labour's Lost*, there are others in *Henry VI*, Parts 2 and 3, and in *A Midsummer Night's Dream* that I think are intriguing, and worth following up. It would be fair to say, however, that they do not add significantly to the case that Shake-speare was one of Lord Strange's men; if the internal evidence of the plays may be invoked to establish the dramatist's company allegi-ance, *Richard III* and *Love's Labour's Lost* are more important than these other plays. I have therefore placed my discussion of *Henry VI* and *A Midsummer Night's Dream*, including a new explanation of the 'Clifford' scenes and new suggestions for the dating of *A Midsummer Night's Dream*, in an appendix (p. 150).

Shakespeare, I repeat, seems to have served Lord Strange for eight or more years – the crucial years of his apprenticeship in the theatre. That may help to explain Robert Greene's furious attack, in 1592, on the 'absolute *Johannes factotum*' who is 'in his own conceit the only Shake-scene in a country'.[22] Why was Greene so angry? Because Shakespeare had supplanted him in popular esteem? No doubt that was one reason. In addition, though,it is relevant that Greene had himself courted the Stanleys, dedicating his *Mirror of Modesty* (1584) to the Countess of Derby, Lord Strange's mother, and making a bid for Lord Strange's favour in 1589 with *Ciceronis Amor* – while at the same time he published, and probably encouraged, Nashe's sneers at the author of a lost Senecan tragedy called *Hamlet* (Nashe's Preface to Greene's *Menaphon*, 1589). Greene's later attack on Shakespeare, in 1592, adopted some of the very phrases of Nashe's diatribe against the author of *Hamlet*, so it seems that Nashe and Greene believed Shakespeare to be the author of the early (lost) *Hamlet* of 1589, and that Greene had looked upon Shakespeare as a rival for some years before his final outburst in *Groat's Worth of Wit* (1592).

I suggested long ago that Nashe's phrasing pointed to Shakespeare as the author of this early *Hamlet*, since Nashe was attacking 'Senecan' dramatists who were not university graduates; Kyd and Shakespeare were the only dramatists of any significance who were not graduates at this time, and both wrote 'Senecan' tragedies – but the author of *Hamlet* is identified as one who *imitates* the Kid in Aesop, i.e. as an imitator of Thomas Kyd rather than Kyd himself. Recent publications arguing that Shakespeare himself revised *King Lear* and *Othello* encourage me in the belief that he probably revised *Hamlet* as well; in other words, that he composed the early *Hamlet* of 1589. This, of course, must remain a conjecture, because the 1589 *Hamlet* has not survived. Nevertheless, Greene's echoing of Nashe's attack on the author of *Hamlet* shows, I think, which way the wind was blowing.[23]

We must now add that in the early months of 1592 Lord Strange's Men produced three of Greene's plays (*Friar Bacon, Orlando Furioso* and *A Looking Glass for London and England*).[24] Then, in the summer of 1592, Greene's former protégé, Nashe, extravagantly praised Lord Strange in *Pierce Penilesse*, and went out of his way to propitiate Lord Strange's dramatist by praising *Henry VI*: 'How would it have joyed brave Talbot (the terror of the French) to think that after he had lain two hundred years in his tomb, he should triumph again on the stage, and have his bones new embalmed with the tears of ten thousand spectators at least, at several times ...' [25] Nashe had changed sides, Lord Strange's Men would not help him, Shakespeare's 'tiger's heart' had turned everyone against him – that must have been Greene's bitter summing-up in 1592. When he finally put pen to paper, however, he wrote in a curiously roundabout way, only identifying his friends and enemies obliquely. ('Young Juvenal, that biting satirist that lastly with me together writ a comedy' is probably Nashe; 'Shake-scene' is Shakespeare.) The reader has to guess the names and, similarly, to puzzle out for himself which troupe of actors has so enraged Greene; contemporaries would know, of course, which was Shakespeare's company, and it may be that another pun obliquely identifies it: 'unto none of you (like me) sought those burrs to cleave: those puppets (I mean) that spake from our mouths, those antics garnished in our colours. Is it not *strange* that I, to whom they all have been beholding; is it not like that you... [shall] be both at once of them forsaken?'[26]

A second problem in Shakespeare's early career is also placed in a new perspective when we identify him as one of the Lord Strange's Men — the apparent suddenness of his conquest of the theatrical world. Greene's 'Shake-scene' passage of 1592 implies that Shakespeare is already a dominant figure in the theatre; and when Strange's Men regrouped in 1594 as the Lord Chamberlain's Men he is clearly one of the leaders of the company. How could this happen so quickly, if he only began to write plays in 1590–1? In an earlier book I suggested that Shakespeare must have started as a playwright in 1586 or so. Having now looked more carefully at the 'Stanley connection' I believe that it may be a mistake to think of Shakespeare as a mere actor and servant, one of ten or so 'Lord Strange's Men'. If I am correct in arguing that *The Phoenix and the Turtle* belongs to 1586 – admittedly, a disconcertingly early date – and in seeing *Love's Labour's Lost* as a good-natured frolic at Lord Strange's expense by a privileged retainer, then we must agree that by 1592 Shakespeare already enjoyed a very special *social* position in Lord Strange's circle, and that could explain why Greene singled him out, maliciously, as the central figure amongst 'those puppets'.

I cannot end this chapter without mentioning another strange story – Spenser's stanzas about 'our pleasant Willy' in *The Tears of the Muses* (1591), a poem dedicated to the Lady Strange. In a section devoted to the decay of comedy, Spenser laments that 'ugly barbarism' has recently displaced 'sweet wits' and 'unhurtful sport'.

> All these, and all that else the comic stage
> With seasoned wit and goodly pleasance graced,
> By which man's life in his likest image
> Was limned forth, are wholly now defaced;
> And those sweet wits, which wont their like to frame,   5
> Are now despised, and made a laughing game.

And he, the man whom Nature self had made
To mock herself, and truth to imitate
With kindly counter under mimic shade,
Our pleasant Willy, ah! is dead of late: 10
With whom all joy and jolly merriment
Is also deaded, and in dolour drent.

In stead thereof scoffing scurrility
And scornful folly with contempt is crept,
Rolling in rhymes of shameless ribaldry   15
Without regard, or due decorum kept.
Each idle wit at will presumes to make,
And doth the learneds' task upon him take.

But that same gentle spirit, from whose pen
Large streams of honey and sweet nectar flow,   20
Scorning the boldness of such base-born men
Which dare their follies forth so rashly throw
Doth rather choose to sit in idle cell
Than so himself to mockery to sell.

As I have argued that Shakespeare belonged to Lord Strange's company in the 1580s and early 1590s, Spenser's 'pleasant Willy' requires some attention. Could Spenser have meant John Lyly, who used to be thought the leading writer of comedy in the 1580s? If so, why 'Willy'? – Or perhaps pleasant Will Shakespeare? (Heywood tells us that many 'modern' poets had their Christian names shortened: 'Mellifluous Shakespeare, whose enchanting quill / Commanded mirth or passion, was but Will'.[27] Compare Sonnet 136, 'And then thou lovest me, for my name is Will'). E. K. Chambers ruled that 1591 'is too early to make a reference to Shakespeare ... at all plausible';[28] but those who contend that Chambers erred in dating the beginning of Shakespeare's writing career as late as 1590–1 will want to re-open this question.

It is, of course, not impossible that 'pleasant Willy' and 'that same gentle spirit' are two different men, and that Willy has literally died. But the usual interpretation is surely the more likely one: *gentle* (line 19) refers back to *kindly* (line 9), therefore Willy is that *same* gentle spirit, and he is *dead of late* figuratively, that is, he chooses to sit in idle cell and not to write. Taking it so, and assuming that *The Comedy of Errors, The Two Gentlemen of Verona* and *The Taming of the Shrew* were already performed by 1591, as many believe, we must ponder Spenser's dedication to Lady Strange. For Shakespeare, as one of Lord Strange's Men, would be known to Lady Strange; and Spenser also knew her, and indeed claimed to be related to her. (She was one of the Spencers of Althorpe – the 'noble family', as he said in *Colin Clout's Come Home Again*, 'Of which I meanest boast myself to be'.) Dedicating *Tears* to Lady Strange, Spenser referred to 'your particular bounties, and also some private bands of affinity, which it hath pleased your ladyship to acknowledge'. Spenser, in short, would be aware of Lady Strange's entourage, and accordingly might give a special prominence to Lord Strange's poet as a writer of comedies, even though those comedies had only been performed, not printed.

I once thought it unlikely that 'pleasant Willy' stood for Shakespeare: Spenser, in *Tears*, laments the decay of learning, and Shakespeare 'did not strike contemporaries as a man of learning'.[29] Perhaps Jonson's dismissive remark about 'small Latin and less Greek' influenced me more than it should have done. I now think that Shakespeare and Spenser could well have met, through Lord and Lady Strange, and that the younger man, a former schoolmaster if not a graduate, is bound to have impressed Spenser as he seems to have dazzled most of his acquaintances. A year or so later Henry Chettle, having encountered Shakespeare for the first time, evidently considered him a 'scholar' and a gentleman.

> How I have all the time of my conversing in printing hindered the bitter inveighing against *scholars,* it hath been very well known; and how in that I dealt, I can sufficiently prove. With neither of them that take offence was I acquainted, and with one of them I care not if I never be ... [As for the other, i.e. Shakespeare] myself have seen his demeanor no less civil than he excellent in the quality he professes.[30]

Spenser's standards may have been more rigorous than Chettle's yet I fancy that the dramatist who was soon to write *Love's Labour's Lost* would have struck Spenser, in conversation, as a 'sweet wit' and as highly sophisticated.

The phrase '*our* pleasant Willy', and Spenser's awareness of Willy's reasons for choosing to remain 'idle', both suggest that the two poets were personally acquainted. Now Shakespeare, it is thought, read the first books of *The Faerie Queene* before they were published in 1590, perhaps in 1587–8;[31] and Spenser, though resident in Ireland, returned to England in 1589–90, and did his best at this time to renew contact with courtly patrons. If Spenser met 'our pleasant Willy' in 1589–90, this was the very period when English comedy became embroiled in the Martin Marprelate controversy, stooping to scoffing scurrility – until the bishops grew so alarmed at the satirical muck-raking of their own supporters that they stopped their activities.[32] The picture fits together, and, in addition, Spenser's stanzas quite remarkably anticipate what others were to say later about Shakespeare's style and personality. (1) The truth and naturalness of his characters was admired, and rated above all competitors, in the seventeenth century. Compare 'And he, the man whom Nature self had made / To mock herself, and truth to imitate' (lines 7–8). (2) Francis Meres commended 'mellifluous and honey-tongued Shakespeare', and Barnfield his 'honey-flowing vein'. Compare 'from whose pen / Large streams of honey and sweet nectar flow' (lines 19–20). (3) Jonson, who knew him personally, called him 'gentle Shakespeare'; and, though there was another side to his character,[33] it is clear that Shakespeare inspired the deepest affection in his friends. Jonson headed his great memorial poem 'To the memory of my beloved . . .', and Heminges and Condell declared that they collected the plays in the First Folio 'without any ambition either of self-profit, or fame: only to keep the memory of so worthy a friend and fellow alive as was *our Shakespeare*'. Compare '*Our* pleasant Willy', 'that same *gentle* spirit' (lines 10, 19). (4) Spenser distinguished between two kinds of comedy, and saw 'pleasant Willy' as a leader of 'unhurtful sport / Delight and laughter', of 'goodly pleasance' and 'jolly merriment', as against 'scoffing scurrility', etc. (lines 2, 11, 13). Shakespeare specialised in celebratory or 'happy' comedy, and avoided the harshly satirical (except for his brief participation in the 'war of the theatres', probably in *Troilus and Cressida*). At least one contemporary noted this decided preference of his.

> To our English Terence, Mr. Will.
> Shake-speare.
>
> Some say (good Will) which I, in sport, do sing,
> Hadst thou not played some kingly parts in sport
> Thou hadst been a companion for a king,
> And been a king among the meaner sort.
> *Some others rail; but, rail as they think fit,*
> *Thou hast no railing but a reigning wit.*
> And honesty thou sow'st, which they do reap,
> So to increase their stock, which they do keep.[34]

(5) Contrasting the 'boldness' of others with pleasant Willy, who 'doth rather choose to sit in idle cell' than stoop to their level (lines 21-4), Spenser described a situation repeated in the Sonnets. When the Rival Poet 'spends all his might / To make me tongue-tied', and the Young Man countenanced this, Shakespeare quite deliberately chose 'silence' (Sonnets 78–86), and likewise refused to compete.

I do not attach the same importance to each of these five 'anticipations'. Shakespeare was not the only poet praised for his honeyed style; and Spenser overused 'gentle', in *Tears* and elsewhere, as a general term of approbation. All the same, Spenser's picture of 'pleasant Willy' agrees in so many particulars with later views of

Shakespeare, and in so few with other accounts of Lyly or the remaining writers of comedy, that the name 'Willy' can no longer be brushed aside as a meaningless coincidence. Nor is it irrelevant, in my opinion, that Spenser's lament for the state of poetry picks out one man as an exception – one solitary poet who deserves several stanzas of praise – and that later centuries agree that one writer achieved pre-eminence in 'the age of Shakespeare'. 'Pleasant Willy', I believe, had abandoned comedy to write history-plays when Spenser composed *The Tears of the Muses* – or, possibly, had stopped writing altogether for a while.

Accepting that 'pleasant Willy' alludes to Shakespeare, I am predisposed to favour another possible allusion in *Colin Clout's Come Home Again* (1595).

> There also is (ah no, he is not now!)
> But since I said he is, he quite is gone,
> Amyntas quite is gone, and lies full low,
> Having his Amaryllis left to moan.
> Help, O ye shepherds, help ye all in this,
> Help Amaryllis this her loss to mourn:
> Her loss is yours, your loss Amyntas is,
> Amyntas, flower of shepherds' pride forlorn.
> He whilst he livèd was the noblest swain
> That ever pipèd in an oaten quill:
> Both did he other, which could pipe, maintain,
> And eke could pipe himself with passing skill.
> And there, though last not least, is Aetion,
> A gentler shepherd may nowhere be found:
> Whose Muse, full of high thought's invention,
> Doth like himself heroically sound.

Spenser's commentators agree that Amyntas must be Ferdinando Stanley the fifth Earl of Derby, who died in 1594, and that Amaryllis is consequently the former Lady Strange, dedicatee of *The Tears of the Muses*; also, that *Colin Clout* was finished in draft form by 27 December 1591, and revised after the Earl's death.[35] The possibility that 'Aetion' stands for Shakespeare has of course been raised before, largely because others later made the same point about his name, i.e. 'the war-like sound of his surname' (Thomas Fuller).[36] But Aetion is more commonly thought to be Michael Drayton, 'who gave himself the heroic name of Rowland'.[37] It should be noted, however, that Spenser introduces Aetion just after praising Amyntas for 'maintaining' others who could pipe, or write poetry – so what would be more natural than that Spenser's thoughts should turn from Lord Strange to one of his most distinguished protégés? There is no evidence that Lord Strange ever supported Drayton, but, as we have seen, several kinds of evidence link Shakespeare and Lord Strange's Men. And of how many other poets could one say that they had names that 'heroically sound', precisely what was later said again about Shakespeare's? Anyone who believes, as I do, that Shakespeare had written five history plays before the end of 1591 (the three parts of *Henry VI*, *Richard III* and *King John*) will conclude that Spenser referred to this astonishing achievement when he applauded a gentle shepherd's heroic muse.

'Pleasant Willy' and 'Aetion' have been considered before as possible allusions to Shakespeare. The tradition, perpetuated by E. K. Chambers, that Shakespeare only began to write plays in 1590-1, has always weighed against them but the tradition is crumbling at last. Once we grasp the importance of Lord Strange in Shakespeare's early career, Spenser's thinly disguised hints about Willy's character and Aetion's heroic name, together with the gentle shepherd's 'strange' connections in each poem, tip the scales the other way. Honour where honour is due: Spenser, a shrewd observer of the literary scene, was almost certainly the first poet to write appreciatively of his great contemporary in print. And Spenser's two tributes, we may add, lend some support – circumstantial but not insubstantial – to the theory that Shakespeare worked for a while for matchless Ferdinando.[38]

VII

The Shakespeare Epitaphs
and the Stanleys

By the middle of the seventeenth century a surprising number of independent witnesses had ascribed to Shakespeare half a dozen epitaphs, not one of which appears in the traditional *Complete Works*. Although their literary quality cannot be described as 'Shakespearian', there are good reasons for believing that some, at least, of these verses were correctly attributed. I am particularly interested in the epitaphs for Sir Thomas and Sir Edward Stanley, which can be seen as another arm of Shakespeare's 'Lancashire connection', but begin with those for John Combe and Elias James.

(1) he had a particular intimacy with Mr Combe, an old gentleman noted thereabouts for his wealth and usury. It happened that ... Mr Combe told Shakespeare in a laughing manner that he fancied he intended to write his epitaph, if he happened to outlive him; and since he could not know what might be said of him when he was dead, he desired it might be done immediately. Upon which Shakespeare gave him these four verses:

> Ten in the hundred lies here engraved,
> 'Tis a hundred to ten, his soul is not saved.
> If any man ask who lies in this tomb
> 'O, ho!' quoth the devil, ''Tis my John-a-Combe.'
> (Rowe's *Life* of Shakespeare, 1709)

(2) When God was pleased, the world unwilling yet,
> Elias James to nature paid his debt,
> And here reposeth; as he lived he died,
> The saying in him strongly verified,
> 'Such life, such death'. Then, the known truth to tell,
> He lived a godly life, and died as well.
> Wm. Shakespeare. (Rawlinson Poet.
> MS. 160, fo. 41, Bodleian Library)

[77]

(3) On the north side of the chancel of Tonge Church, in the county of Salop, stands a very stately tomb, supported with Corinthian columns. It hath two figures of men in armour thereon lying ... and this epitaph upon it: 'Thomas Stanley, Knight, second son of Edward, Earl of Derby,' etc. These following verses were made by William Shakespeare, the late famous tragedian.

Written upon the east end of the tomb

Ask who lies here, but do not weep;
He is not dead, he doth but sleep.
This stony register is for his bones,
His fame is more perpetual than these stones;
And his own goodness, with himself being gone,
Shall live when earthly monument is none.

Written upon the west end thereof

Not monumental stone preserves our fame,
Nor sky-aspiring pyramids our name;
The memory of him for whom this stands
Shall outlive marble and defacers' hands;
When all to Time's consumption shall be given,
Stanley, for whom this stands, shall stand in heaven.
(Sir William Dugdale, 1664)[1]

According to E. K. Chambers, little reliance can be placed on ascriptions found in seventeenth-century manuscripts. Of (1) he said 'if there is anything in the story, Shakespeare can at most ... have adapted verses which he knew from Hoskins or another', because similar verses on a usurer had been printed in 1608 ('Ten in the hundred lies under this stone, / And a hundred to ten to the devil he's gone'), and another version was described by Camden in 1614 as 'composed by Master John Hoskins [1566–1638] when he was young':

Here lies ten in the hundred
In the ground fast rammed.
'Tis an hundred to ten
But his soul is damned.

Of (3) Chambers wrote, even more dismissively, that 'it is clear that one set of the verses cannot be Shakespeare's, if it relates to the Sir Edward who owned Tong [he died in 1632], and on internal evidence there is no temptation to accept either of them as his'.[2]

I have grouped these epitaphs together because in each case new information has come to light, after the epitaphs were attributed to Shakespeare, some of it unknown to Chambers, confirming a 'special relationship' between the poet and those he allegedly wrote about.

[78]

(1) 'An Epitaph upon one John Combe of Stratford upon Avon' was first printed, without naming an author, in 1619; and was ascribed to Shakespeare by Hammond (1634) and others before Rowe printed his version in 1709. Yet neither Rowe nor his predecessors knew about Combe's will or about Shakespeare's, which came to light later; and the wills confirm a 'particular intimacy' between the two families. (Combe left Shakespeare £5 in 1613, and Shakespeare bequeathed his sword to Thomas Combe in 1616; Thomas was John Combe's nephew and heir.) (2) Leslie Hotson showed in 1949 that Elias James, whose will was proved 26 September 1610, was connected with Shakespeare's friend John Jackson. (The Blackfriars Gate-House was conveyed in 1613 to Shakespeare, William Johnson, vintner, and 'John Jackson and John Hemmyng of London, gentlemen'.) Jackson later married Jane, the widow of Elias James's brother Jacob (died 1613), and before that, in 1611, Thomas Savage (for whom see p. 84) had appointed as overseer of his will 'my very loving friend John Jackson'.[3] The unknown Elias James turns out to be a friend of one of Shakespeare's friends – a discovery that compels us to take the mid-seventeenth-century ascription of the epitaph more seriously.

(3) Next, Sir Thomas and Sir Edward Stanley and Shakespeare's 'Lancashire connection'. The Stanley tomb at Tong, in Shropshire, carries the inscription 'Thomas Stanley, Knight, second son of Edward Earl of Derby ... had issue two sons, Henry and Edward. Henry died an infant, and Edward survived, to whom those lordships descended', and goes on to name Edward's wife and one son and seven daughters. The relevant part of the Stanley pedigree is as follows:

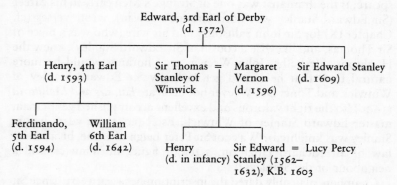

I agree with Chambers that the verse epitaphs were intended for the younger Sir Edward and for his father, but not entirely with his reservation that, since this Sir Edward died in 1632, 'his figure, if it is his, and the verses on him must have been added to the tomb after that date, and incidentally after Shakespeare's death'. The implication seems to be that Shakespeare, being dead, could not have been involved; and it is spelt out in the *Shakespeare Encyclopaedia:* if Sir Edward is Sir Thomas's son 'there can be no question that Shakespeare did not write the epitaphs, since Sir Edward died in 1632, 16 years after Shakespeare'.[4] At this time, however, tombs with all their accessories were not infrequently ordered by the living, for themselves – as in the case of Edmund Tilney, the Master of the Revels, who asked in his will (1 July 1610) 'that there be a monument erected and set upon the place where I with the consent of the parson and churchwarden there have appointed ... if myself in my life-time do not finish the same'.[5] So, too, Bess of Hardwick arranged for her own burial 'in the place appointed', beneath her tomb, which was 'finished and wants nothing but setting up'.[6] As John Weever explained, 'It was usual in ancient times, and so it is in these our days, for persons of especial rank and quality to make their own tombs and monuments in their life-time; partly for that they might have a certain house to put their head in ... and partly to please themselves, in the beholding of their dead countenance in marble.'[7] Since Shakespeare is said to have jokingly given John Combe his epitaph, and to have composed one for himself, there is no reason to believe that he could not have written, before 1616, the epitaph for Sir Edward Stanley.

That he actually did so seems much likelier now that we begin to understand the 'Lancashire connection'. Sir Thomas and Sir Edward cease to be two mere names, otherwise unconnected with Shakespeare; if the dramatist was one of Strange's Men early in his career (Sir Edward Stanley was Lord Strange's cousin), wrote verses (cf. Chapter IX) for Sir John Salusbury and his wife (who was a niece of Sir Thomas, and likewise a cousin of Sir Edward Stanley), knew the Hoghtons, Heskeths, John Weever, etc., nothing would be more natural than that he would get to know Sir Edward Stanley of Winwick and Tong. Did Weever not dedicate *Faunus and Melliflora* (1600) 'to the right valorous and excellent accomplished gentleman, master Edward Stanley of Winwick, Esq.' (i.e. three years before Stanley was knighted)? Was not Sir Peter Leigh of Lyme, brother-in-law of Sir Richard Hoghton, a major figure in Winwick and a neighbour of the Stanleys?[8]

Chambers plausibly dated the inscription between 1603 (since Sir Edward is not referred to as a knight) and 1600 (when Sir Edward's daughter, Venetia, named in the inscription, was born). Would not this be 'rather late to put up a monument to persons who died in 1576 and 1596 respectively [i.e. Sir Edward's parents]?'[9] A good question, which can now be answered. We learn from *Inhabitants of Winwick v. Stanley* (26 Elizabeth)[10] that Sir Thomas Stanley in his later years was in financial difficulties; one deponent, Thomas Heye, declared that most of the complainants gave a year's rent to Sir Thomas 'of their benevolences when he was in trouble' (9th interrogatory). There are no clues in Sir Thomas's will,[11] but his widow's[12] reveals another relevant fact: she married again, and might have wished to be buried with her second husband. In the event, however, she snubbed her second husband, leaving him no token of her love, decreeing 'my body to be buried in the Parish Church of Tong by my husband Sir Thomas Stanley'; her will states, cryptically, that it was 'made by the consent and agreement' of her second husband, William Mathe, Esq. The tomb, therefore could have been delayed because the family was short of funds and, later, because there would be some doubt as to the figures to be represented.

The discovery that John Combe, Elias James and Sir Edward Stanley were friends of Shakespeare, or of his friends, appears to vindicate the near-contemporary attribution of their epitaphs to the dramatist. But – are they good enough to be his? Before we dismiss them as unworthy of the sweet swan of Avon, let us compare some other epitaphs that have also been ascribed to him.

(4) Mr Ben. Johnson and Mr Wm. Shake-speare being merry at a tavern, Mr Jonson having begun this for his epitaph:

Here lies Ben Johnson that was once one

he gives it to Mr Shakspear to make up, who presently writes:

Who while he lived was a slow things [*sic*]
And now being dead is nothing.
(Ms. collection by Nicholas Burgh, *c.* 1650)

(5) Good friend, for Jesus' sake forbear
To dig the dust enclosèd here!
Blessed be the man that spares these stones,
And cursed be he that moves my bones.[13]

It was in 1693 that Dowdall first recorded that Shakespeare's epitaph (5) was 'made by himself a little before his death'; he added that 'the clerk that showed me this church is above 80 years old', which might have inspired confidence, except that the same clerk said 'that this Shakespeare was formerly in this town bound apprentice to a butcher; but that he ran away from his master to London'.[14] While it seems unlikely, though not impossible, that Shakespeare was apprenticed to a butcher (cf. p. 2), we have no compelling reason to disbelieve the clerk about the epitaph, any more than to dispute his story that Shakespeare's 'wife and daughters did earnestly desire to be laid in the same grave with him' – unless it be that, again, we think the verses not good enough. What, then, would be 'good enough'? Two more epitaphs, undoubtedly from Shakespeare's pen, indicate that, like other practitioners in this sub-genre, he could be content with the epitaph's traditional near-doggerel style, and did not always aim at the 'powerful rhyme' of gilded monuments.

(6) Here lies a wretched corse, of wretched soul bereft;
Seek not my name. A plague consume you wicked caitiffs left!

(7) Here lie I, Timon, who alive all living men did hate.
Pass by, and curse thy fill; but pass, and stay not here thy gait.

Shakespeare copied Timon's epitaphs almost verbatim from North's Plutarch, presumably intending to delete one – and that has a bearing on other epitaphs that are not thought sufficiently 'Shakespearian'. He did not wish to make them recognisably his own –

That every word doth almost tell my name
Showing their birth, and where they did proceed
(Sonnet 76)

– because that would be inappropriate. Sometimes

– my nature is subdued
To what it works in, like the dyer's hand.
(Sonnet 111)

If he 'gave' Combe verses adapted from someone else's model, and possibly did the same in composing his own epitaph,[15] and more or less transcribed Timon's epitaphs from Plutarch, it becomes clear that he wished to conform to tradition, rather than 'make it new'. Accordingly (1) and (4) are comic epitaphs that could have been written by anyone, and (5), his own, is appropriate for the grave of any mortal who has no special claim to fame.

I must pause to underline this last point. The best reason for accepting Shakespeare's authorship of (5) is, surely, that it differs so markedly from the adulatory tone of the verses inscribed on his monument, and the respect shown to him by all the poets who paid tribute to him after his death, and in the Folio. In 1616 no one except Shakespeare himself could have omitted all mention of his achievements as a poet; and only the fact that he himself commanded it can explain why his family had such a modest epitaph inscribed on his grave-stone. It could seem 'appropriate' only to Shakespeare.

The failure of the epitaphs to impress us as 'Shakespearian' must not, I suggest, be allowed to weigh too heavily against them. If we were considering an anonymous seventeenth-century play this 'internal evidence' would be all-important, but not so with the epitaphs. The really significant factor is that those who first attributed (1) to (3) to Shakespeare could not know that, in each case, other 'connections' would one day be discovered. Why should he celebrate Elias James? Why write in honour of Sir Thomas Stanley, long dead, and of Sir Edward Stanley, who remained inconveniently alive until 1632? Why Tong in Shropshire? Such questions once stopped all further discussion – quite needlessly, it now appears.

To return to the Stanley epitaphs: though the tomb was erected between 1600 and 1603 (cf. p. 80), Shakespeare could have been asked to compose his verses either at this time, which would chime in well with his other 'Lancashire' contacts (cf. p. 85), or earlier – or later. Years of planning can precede the building of a tomb, and the verses might have been ready long before they could be inscribed; and verses can be added later as well. I assume that the epitaph for Sir Edward Stanley was kept 'in storage' until 1632 or that perhaps both epitaphs were inscribed then. What we are not entitled to assume is that the poet of *Hamlet* would be too haughty to stoop to such trifles. After all, the steward of the Earl of Rutland recorded in 1613, 'to Mr Shakespeare in gold about my Lord's ''impreso'', xliijs; to Richard Burbage for painting and making it, in gold, xliiijs.'[16] If Shakespeare wrote the verses or mottoes for Rutland's *imprese* (painted shields), as is generally accepted, why not the Stanley epitaphs?

VIII

Thomas Savage of Rufford

Leslie Hotson first pointed out, less than forty years ago, that Thomas Savage, the London goldsmith who acted as trustee for Shakespeare and four colleagues in 1599, came from Rufford in Lancashire – and that Sir Thomas Hesketh, to whom Alexander Hoghton recommended William Shakeshafte in 1581, lived in the same small town or village (cf. p. 34 above). Hotson's important discovery has already been misreported, and may pass into popular mythology beautified with others' feathers. 'Savage was a native of Rufford in Lancashire', states the *Shakespeare Encyclopaedia*. 'His cousin, whom he mentions in his will, was the widow of Sir Thomas Hesketh, in whose acting company Shakespeare might have spent the early years of his career'.[1] Schoenbaum made the same assertion in *Shakespeare's Lives*, i.e. Savage left a bequest in his will 'to the widow of Thomas Hesketh of Rufford – the same Hesketh to whom William Shakeshafte was recommended in 1581'.[2] There is of course no good reason for identifying Thomas Hesketh, the deceased husband of Savage's Rufford cousin, and Sir Thomas Hesketh. And there is one very good reason for not doing so: 'I, Dame Alice Hesketh, widow, late wife of Sir Thomas Hesketh of Rufforth in the County of Lancaster', made her will in November 1604, and an inventory of all her goods and chattels was prepared after her death, in March 1605.[3] Savage would not leave a bequest in 1611 to Dame Alice, who died in 1605. Who, then, was the Thomas Hesketh referred to by Savage? Two of Sir Thomas's sons were also called Thomas – his second legitimate son, and a bastard son (cf. p. 36). Though other Thomas Heskeths may have lived and died there before 1611, Rufford was not a large place, and Savage's cousin may well have been Sir Thomas's daughter-in-law. I have not so far managed to track down the dates when the two Thomases died, or the names of their wives; perhaps others will return to these questions and will show how, if at all, Thomas Savage and Sir Thomas were related by marriage.

[84]

Another Rufford clue that needs to be followed up is an entry in the registers of the parish church of Croston (Rufford was in the parish of Croston): the wedding, on 9 August 1551 of Jeffry Savage and Jenett Hesketh.[4] Thomas Savage named his mother in his will as 'Jennette Savadge', so it looks as if we have identified his father. In the unpublished records of the Goldsmiths Company there is an entry that Peter Savage, the son of Geoffrey Savage in the town of 'Rofforth' in the county of Lancaster, weaver, binds himself apprentice for seven years (1583);[5] it could well be that Peter followed his older brother Thomas to London, and that Thomas Savage's father was nothing more than a humble weaver. Even so, his mother might have been related to Sir Thomas Hesketh – for in Sir Thomas's will there are references not only to his own bastard sons but to his 'bastard brethren'. The Heskeths certainly believed that the world must be peopled, and they made their contribution; Thomas Savage's mother, Janet Hesketh, could have been a sister or a niece of Sir Thomas.

Thomas Savage of Rufford enters our story in 1599, the year of the Globe. In the same year John Weever published his *Epigrammes*, with a sonnet addressed to Shakespeare as well as many other verses that celebrated the Hoghtons and their northern friends; a year or two later Robert Chester collected poems in honour of Sir John Salusbury, published in 1601 in *Love's Martyr*, and included Shakespeare's *The Phoenix and the Turtle*; and the Stanley epitaphs ascribed to Shakespeare are also thought to date from this period (cf. p. 80). Whatever had happened in the intervening years, by the turn of the century the 'Lancashire connection' seems to have caught up with Shakespeare, and consequently Thomas Savage of Rufford deserves our most careful attention.

What more can be added to Hotson's very brief account of the goldsmith from Lancashire? First we must visit Goldsmiths Hall, where we learn that from the 1580s till his death in 1611 Thomas Savage took nine apprentices (one being George, the son of Roger Starkie of Croston, Lancashire; that is, he came from Savage's native parish). Savage seems to have been less interested in playing a leading part in the Goldsmiths Company than one might have expected from his will, for by the year of his death he had risen only to the rank of Renter Warden which, I am told, was regarded as a 'probationary' office for those who wished to go higher. The Court Minutes and Wardens' Accounts for 1579–92 are missing, so we know nothing about the date of Thomas Savage's commencement as a goldsmith. The extant volumes tell us, however, that his son, Richard Savage, was apprenticed in 1601. The most character-revealing entry dates from 1599, when Mr Savage (almost certainly our man, though a Richard Savage was also a goldsmith at this time; but Richard seems never to have been 'Mr' Savage) was fined forty shillings for slandering Mr Newman (a warden), and for saying 'very malapertly' that Mr Newman forgot himself, and for 'pressing Mr Newman with very violent words'.

Next, we may add that Savage's connection with Rufford was even closer than Hotson indicated. He was born there, his widowed cousin lived there; in addition, though, at least one sister and her family also lived there, as well as 'my cousin Francis Savage of Rufforth' and, probably, 'my mother Janet' (whose legacy of £10 was to be paid within two months, which suggests that she lived at some distance from London). Because of these family connections, Thomas Savage clearly remained in touch with Rufford and its affairs – as is also indicated by his directions for payments to 'the poor people of the town of Rufforth', 'at the discretion of my brother-in-law John Palmer, Thomas Spencer, Thomas Awly and Hugh Watkinson'. Thomas Spencer is probably the father of Jane Spencer (cf. p. 37), the third wife of Robert Hesketh, Esq. (son and heir of Sir Thomas.[6]

A second significant feature of Savage's will is its religious slant. Apart from his bequests to the poor in Rufford, and in his parish in London, and his unusually generous bequests to the 'parson and churchwardens' of his parish in London, and to their successors (that is, a house or inn called The George, in St Sepulchre's, London, together with four shops and gardens, etc.), it is the phrasing of the will's preamble that immediately reveals an unusual man. These are not words dictated by a lawyer, or merely echoes of a legal stereotype: the will speaks to us with a solemnity, a conviction, that is deeply moving. '. . . first, I bequeath my soul into Thy hands, O God – Father, Son and Holy Ghost. Thou hast first made me, and Thou hast given Thy Son to become man, who died for my sins and for the sins of the people. O Father, for this Thy Son's sake, have mercy upon me. O Lord Jesus Christ, Thou Son of God which hast bought me with Thy precious blood by one oblation sufficient for all, I believe in Thee. . . .'

Thomas Savage must have been married at least twice. In his will he mentions a house of his in which 'Mr John Wotton, gent., now dwelleth' and also 'my mother-in-law, Mrs Wootton' – which may reveal his wife's or a previous wife's maiden name. A badly damaged bill of complaint by Thomas Savage, citizen and goldsmith of London, and Alice his wife, refers to Alice's four children by at least two previous husbands, (1) the father of her son John Perryman, probably also John Perryman; (2) Hugh Myldner. The will of Hugh 'Myldener', citizen and freemason of London, survives and mentions 'my loving wife Alice'.[7] It is dated 10 September 1605, so at least some of Thomas Savages's five children will not have been Alice's. Hugh Myldner, incidentally, had many servants and owned a good deal of property: he seems to have been a substantial businessman, like Thomas Savage (though not, I think, on quite the same scale).

Exactly how Thomas Savage amassed his very considerable fortune – starting, probably, in 1580 or so with little or nothing – we can only guess. I think it likely that he gave only some of his time to his work as a goldsmith, and engaged in other ventures as opportunity offered – like William Shakespeare, and so many enterprising men of his time. Savage left bequests to 'the worshipful company of Goldsmiths in London, whereof I myself am a free member', including £8 'to make them a supper'; he also left 'unto my fellows' in the sea-coal trade, of the city of London, £3 for a dinner – a smaller sum, perhaps because fewer men would be invited, but 'my fellows' implies a close involvement. Savage seems also to have invested in property (again, like Shakespeare): in his will he bequeathed five houses, in Silver St, Great Wood St, two in Addle St, and The George in St Sepulchre's, a very recent purchase. In addition he apparently married a rich widow – a born businessman! It is clear from his will, however, that he was also a devoted family man.

Thomas Savage's name is linked for all time with that of William Leveson, these being the two trustees to whom William Shakespeare and four colleagues assigned their half-share in the gardens and grounds when the Globe was built in 1599. Although Leveson was not himself a Lancastrian, students of Shakespeare will want to know more about the man who was bracketed with Thomas Savage of Rufford.

Leslie Hotson gives us a good start by identifying Leveson as a churchwarden at St Mary's, Aldermanbury, in 1599; a churchwarden, that is, in 'the parish of Digges, Heminges and Condell'.[8] According to Hotson, Leveson 'lived first in Aldermanbury and afterwards in Philip Lane. ... His father was an esquire of the Leveson family of Staffordshire Shropshire, and Kent. ... His elder brother was Sir John Leveson, M.P.' A member of the Mercers' Company, the old Merchant Venturers, and of the Muscovy Company, William Leveson greatly exerted himself on behalf of the Virginia Company and, as depicted by Hotson, was a man of substantial means at the turn of the century: in 1597 'he lent the Queen some hundreds of pounds to pay the expeditionary forces in Picardy'.

Several new facts can now be added. Leveson's wealth in the 1590s is corroborated by a bill of complaint in the Court of Requests (34 Elizabeth) lodged by William Leveson of London, mercer, and William Chapman of London, salter, against Roger James the elder and Roger the younger, two London brewers. The brewers claimed that their deceased beer-clerk had fallen behind in his accounts, and that Leveson and Chapman owed them £200. For us the chief interest of this suit lies in the sums involved: William Leveson was already operating on a large scale in 1592.[9]

On the other hand, Leveson's will (8 January 1621) seems to me to tell a different story.[10] It is dangerous to read too much into specific bequests, but my general impression is that when he made the will Leveson was considerably less well off than he had been twenty-five years earlier. William Leveson, mercer, bequeathed 'to the parson and churchwardens of the parish of Aldermanbury, where I was sometime an inhabitant', £4; to the poor of the parish where he now dwells, £1; to Susan Hall, Robert Harris, Ann Curl ⟨...⟩, probably all servants, ten shillings each; to Robert Hall, 'for soliciting my business', £4; one third of his estate to his sons, Thomas and James; one third to his wife, Mary, his executrix. Compared with Thomas Savage's magnificent bequest to the parson and churchwardens of his parish (cf. p. 86), not to mention his other bequests, Leveson's estate now seems to be on an altogether smaller scale.

William Leveson (or Lewson or Luson, common variants of the family name) must have been well known to the Privy Council. In 1586 the Council sent a supporting letter to the Company of Merchant Adventurers 'that whereas they have refused to admit into the full freedom one William Lewson, a young man having served as an apprentice Robert Roe of London, a merchant of their society alleging that he is incapable of their said freedom because he was contrary to their ordinances received to be an apprentice' – urging the company to admit Leveson, who had committed no fault.[11] In 1595 Leveson infuriated Richard Carmarthen, the newly-appointed surveyor of the Port of London, by 'most obstinately and violently' resisting his authority, refusing to let him inspect his 'packs and fardels of clothes', beating his officers and 'with wild words despising the Queen's letters patents' (Hotson knew and summarised these complaints). It may have been these events that introduced Leveson to Sir Robert Cecil, who now began to use him as a 'post office' for agents abroad: letters for Cecil were addressed to 'Mr William Lewson, merchant, at London'.[12] Or perhaps Cecil came to know Leveson through William Waad, Clerk of the Privy Council and later Lieutenant of the Tower; Waad was Leveson's cousin.[13] As Hotson pointed out, Leveson was also a cousin of Sir Richard Leveson, the naval commander, husband of Mary Fitton (born 1562), aunt of the notorious Mary Fitton (born 1578), who has been thought to be the 'dark lady' of Shakespeare's sonnets.

IX

The Phoenix and the Turtle

Let the bird of loudest lay
On the sole Arabian tree
Herald sad and trumpet be,
To whose sound chaste wings obey.

5 But thou shrieking harbinger,
Foul precurrer of the fiend,
Augur of the fever's end,
To this troop come thou not near.

From this session interdict
10 Every fowl of tyrant wing,
Save the eagle, feather'd king:
Keep the obsequy so strict.

Let the priest in surplice white,
That defunctive music can,
15 Be the death-divining swan,
Lest the requiem lack his right.

And thou treble-dated crow,
That thy sable gender mak'st
With the breath thou giv'st and tak'st,
20 'Mongst our mourners shalt thou go.

Here the anthem doth commence:
Love and constancy is dead;
Phoenix and the turtle fled
In a mutual flame from hence.

25 So they lov'd, as love in twain
Had the essence but in one:
Two distincts, division none;
Number there in love was slain.

Hearts remote, yet not asunder;
30 Distance and no space was seen
'Twixt this turtle and his queen:
But in them it were a wonder.

So between them love did shine
That the turtle saw his right

35 Flaming in the phoenix' sight;
Either was the other's mine.

Property was thus appalled
That the self was not the same:
Single nature's double name
40 Neither two nor one was called.

Reason, in itself confounded,
Saw division grow together,
To themselves yet either neither,
Simple were so well compounded:

45 That it cried, How true a twain
Seemeth this concordant one!
Love hath reason, reason none,
If what parts, can so remain.

Whereupon it made this Threne
50 To the phoenix and the dove
Co-supremes and stars of love,
As Chorus to their tragic scene.

THRENOS
Beauty, truth and rarity,
Grace in all simplicity,
55 Here enclos'd, in cinders lie.

Death is now the phoenix' nest,
And the turtle's loyal breast
To eternity doth rest.

Leaving no posterity,
60 'Twas not their infirmity,
It was married chastity.

Truth may seem, but cannot be;
Beauty brag, but 'tis not she;
Truth and beauty buried be.

65 To this urn let those repair
That are either true or fair:
For these dead birds sigh a prayer.

An untitled poem now known as *The Phoenix and the Turtle*, first published in Robert Chester's *Love's Martyr* (1601), proves indisputably that Shakespeare was in some way connected with the Stanley family. The poem, signed 'William Shake-speare', was one of several 'poetical essays' by 'the best and chiefest of our modern writers' consecrated (with many flourishes) 'to the love and merit of the true-noble knight, Sir John Salusbury'. Chester's own poems record the lamentations of the turtle and the phoenix, and leave us in no doubt that these two excessively talkative birds represent Sir John Salusbury of Lleweni (in Denbighshire) and his wife, Ursula Halsall or Stanley, an illegitimate daughter of Henry Stanley, fourth Earl of Derby.[1]

Though illegitimate, Ursula was an acknowledged child of the earl, and after her marriage (in December 1586), she and her husband remained in close touch with her father and half-brothers. In *The Derby Household Books*, the accounts of the earl's steward, we find 'Mr Salusbury' (as he then was) to have been a visitor at his father-in-law's, now and then at the same time as Hoghtons, Heskeths and others who probably knew William Shakeshafte at Lea or Rufford.[2] According to Robert Parry's *Diary*, William Stanley, the sixth Earl, and his countess 'came to Lleweni and were very royally entertained'[3] in 1597. Perhaps, then, the tendency of commentators to dismiss Shakespeare's poem as obscure and totally baffling needs to be reconsidered. Could it be that the poet was personally acquainted with Sir John Salusbury and his wife, instead of being, as is usually assumed,[4] a stranger who for unexplained reasons agreed to contribute complimentary verses, which, so far as we know, he did for no one else? If the phoenix and the turtle are part of the 'Lancashire connection' it should be possible to throw new light on Shakespeare's fascinating poem.

Before I proceed to new information about Sir John Salusbury, and new explanations of *Love's Martyr* and *The Phoenix and the Turtle*, it will be useful to summarise what is already known, and Carleton Brown's excellent edition of *Poems by Sir John Salusbury and Robert Chester* (1914) remains an indispensable starting-point.[5] John Salusbury of Lleweni was born in 1566 or 1567, the second son of John Salusbury, Esq., and Catherine of Berain (a granddaughter of Sir Roland Velville, illegitimate son of Henry VII). His father died in 1566, before John was born; and John's older brother, Thomas, took part in the Babington conspiracy and was executed on 21 September 1586; at this date, consequently, John became the heir of Lleweni. Three months later he married Ursula Stanley (December 1586), and the local parish registers record the baptisms of their children: Jane (10 October 1587), Harry (26 October 1588: he died the same day), Harry (24 Sepember 1589), John (27 July, 1590: he died the same day), John (8 November 1592), and five more. A productive family! John Salusbury evidently took after his mother, who married three more husbands and had several more children: her second husband was Sir Richard Clough, reputedly the wealthiest commoner in England; next came Morris Wyn of Gwydir, Esq., thrice Sheriff of Caernarvonshire; and lastly Edward Thelwall, Esq., of Plas-y-Ward, Sheriff of Denbighshire in 1590, who played an important role in John Salusbury's later life, even though Catherine of Berain died in 1591.

Despite some dangerous quarrels in Denbighshire, to which we shall have to return, John Salusbury had friends in London and they helped him to advance in the world. Apart from his father-in-law, who died in 1593, and his brothers-in-law, the fifth and sixth Earls of Derby, he also had influential London connections through his stepfather, Edward Thelwall. In March 1595 he was appointed one of the Esquires of the Body to the Queen, and in the same month he was admitted to the Middle Temple. (He had matriculated at Oxford in 1581, but we do not know whether he took a degree.) The Privy Council appointed him, in 1597, Deputy Lieutenant for Denbighshire. In June 1601 he was knighted by the Queen, and in the same year Robert Chester dedicated *Love's Martyr* to him. Then, quite suddenly, his fortunes declined; one has the impression that his many enemies at last proved too much for him, and that he ran into financial difficulties. He died in 1612; Dame Ursula, the 'phoenix', lived on till 1636.

A fairly conventional life, it may be thought, but not so. Sir John Salusbury was also a poet, and a friend and patron of poets. Shakespeare, Jonson, Chapman and Marston contributed verses in his honour to *Love's Martyr*. It is likely, though, that Robert Chester, the author of *Love's Martyr*, was Sir John's closest literary associate, and lived with him or near him in Denbighshire, perhaps as his chaplain or secretary, for many years. Chester and Sir John Salusbury shared a taste for 'mystical' verse – that is, verse that alludes obscurely to people they knew, sometimes in acrostics – and they both wrote in this style about Dorothy Halsall, Sir John's sister-in-law, lavishly praising her physical and other perfections. Some of these poems of her husband might well have seemed too enthusiastic to Dame Ursula, if she ever saw them. Brown thought that the Halsall acrostics 'show that Sir John's infatuation for his sister-in-law began before 1597, but we have no means of knowing how long it continued. Several allusions in the poems addressed to her make it clear that she was already married' (p. xxxix). Infatuation may be the right word, but Sir John wrote acrostics in a like vein for Blanche Wynn, the wife of his half-brother,[6] so it could be that it was simply the fashionable thing to do in polite society. (Shakespeare's sonnets are similarly 'infatuated'.) For our purposes it is more important to note the cultivated obscurity of some of these poems – a special feature found again in *Love's Martyr* and in Shakespeare's *The Phoenix and the Turtle*, as well as in other volumes connected with the same patrons (e.g. Richard Robinson's *A Golden Mirror* (1589), a celebration of Cheshire and Lancashire worthies of the Stanley circle, or Robert Parry's *Sinetes* (1597), dedicated to John Salusbury).

Carleton Brown also gave an account of Sir John Salusbury's many skirmishes – physical and legal – with other leading figures in Denbighshire; and, as I shall suggest shortly, this local rivalry helps to explain the publication of *Love's Martyr*.

> The leaders in this hostile movement were Sir John Lloyd of Llan-rhayader and his brothers-in-law, Sir Richard Trevor of Trevallyn and Captain John Salusbury, together with Thomas Trafford, Esq. ... Their unfriendliness toward Salusbury probably had its origin in some neighbourhood feud, though it may have been aggravated by political differences. Lloyd and Captain Salusbury, at least, had been conspicuous among the adherents of Essex. ... Quite aside from political controversies, however, there is abundant evidence of strained relations for several years previous between Sir Richard Trevor, Sir John Lloyd, and Captain Salusbury on the one hand, and the Thelwalls, with whom Sir John Salusbury was allied by his mother's fourth marriage, on the other. (p. xix)

(Captain John Salusbury was Sir John Salusbury's cousin: see Appendix B(4) for the Salusbury family tree). All these animosities erupted in the Parliamentary election of October, 1601. A vivid chapter of J. E. Neale's *The Elizabethan House of Commons* (1949) on 'County Elections: the Denbighshire Elections of 1588 and 1601' picks up the story, and confirms Brown's surmise about a 'neighbourhood feud ... aggravated by political differences'. The county, Neale explained, was split into two halves, east and west, and their rivalry had continued for many years. In the 1590s Edward Thelwall and his stepson John Salusbury (later Sir John) were the leading figures in the west, and Richard Trevor, John Lloyd and others in the east; the east aligned itself with the Earl of Essex (John Lloyd and his brothers-in-law, and Trevor's brother, served with Essex in Ireland), the west with Sir Robert Cecil. The 'Essex rebellion', in February 1601, seriously implicated the eastern party: 'they had hitched their fortunes to the Earl of Essex, and fell with him'. Nevertheless, in the election later that year Sir Richard Trevor stood against Sir John Salusbury – and, on the fateful day, what could almost be called two private armies faced each other at Wrexham. If we may believe Trevor's witnesses, Sir John Salusbury openly boasted that he would be chosen knight of the parliament, or it would cost five hundred lives; he and his men terrified the voters, and he vaunted that he would take precedence of Trevor and Lloyd at the county court or die for it.

The events of that day concern us because they reveal two very different 'images' of Sir John Salusbury – as his enemies saw him, and as he saw himself – in the year of *Love's Martyr*. Let us pause and hear what the two sides have to say, always remembering that there may be some slight exaggeration when hot-tempered Welshmen air their grievances. According to Salusbury, Trevor proclaimed a general muster in his area, and pressed Salusbury's supporters for the wars in Ireland – ordering them to a distant place on election-day, so that they could not vote; he then took two hundred armed men to Wrexham, while Sir John Lloyd brought one hundred, and other allies came with more than three hundred, marching through the county and terrorising the inhabitants. According to Trevor, Salusbury entered Wrexham with a similar army, with trumpets sounding. Next day the sheriff, fearing riots, asked the two principals to stay away from the election, which he proposed to hold in the open, at the High Cross. Trevor had assembled three hundred of his men in the church, and Salusbury decided that he too would go to church.

> Whatever his motive – whether to brave Trevor, or, as he argued, to make his devotions – he walked to the church, accompanied by some friends, baring his head as he went by the county court. At the churchyard, he and Trevor passed each other, one going out as the other came in. Trevor quickly turned back. Soon they were bidding each other keep the peace, Salusbury doffing his hat and crying 'God save the Queen!'; until, by repeated and mutual injunctions to peace, they warmed themselves into drawing their swords. Then, says Salusbury, a warning piece was shot off, which brought Trevor's men pouring into the churchyard. Among them was Captain John Salusbury who demanded where the villain was, 'swearing outrageously that he would shoot him through'.

That is J. E. Neale's impartial reconstruction. Sir John Salusbury painted a different picture of himself as one who, 'accompanied only with two aged gentlemen and about six other persons', went to church 'in a very peaceable manner', the most inoffensive of men!

The sheriff separated the two factions, and no election took place. Salusbury immediately complained to Cecil about 'the most outrageous abuse offered not only to me but to the whole commonalty of this County of Denbigh',[7] and lodged a formal complaint in the Star Chamber; and in December 1601 he was after all elected to Parliament. Moreover, wrote A. H. Dodd in another pioneering study, 'by timely intervention with Cecil he [Sir John Salusbury] prevented the nominations both of Trevor as sheriff and of Trevor and Lloyd as deputy lieutenants';[8] and 'meanwhile it rained Star Chamber cases', the two sides accusing each other of oppression, fraud, riot, murder, etc.

As if these political frictions were not enough, the Salusbury–Trevor feud must have been exacerbated by another event of the greatest concern to both parties – the death of Sir Robert Salusbury of Rug. Carleton Brown and J. E. Neale seem not to have known of this complication, but it exercised many minds from 1599 to 1601. Sir Robert, Sheriff of Denbigh in 1597, an Essex supporter knighted in Ireland, was a cousin of Sir John Salusbury (Sir John's father was the brother of Sir Robert's mother)[9] and also a brother-in-law of Sir John Lloyd (Lloyd married Sir Robert's sister, Margaret). Sir Robert's son and heir being still a minor, the two Denbigh factions must both have wanted to secure this wealthy ward, which would have entitled them to arrange his marriage and firmly attach him to their interest. But other vultures were also attracted. On 24 May 1599, Margaret Lady Hoby wrote to Sir Robert Cecil: 'It was my evil fortune to desire and obtain of her Majesty the wardship of Sir Robert Salusbury's [Salsberey's] son and heir, who then by the report of his brother captains was supposed to be dead, though since fallen out contrary, yet it is certainly thought that his disease, though lingering, is not recoverable. I entreat you that I may receive some benefit of my first obtained suit at court'.[10] Sir Robert Salusbury 'lingered' for a while, at the house of Gabriel Goodman, Dean of Westminster, who reported to Cecil on his illness.[11] Now Goodman, a native of Ruthin in Denbighshire, had been for many years chaplain to Sir William Cecil (Lord Burghley), and was the son of Cecily, daughter of Edward Thelwall of Plas-y-ward; that is, he was a cousin of Sir John Salusbury's step-father.[12] In his will (1601) Goodman left 'to my brother-in-law and cousin Edward Thelwall' a ring of gold, and other bequests to Thelwall's sons; and his bequests to Sir Robert Cecil and his brother reveal his closeness to Master Secretary's family. Sir Robert Salusbury himself made 'my dear and loving cousins, Edward Thelwall, Esq., and Edward Puleston, Esq.' his executors (Edward Puleston was Sir Richard Trevor's brother-in-law), and devised lands to them in Denbigh and Merioneth in trust for his son and heir, John Salusbury (1599).[13] In his last illness, therefore, Sir Robert Salusbury could probably be considered to be in the hands of the Thelwall–Lleweni faction, and of the 'Cecil party'; when he died, Thomas Marbury, a Cecil protégé, was granted the wardship of his son (30 November 1600);[14] yet the inventory of Sir Robert's goods and chattels in Denbigh and Merioneth was apparently made out by Sir Richard Trevor, Piers Salusbury and Roger Williams.[15] At this very time the fortunes of the 'Essex party' were sinking, and in February 1601 Sir John Lloyd and other Denbighshire supporters of the earl were implicated in his 'rebellion'.

Having traced some of the troubled events of 1599 to 1601 in Denbighshire and London, and the affiliations of the two factions to Essex and Cecil, we are now ready to consider the publication of Love's Martyr in 1601. Why should Chester's dated and culpably long-winded poems have been offered to an indifferent world in this particular year? Brown has shown, we shall see shortly (p. 99), that Love's Martyr, 'or at least that portion of it which is concerned with the story of the Turtle and Phoenix, must have been written more than a decade before its publication in 1601'.[16] Why then publish in 1601? Brown's explanation seems to me to miss the point entirely.

> One may most easily account for the publication of Love's Martyr . . . by supposing that Sir John Salusbury, in order to gratify the literary ambition of Chester, who was his friend as well as his dependant, took the manuscript of the poem with him on one of his journeys from Lleweni to London, asked a few of the most prominent poets . . . to lend their names and verses to the success of the volume, and then sent it to the printer. (p. liv)

Salusbury, we must recall, was engaged in a bitter struggle with his east Denbighshire rivals, which reached its crisis in 1601. In the first half of the year Salusbury's enemies lost an important round, as supporters of Essex, and Sir John seemed to be in the ascendant: the Queen knighted him in June; but they were still strong enough to thwart him, with 'unlawful troops assembled', in the October election, and the battle was by no means over. At this time several Star Chamber suits were pending, one probably instigated in 1600 by Sir John, whose complaints inspired the interrogatories prepared for Attorney General v. Sir Richard Trevor (44 Elizabeth). In all of these disputes the two parties claimed, as was not unusual in such cases, that their opponents were violent, overbearing men who took the law into their own hands, whereas they themselves were peace-loving and long-suffering, etc., etc.; and of course the legal authorities, having to deal with so many riots and assaults alleged by both sides, were naturally interested in Sir John's and Sir Richard's character. Which was the man of violence? Which was the aggressor? I think that we may fairly say that they were one as bad as the other. Sir John Salusbury, known as the Strong, impressed those who knew him as formidable and ungovernable,[17] as when Sir Richard Lewkenor, Chief Justice in Chester, complained in 1602 of 'the indirect and unjust courses of Sir John Salusbury, who cannot be pleased except he rule the country, and judges and justices also'.[18] Lewkenor, himself a proud and difficult man, disliked Sir John Salusbury, but his view is confirmed by Lord Zouche, the new Lord President of Wales, who wrote to Cecil in the same year, 'I received this day a letter from you concerning Sir John Salusbury. If he will be ordered, I will do him all the kindness I may. It may be, I will go to the Assizes to see if I can make a friendship amongst them in that shire'[19] – which, incidentally, confirms that Cecil still exerted himself on behalf of Sir John.

Sir John Salusbury 'cannot be pleased except he rule the country': that is certainly how his opponents saw him. Yet, as his own depositions and pleadings prove, that was not how he saw himself. How fortunate, therefore, that Robert Chester had chosen, years ago, to depict him as the turtle, or turtle-dove, humblest and gentlest of birds, in an unpublished poem that might set the record straight! Dedicated by Chester 'To the honourable, and (of me before all other) honoured knight, Sir John Salusbury, one of the Esquires of the Body to the Queen's most excellent Majesty', *Love's Martyr* describes Salusbury as 'true honour's lovely squire' (i.e. before he was knighted in June 1601) and continues –

> His name is *Liberal honour*, and his heart
> Aims at true faithful service and desert.
>
> Look on his face, and in his brows doth sit
> Blood and sweet mercy hand in hand united:
> Blood to his foes, a precendent most fit
> For such as have his gentle humour spited:
> His hair is curled, by nature mild and meek,
> Hangs careless down to shroud a blushing cheek. (pp. 11–12)

The turtle could not accuse Robert Chester of backwardness in praise, for the poet presents his master as the incarnation of honour, constancy, chastity – indeed, all the virtues.

How convenient, then, that this half-forgotten poem (Chester calls it 'my long expected labour') could give the world a more flattering portrait of Sir John than that painted by his enemies! The idea was not a new one – Spenser had written mystical-allegorical poems that attempted to influence public opinion (*The Shepherds' Calendar, Mother Hubbard's Tale, The Faerie Queene*), and even prose works were suspected of hidden meanings that reflected on state affairs. For example: 'The treatise of Henry IV is well written', John Chamberlain reported on 1 March 1599. 'The author is a young man of Cambridge, a lawyer. There is much talk about it, why such a story should come out now, and exception is taken to the Latin epistle, dedicated to the Earl of Essex. I can find no harm in it, but it was commanded to be cut out of the book'.[20] Sir John Salusbury, bidding to overthrow his enemies in Denbighshire, no doubt hoped that there would be 'much talk' about *Love's Martyr* in 1601 and speculation 'why such a story should come out now.' To put it in a nutshell, it suited the turbulent Sir John not only to masquerade as a turtle-dove, but also to remind the world that he had married a phoenix (a princely bird, related to the Earl of Derby). I believe that *Love's Martyr* was published to influence public opinion – hence the unusual addition of 'poetical essays' by 'the best and chiefest of our modern writers', apparently as an after-thought, at the end of the volume.

We must now consider a strange inconsistency in these appended 'poetical essays'. It is clear, said Carleton Brown, 'that to Jonson both Turtle and Phoenix were living persons – man and wife – with whom he stood on terms of acquaintance, perhaps even friendship'.[21] So, too, Marston knew the Salusbury family, for he wrote 'A narration and description of a most exact wondrous creature, arising out of the Phoenix and Turtle Dove's ashes', and mentions that this offspring 'now is grown unto maturity'; Jane Salusbury, the oldest child, was 14 in 1601 and could count as mature. Only Shakespeare seems to have composed his finely chiselled verses sublimely indifferent to the facts, representing the Phoenix and Turtle (who, we have seen, had produced an enormous brood of children at the rate of about one a year) as childless!

> Leaving no posterity,
> 'Twas not their infirmity,
> It was married chastity.

Brown concluded that one searches in vain in Shakespeare's poem for such familiarity with the Salusbury family as is displayed by the other poets; his relations with Sir John 'were less close than those of Jonson, Marston, and Chapman'.[22]

This is not what we would expect if Shakespeare had indeed served for some years as one of Derby's or Strange's Men (in short, as a retainer of the phoenix's father or brother); at the very least, one would think, he should have known that Sir John and Dame Ursula were not childless. Brown did not notice, however, that his account of Shakespeare's ignorance of the facts does not square with a point he had previously made – namely that Shakespeare's poem was influenced by *Love's Martyr*, and particularly by the Pelican's speech (p. 131 ff.). Why, I wonder, would Shakespeare read this obscure and interminable collection of poems, unless he was interested in the Salusbury family, in whose honour it was composed?

Brown helps us to solve these problems on an earlier page, where, as I have mentioned, he showed that *Love's Martyr*, or at any rate the poems about the turtle and the phoenix, must have been written 'more than a decade before its publication in 1601'.[23] Chester's story describes the first meeting of the phoenix and the turtle, at a time when the turtle grieves for 'my turtle that is dead'.[24] The phoenix offers to share this sorrow –

> Come, poor lamenting soul, come sit by me,
> We are all one, thy sorrow shall be mine

– and more astonishingly, to be the turtle's love ('For thou shalt be my self, my perfect love'). The turtle responds respectfully:

> (*Turtle.*) How may I in all gratefulness requite
> This gracious favour offered to thy servant?
> The time affordeth heaviness, not delight,
> And to the time's appoint we'll be observant;
>   Command, O do command, whate'er thou wilt;
>   My heart's blood for thy sake shall straight be spilt.
>
> (*Phoenix.*) Then I command thee on thy tender care,
> And chief obedience that thou ow'st to me,
> That thou especially, dear bird, beware
> Of impure thoughts, or unclean chastity:
>   For we must waste together in that fire
>   That will not burn but by true love's desire.[25]

The turtle flings himself into the flames, and the phoenix follows, hoping that 'another creature' will be born of their ashes. Brown comments:

The marriage of Salusbury and Ursula Stanley occurred in December, 1586, only three months after the execution of Thomas Salusbury. According to all accounts, John Salusbury was deeply affected by his brother's tragic death. Indeed, in a 'poysie' composed for the wedding festivities the hope is expressed that his marriage might serve 'to delighte his doulfull mynde'. This fits well, it will be observed, with the dejection in which the Phoenix finds the Turtle-dove ... [which] is the result, as we are expressly told, of a bereavement.[26]

Brown finally reminds us that Salusbury's eldest child, Jane, was born in October 1587, and that 'Harry, the next child [i.e. the next one to survive] was born in September, 1589, but the poem makes no reference to any male issue of the Turtle and Phoenix as might perhaps be expected if it had been composed after this date'.

Brown's date for the 'phoenix and turtle' portions of *Love's Martyr*, implied rather than stated, seems to fall between October 1587 and September 1589. This dating depends on Chester's cryptic references to 'a second phoenix', which become explicit in a section headed 'Conclusion' (pp. 133–4):

> From the sweet fire of perfumed wood
> Another princely phoenix upright stood,
> Whose feathers purified did yield more light
> Than her late burned mother out of sight;
> And in her heart rests a perpetual love
> Sprung from the bosom of the turtle-dove.
> Long may the new uprising bird increase
> Some humours and some motions to release ...

It could be, though, that the 'Conclusion' was added in 1601, when Chester at last finished his 'long expected labour' (as he explained in his dedication); what would be more natural, after all, than to finish by writing a 'Conclusion'? In that case the cryptic earlier references to a second phoenix could be seen as an inevitable by-product of the phoenix-legend, that is, as hopeful forward-looking rather than as irrefutable proof of the birth of Jane Salusbury. I prefer this slight modification of Brown's date because Chester's poem, first and foremost, celebrates the union of the phoenix and the turtle, and its heavy emphasis on the turtle's grief (the most unusual twist of this strange love-story) accords with what is known of John Salusbury's state of mind in December, 1586. A masque and other entertainments were presented at Salusbury's marriage, and the 'phoenix and turtle' portions of *Love's Martyr* are best explained as another offering of the same date.

And if that seems the likeliest date for Chester's poems, why not for Shakespeare's *The Phoenix and the Turtle*? I can anticipate several swift replies: he had not begun to write at this time; or, if he had, he could not have written so well; and – the title-page of *Love's Martyr* describes the poems appended at the end of the volume (including Shakespeare's) as *new*, the work of modern writers. Let us take this last point first, and begin by observing that the complete text of Chester's title-page (shortened by E. K. Chambers and others) reveals that *new* and *modern* need not be taken literally.

Love's Martyr: Or, Rosalin's Complaint. Allegorically shadowing the truth of love, in the constant fate of the Phoenix and Turtle. A poem interlaced with much variety and rarity; now first translated out of the venerable Italian Torquato Caeliano, by Robert Chester. With the true legend of famous King Arthur, the last of the nine Worthies, being the first essay of a new British poet: collected out of divers authentical records. To these are added some new compositions, of several modern writers, whose names are subscribed to their several works, upon the first subject: viz. the Phoenix and Turtle.

The title-page distinguishes between up-dated and translated works of long ago ('translated out of the venerable Italian', 'collected out of divers authentical records') and poems of a more 'modern' period; and if Chester himself qualifies as 'a new British poet', because he now first publishes verses written in the 1580s, Shakespeare's *The Phoenix and the Turtle* could likewise count as new and modern, even though also written in the 1580s. In short, I suggest that we should consider the possibility that Shakespeare, if he was one of Lord Strange's Men at the time, wrote his verses for Lord Strange's sister in 1586, influenced by Chester's 'allegorical shadowing'; that a copy of Shakespeare's poem survived amongst Chester's 'phoenix' papers; and that, returning to these papers in 1601, Chester luckily came across Shakespeare's poem and thereupon solicited further poetical essays from Jonson, Chapman and Marston. (Of the fourteen poems by 'the best and chiefest of our modern writers' printed at the end of *Love's Martyr*, Shakespeare's is the only one without a heading. This, and the oddity that the next poem half-apologises because Shakespeare got his facts wrong (cf. p. 108, below), suggests that Shakespeare's poem belongs to an earlier date than the rest).

Could Shakespeare have written in such masterly fashion as early as December 1586? More and more experts now agree that he must have begun to write plays before 1590, the once fashionable date for his commencement as a dramatist.[27] By all accounts, Shakespeare wrote with exceptional ease; Heminges and Condell testified that he composed 'with that easiness, that we have scarce received from him a blot in his papers'.[28] An exaggeration, perhaps – but would so fluent a writer, a 'natural' if ever there was one, have waited till he was 26 before discovering his extraordinary talent? Other poets almost invariably begin to write in their teens: are we to imagine a Shakespeare so dim-witted that he failed to recognise his own most precious asset, even though we believe him to have been brilliantly perceptive where other people were concerned? Once we grant that it is not inherently unlikely that Shakespeare, at the age of 22 – already a married man and father of three – might wish to show what he could do in courtly poesy, we are not entitled to argue that *The*

Phoenix and the Turtle is technically too clever to have been written by so young a poet. For *The Phoenix and the Turtle* is unique, and cannot be judged against any comparable work from his pen. We know from *Love's Labour's Lost*, however, that he could dazzle with verbal pyrotechnics from an early age;[29] in *The Phoenix and the Turtle* the one thing that is certain is that he did his utmost to impress – and I think it perfectly possible that the young Shakespeare, when he really tried, could rise to this level. Did Milton not produce a 'show-piece' poem, his *Nativity Ode*, at 21, and Pope another, the *Essay on Criticism*, at 23?

It is, of course, the 'Lancashire connection' that prompts us to ask whether *The Phoenix and the Turtle* could have been written in December 1586, rather than in 1600 or 1601. For if Shakespeare knew the Hoghtons and Heskeths, Thomas Savage, Edward Stanley and the inquisitive John Weever, who seems to have kept a weather-eye upon all potential patrons in the north and west; or even if he had merely served for a while as one of Lord Strange's Men, a strongly-backed hypothesis quite independent of the other Lancashire connections that I have suggested – then one would have thought that Shakespeare would know better than to assert that the phoenix and the turtle left 'no posterity'. I would go further: the fact that Sir John Salusbury was an Esquire of the Body while Shakespeare's master was the Lord Chamberlain, a principal officer of the royal household, makes it unlikely that Shakespeare was unacquainted with Sir John and his circumstances in 1600–1. Even discounting the 'Lancashire connection', therefore, I think it improbable – though not impossible – that he would have erred so disastrously in a poem that, I feel, was written carefully and was meant to please.

How, then, can we explain that disconcerting phrase, 'leaving no posterity'? Shakespeare's poem as a whole, and this phrase, really only make sense as a pendant to Chester's allegory. And Chester had boldly decided that his congratulatory poem should not shirk the tragic death of Thomas Salusbury, a bereavement that overclouded the marriage of John Salusbury and Ursula Stanley. (We read in Camden's *Annals* that the first seven Babington conspirators were hanged, 'cut down, their privities cut off, bowelled alive and seeing, and quartered, not without some note of cruelty'; Thomas Salusbury and six more suffered the next day, not quite so inhumanly 'for they all hung till they were quite dead, before they were cut down and [disem] bowelled'.[30] Thomas's mutilated head was probably still publicly displayed in London three months later, at the time of John Salusbury's marriage.) But how was Chester to combine dirge and marriage, 'in equal scale weighing delight and dole'? He hit upon the solution that the bride and groom 'die' in the flames of love, destroying themselves as individuals in order to become 'one name'.

> (*Phoenix.*) Then to yon next adjoining grove we'll fly
> And gather sweet wood for to make our flame,
> And in a manner sacrificingly
> Burn *both our bodies*, to revive *one name* ... (p. 128)

> (*Phoenix.*) O holy, sacred and pure-perfect fire,
> More pure than that o'er which fair Dido moans,
> More sacred in my loving kind desire
> Than that which burned old Æson's aged bones.
>   *Accept* into your ever-hallowed flame
>   *Two bodies*, from the which may spring *one name*. (p. 130)

> (*Turtle.*) O sweet perfumed flame, made of those trees
> Under the which the Muses nine have sung,
> The praise of virtuous maids in mysteries
> To whom the fair-faced nymphs did often throng.
>   *Accept my body* as a sacrifice
>   Into your flame, of whom *one name* may rise. (p. 131)

(Compare *The Phoenix and the Turtle*, 39–40: 'Single nature's double name / Neither two nor one was called'.) The same familiar conceit, that lovers in effect 'die' in their union, and that this transforms them into a new soul, is found in Donne's *The Extasie*.

> But as all several souls contain
>   Mixture of things, they know not what,
> Love, these mixed souls, doth mix again,
>   And makes both one, each this and that ...

> When love, with one another so
>   Interinanimates two souls,
> That abler soul, which thence doth flow,
>   Defects of loneliness controls.

> We then, who are this new soul, know,
>   Of what we are composed, and made ...

Resorting to the conceit that true lovers must destroy themselves to become 'one', Chester elaborated the 'funereal' note in his poem, and muted the traditional rejoicing of an epithalamium – in keeping with the very special circumstances and mood of the Salusbury–Stanley marriage. Perfect love, as the pelican explains more fully, is only possible after the extinction of self; the two lovers immolate themselves in the flames of their love, and the 'two in one' become 'a more perfect creature'. The pelican's speech (pp. 131–3), I suspect, was the original summing-up, and the 'Conclusion' (pp. 133–4) was added later, in 1601; the pelican standing, in all probability, for Chester himself.

(*Phoenix*.) I come, sweet turtle, and with my bright wings
I will embrace thy burnt bones as they lie;
I hope of these another creature springs
That shall possess both our authority:
 I stay too long, O take me to your glory!
 And thus I end the turtle-dove's true story.
                                        Finis. R. C.

Pelican.
   What wondrous heart-grieving spectacle
   Hast thou beheld, the world's true miracle?
   With what a spirit did the turtle fly
   Into the fire, and cheerfully did die?
5 He looked more pleasant in his countenance
   Within the flame, than when he did advance
   His pleasant wings upon the natural ground.
   True perfect love had so his poor heart bound,
   The phoenix, Nature's dear adopted child,
10 With a pale heavy count'nance, wan and mild,
   Grieved for to see him first possess the place
   That was allotted her, herself to grace,
   And follows cheerfully her second turn,
   And both together in that fire do burn.
15 O, if the rarest creatures of the earth,
   Because but one at once did e'er take breath
   Within the world, should with a second he,
   A perfect form of love and amity,
   Burn both together, what should there arise
20 And be presented to our mortal eyes
   Out of the fire, but a more perfect creature?
   Because that two in one is put by Nature
   The one hath given the child enchanting beauty,
   The other gives it love and chastity,
25 The one hath given it wit's rariety,
   The other guides the wit most charily;
   The one for virtue doth excel the rest,
   The other in true constancy is blessed.
   If that the phoenix had been separated
30 And from the gentle turtle had been parted
   Love had been murdered in the infancy;
   Without these two no love at all can be.
   Let the love-wandering wits but learn of these
   To die together, so their grief to ease.
35 But lovers nowadays do love to change
   And here and there their wanton eyes do range,
   Not pleased with one choice, but seeking many,
   And in the end scarce is content with any.
   Love nowadays is like a shadowed sight

40 That shows itself in Phoebus' golden light:
    But if in kindness you do strive to take it,
    Fades clean away, and you must needs forsake it.
    Lovers are like the leaves with winter shoken,
    Brittle like glass, that with one fall is broken.
45 O fond corrupted age, when birds shall show
    The world their duty, and to let men know
    That no sinister chance should hinder love,
    Though, as these two did, death's arrest they prove.
    I can but mourn, with sadness and with grief,
50 Not able for to yield the world relief,
    To see these two consumed in the fire
    Whom love did copulate with true desire.
    But in the world's wide ear I mean to ring
    The fame of this day's wondrous offering,
55 That they may sing, in notes of chastity,
    The turtle and the phoenix' amity.

Conclusion.
Gentle conceivers of true-meaning wit
Let good experience judge what I have writ ...

The pelican, it should be noted, in emphasising 'this day' and promising to ring out its fame to the wide world, adopts one of the conventions of the epithalamium, a nuptial song or poem presented to the bride and groom on their actual wedding-day (line 53 ff.). That, and Chester's decision to focus on the phoenix and turtle before their marriage, and to end the story with the consummation of their love, persuades me that Chester's 'phoenix and turtle' poems date from December 1586, rather than from 1587-9 (cf. p. 100). What, then, are we to make of the 'more perfect creature' or 'child' (lines 21, 23) mentioned by the pelican? Coming immediately after the phoenix's dying words (quoted p. 104, above), '*I hope* of these another creature springs', the pelican's continuation of this idea ('what should there arise ... but a more perfect creature') is equally hypothetical, and it is significant that, listing the blessings that the 'creature' inherits from each parent, the pelican next refers to it as 'the child' — that is, remains unspecific about its sex, a necessary vagueness if it has not yet been born. The first clear reference to the sex of the child occurs in the 'Conclusion', which compares the child and 'her late burned mother' (cf. p. 100); and this poem, I have suggested, was added much later, in 1601.

We must now look more closely at Shakespeare's *The Phoenix and the Turtle*, to see whether the events of December 1586 help us to penetrate its 'allegorical shadowing'. First of all, this date absolves the poem of the seeming inaccuracy of line 59 ('Leaving no posterity'). No child had yet been born, and it may well have been thought in December 1586 that the marriage would not be consummated immediately, either because of the bridegroom's depression or because the bride was too young. (At this time marriages were sometimes arranged between children or adolescents, and consummation was deferred till much later.) Next, the poem's extraordinary death-emphasis becomes more comprehensible: the Salusbury-Stanley marriage being overshadowed by the recent execution of Thomas Salusbury, Shakespeare chose to develop Chester's conceit of the two birds that plunge into the flames of love, dwelling more fully on the extinction of the lovers as individuals – 'Property was thus appalled / That the self was not the same' – and, indeed, imagining the total extinction of John Salusbury and Ursula Stanley. That is, he abandoned Chester's idea of a 'happy tragedy' (*Love's Martyr*, p. 130), one that would in the natural course of things produce offspring, and instead chose to make 'defunctive music', a dirge, in deference to the solemn mood of the bereaved Salusbury family.

J. E. Neale wrote of this bereavement and its political implications, and, though he did not comment on Shakespeare's poem, he helps us to understand the mood at Lleweni, and some of the poem's obscurities. As late as 1588 and thereafter, according to Neale, the house of Lleweni remained 'under a cloud' because of Thomas Salusbury's execution as a traitor in 1586. 'It is indicative of the gloom cast on Llewenny by this catastrophe that when a new Deputy-Lieutenant was appointed [in 1588] from western Denbighhire, the office went to a kinsman, Robert Salusbury, two years younger than John and head of a cadet branch of the family, whose principal residence was at Rug'.[31] For the Earl of Derby, the phoenix's father, his daughter's imminent marriage to the brother and heir of a Roman Catholic 'traitor' must have been a most unwelcome turn of fortune's wheel – all the more so since several of the Earl's closest relatives were known or suspected Catholics.[32] Camden informs us that the details of the Babington conspiracy 'were most commonly known all over England':[33] that being so, we may suppose that efforts would be made to stop or postpone the marriage. There are many hints of this in *Love's Martyr*, beginning with a dialogue between Nature and the phoenix (p. 16 ff.), who lament that Envy, Malice, Hate and Suspicion prevent the phoenix from joining the turtle – 'Upon the Arabian mountains I must die, / And never with a poor young turtle graced.' Nature encourages the phoenix to resist, 'and thou shalt triumph o'er thine enemy', and later conducts the phoenix to meet the turtle. The pelican also alludes to the phoenix's difficulties before her marriage (lines 29–31):

> If that the phoenix *had been separated*
> And from the gentle turtle *had been parted*
> Love had been murdered in the infancy.

And these difficulties surely explain Chester's otherwise excessive insistence on the lovers' *constancy*, a word also given prominence by Shakespeare: 'Here the anthem doth commence: / Love and constancy is dead.' *Constancy* implies that John Salusbury and Ursula Stanley were kept apart for a while, and that their love triumphed nonetheless; and the 'Paphian Dove' (John Salusbury) hints at something similar when he says 'Come, come sweet Phoenix, I *at length* do claim thee' (p. 135). It may be that the phoenix takes the initiative in offering herself to the turtle (cf. p. 99) because the Salusbury family was in disgrace, and could not compel the Earl to honour an engagement that was not yet binding. Shakespeare, I think, darkly alludes to these difficulties:

> Two distincts, *division none.*
>
> *Hearts remote, yet not asunder;*
> *Distance, and no space was seen*
> 'Twixt this turtle and his queen.
>
> Reason, in itself confounded,
> *Saw division grow together.*
>
> Love hath reason, reason none,
> *If what parts, can so remain.*

Shakespeare's third stanza probably refers to the special circumstances of the marriage as well.

> *From this session interdict*
> *Every fowl of tyrant wing,*
> *Save the eagle, feathered king;*
> Keep the obsequy so strict.

Salusbury's own poems describe the Earl of Derby as 'the eagle' (the Derby crest was an eagle carrying a child);[34] and we may assume that the Earl would attend his daughter's wedding. Other members of the nobility ('fowl of tyrant wing', birds of prey), on the other hand, could not be expected to honour the treason-stained Salusbury family at their seat in Wales, where the festivities took place, and the poet actually states that they have been forbidden to come (line 9) – which no doubt grieved the Salusbury family, for Ursula Stanley's status, as one of the 'nobility', seems to have been immensely important to them. When Catherine of Berain died in 1591, Robert Parry's (unpublished) poem described John Salusbury's sorrow, adding 'His loving spouse *of noble blood* associates him in moan';[35] Robert Chester made Ursula's high status equally clear, as did Shakespeare in adopting Chester's bird-allegory: any lover could be a turtle, but a phoenix, it goes without saying, was unique.

Many of the ideas and words of *The Phoenix and the Turtle* quite evidently derive from the pelican's speech and adjacent matter in *Love's Martyr*. Could Shakespeare then have written his poem in 1601, following this purely literary source, and ignorant of the events of 1586? It is not impossible but, I think, unlikely. He seems to be aware of the special circumstances of 1586 that are not spelt out by Chester, particularly in making so much of a 'division' that brings together – an embarrassment of long ago that no one could wish to draw attention to in 1601, though Chester proves it to have been important earlier – and in choosing to stress death as much as the union of lovers. Of the 'modern' poets who supplied poetical essays for *Love's Martyr* he was the only one to hark back to this earlier *division*, and to strike so lugubrious a note; the others all congratulate Sir John Salusbury or his wife or daughter on their 'high merits', perfection, etc., as would be appropriate in 1601. The anonymous poet who immediately followed Shakespeare felt it necessary to point out, respectfully, that his predecessor had got his facts wrong (from the perspective of 1601), which again suggests that Shakespeare's poem belonged to an earlier date: the inappositeness of 'Leaving no posterity' was all too obvious, and had to be explained away.

> O, 'twas a moving *epicedium*!
> Can fire? can time? can blackest fate consume
> So rare creation? *No, 'tis thwart to sense*:
> Corruption quakes to touch such excellence;
> Nature exclaims for justice, justice fate:
> Ought into nought can never remigrate.
> Then look: *for see, what glorious issue, brighter*
> *Than clearest fire, and beyond faith far whiter*
> *Than Dian's tier, now springs from yonder flame!*

There are, then, good reasons for dating *The Phoenix and the Turtle* in December 1586. The poet knows too much about the circumstances of the Salusbury–Stanley wedding to make it at all credible that he would not know, if he was writing in 1601, that the happy couple was blessed with many children. And if he did indeed write the poem in 1586, it would have been as a follower of the Earl of Derby or of Lord Strange – which, I need hardly add, fits in well

[108]

with all the other evidence adduced in Chapter VI. It comes as a surprise that he could write so brilliantly at so early a date, perhaps at the very time when he composed *The Two Gentlemen of Verona* or *Titus Andronicus*; yet if we read the poem as a bid for recognition, a show-piece by an ambitious young man who wants to make his mark on a special occasion, we can understand that he would take very special pains, whereas in writing dramatic dialogue 'he flowed with that facility' so much regretted by Ben Jonson.

The offering of poems on special occasions seems to have been a tradition in the Salusbury family. English, Welsh and Latin poems were presented at Christmas, New Year and Easter; the death of Catherine of Berain did not pass without poetical effusions, and we know that the Salusbury–Stanley marriage of 1586 was graced with a masque, and that at least one family friend wrote 'posies' or verses for this masque.[36] That is why I have suggested that the most likely occasion for Chester's 'phoenix and turtle' poems, later published in *Love's Martyr*, would also be the Salusbury–Stanley marriage. Let us suppose that William Shakespeare arrives with the Derby entourage a few days before the wedding, perhaps to take part in an entertainment on the wedding-day, hears that various family friends have written poems for the bride and groom, meets Robert Chester, reads Chester's verses – and decides that this is an opportunity to show what he can do. Characteristically, he competes with the poetical opposition on its own terms, adopting the 'phoenix and turtle' story and the mystical-allusive manner of Robert Chester (just as he vied with the University Wits as a playwright, beating them at their own game as an imitator of Plautus, and larding his early work with classical allusions). It is likely, indeed, that Chester himself wrote as he did because the Salusbury circle favoured a 'learned' style, one that could degenerate, as sometimes in John Salusbury's own verses, into the obscurely 'clever' – into riddling allusiveness or acrostics. The family's more sober bookishness is hinted at in the will of Simon Thelwall, Esq., Edward Thelwall's father: 'Item. My will is that all my books shall remain always in my house at Plasward'. (Both of Edward Thelwall's parents died in 1586, the year of Thomas Salusbury's execution – a black year for the family.)[37] And these bookish inclinations are spelt out in the autobiography of Herbert of Cherbury, whose parents 'thought fit to send me to some place where I might learn the Welsh tongue ... whereupon I was recommended to Mr Edward Thelwall, of Plas-y-ward in Denbighshire'. (Herbert was nine at the time, so he refers to John Salusbury's stepfather in the year 1591 or thereabouts.) 'This gentleman I must remember with honour, as having of himself acquired the exact knowledge of Greek,

Latin, French, Italian, and Spanish, and all other learning, having for that purpose neither gone beyond seas, nor so much as had the benefit of any universities.'[38] An intimidatingly talented family for the young man from Stratford to measure himself against! But – he was not entirely 'unlettered' himself, he had been 'a schoolmaster in the country', and, we gather from Robert Greene's attack of 1592 (he 'supposes he is as well able to bombast out a blank verse as the best of you', he 'is in his own conceit the only Shake-scene in a country') as a young writer he struck at least one contemporary as highly competitive. All of which helps to throw light on the self-conscious cleverness and riddling obscurity of *The Phoenix and the Turtle*. And it also gives us, in passing, an insight into Shakespeare's social standing at this time, since the other poetical offerings came from gentlemen or (as in the case of Robert Chester) from scholarly retainers. The poem indicates that young William Shakespeare saw himself not as a mere servant but as a retainer who could mix with his social superiors.

I conclude with some brief remarks about the later history of Sir John Salusbury and his family. First there is the mystery of Sir John's decline after 1601, just as he seems to have got the better of all of his enemies. There were probably two reasons for it – Cecil's growing awareness of Sir John's quarrelsome and ungovernable temper, and the rising fortunes of the Trevor family. Sir John's many complaints, in the law-courts and in private letters, must have exhausted Cecil's patience; and Sir John's letter to Cecil of 15 April 1603, printed by Carleton Brown,[39] reveals to us, though not to the writer, which way the wind was blowing: 'And not being called upon by your honour, I am at this time bold to signify unto you the continuance of my dutiful love towards your honour, humbly praying your honour that I may hear from you, whether it is your pleasure that I should make my repair to attend your honour.' Four 'your honours' in one sentence are too many; and it seems that Cecil did *not* ask Sir John to attend upon him. This could have been because Sir Richard Trevor's younger brother, John, was a rising star in the government's service; and in my view Sir Richard, even more than Sir John Lloyd, was Sir John Salusbury's principal opponent in Denbighshire.[40] John Trevor, formerly the Lord Admiral's secretary, became Surveyor of the Navy in December 1598; and the grant, on 6 June 1603, of the office of Steward and Receiver at Windsor Castle to Sir John Trevor,[41] may be read as Cecil's silent reply to Salusbury's letter of 15 April.

Shortly after this rebuff Sir John Salusbury negotiated with Sir Richard Molyneux of Sefton (cf. p. 52) for the marriage of his son and heir, Henry Salusbury, to the latter's daughter, Bridget. A letter of attorney, dated 18 January 1604, empowered Griffith Pierce, gent., and John Heaton, servant to Salusbury, to receive 1000 marks from Sir Richard (the bride's dowry?); the witnesses include Edward Thelwall (Sir John's stepfather, and clearly a close associate of his over many years) and 'Robert Chester'. But Henry and Bridget did not marry, and the result was *Sir Richard Molyneux v. Sir John Salusbury*.[42] The two disappointed fathers had known each other for years, as visitors of Henry Earl of Derby named in the *Derby Household Books*; and the proposed marriage (overlooked by Carleton Brown and others) proves that the phoenix and the turtle were still in touch with the Stanley circle in Lancashire.

Carleton Brown mentioned that in his last years Sir John 'appears to have been harassed ... by petty creditors'. It is even more interesting, I think, that Sir John had to raise loans, and far from petty ones, in the very year of *Love's Martyr*, which shows that he had to struggle against mounting financial pressures, as well as political opponents, in this year of crisis. On 30 September 1601 Sir John Salusbury made an assignment of a lease of lands etc. to Roger Salusbury of Bachegraig and others, for the purpose of paying his debts and to make provision for his daughters: he borrowed £1,000 towards the payment of his debts; £1,500 for the advancement in marriage of Jane, his eldest daughter; £1,000 each for Arabella and Oriana, his other daughters.[43] Sir John's debts were already beginning to get out of hand, and clearly things went from bad to worse, as we learn from a paragraph in the will of Richard Parry of Twyssog, Denbighshire, dated 28 June 1613, which bluntly exposes Sir John's financial difficulties and his unusual methods of raising cash. (Richard Parry was the husband of Blanche, the daughter of Edward Thelwall.[44])

And where I have lent now long sithence to Sir John Salusbury, Knight, late deceased, the sum of six pounds, as by a bill of his hand, in my custody, may appear. And where also I lent my lady his wife, by the hands of my brother Robert Parry, the sum of five pounds, as by her letter may appear. And where also I delivered to the hands of the said Sir John Salusbury the sum of twenty pounds, to the king's majesty's use, upon a privy seal received requiring the same, which he never paid over to his Majesty's use, and therefore I have been enforced to sue in th'Exchequer Chamber for the same. And for other twenty pounds lent by my brother-in-law ... to his highness' use, which several sums we have recovered by a decree in th'Exchequer Chamber, together with twelve pounds for costs of the suit, by reason whereof six and twenty pounds doth belong unto me. Which said sums of six and twenty pounds and eleven pounds being in the whole seven and thirty pounds ... I do give ... to my two youngest sons ... well hoping and trusting that Mr Harry Salusbury [Sir John's heir] will not fail to pay the said several sums of money to the poor infants without delay, the rather for that I have spent in his late good father's occasions great sums of money, which I do wholly remit and forgive if the sums aforesaid be duly paid without sinister delay.

A marginal note was added in the copy of the will: 'Mr Harry Salusbury gave me due satisfaction for the £11 and bound himself to pay the £26 May Anno 1613. Which I do bequeath to my said sons Harry and Richard Parry.'

Sir John Salusbury died in 1612, and his enemy Sir Richard Trevor died at the age of eighty in 1638. The conclusion of Sir Richard's will, dated 1636, reminds me of the turbulent passions of earlier years. After many loving and thoughtful bequests, Sir Richard suddenly flares up: 'And I charge you upon my blessing [addressing his daughter, Magdalen] that Dorothy St John have no pennyworth of mine'![45] Yet Sir John Salusbury's son, Sir Henry, seems to have patched up the family quarrel, for in his will (1621) he conveyed some of his lands in Denbigh, Flint and Anglesey in trust to various friends, including Sir Richard Trevor.[46] Sir Henry lived on till 1634, and it has been claimed that he wrote the congratulatory verses to Heminges and Condell, on the publication of Shakespeare's First Folio, in a manuscript that once belonged to the Salusbury family of Lleweni.

To my good friends Mr John Heminges and Henry Condell.

> To you that jointly, with undaunted pains,
> Vouchsafed to chant to us these noble strains,
> How much you merit by it is not said,
> But you have pleased the living, loved the dead,
> Raised from the womb of earth a richer mine
> Than Curtis could with all his Castiline
> Associates: they did but dig for gold,
> But you for treasure much more manifold.[47]

The same manuscript contains an autograph version of one of Ben Jonson's poems printed in *Love's Martyr*, and proves, if further proof is needed, that the Salusbury family was genuinely interested in the poets who contributed to Chester's volume. How appropriate that the son of the phoenix and the turtle wrote verses in Shakespeare's honour! And how interesting that *two* Denbighshire poets did so in 1623: for Hugh Holland, whose sonnet on 'the famous scenic poet, Master William Shakespeare', was printed in the First Folio, is also known to have been a native of Denbighshire.[48] In fact,

Holland was possibly related to Sir John Salusbury's family; Sir Robert Salusbury's younger brother, John Salusbury of Rug, Esq. (formerly known as Captain John Salusbury: cf. p. 93), bequeathed 'to my cousin Hugh Holland a gold ring' (PCC, 11 September 1611), and, as we have seen, Sir Robert and John Salusbury were cousins of Sir John Salusbury of Lleweni.

X

Shakespeare's religion

A momentous consequence of the 'Shakeshafte theory' propounded in the opening chapters of this book is, without doubt, that we would have to assume that young William Shakespeare was a Catholic. Neither Alexander Hoghton nor Sir Thomas Hesketh would have engaged him as a 'servant', in those perilous times, unless they felt certain about this; and if he lived with Alexander as a schoolmaster, his employer's chief reason for having a resident schoolmaster must have been that he wanted one of his own faith.

How does the theory of Shakespeare's Catholicism square with the other known facts? I have already indicated that, in my view, he must have changed his religion, probably before the end of the 1580s, as many Catholics did towards the close of Queen Elizabeth's reign. The government put more and more pressure on Catholics – legal, financial and moral – and the threat of a Spanish invasion, in the Armada years, pinched many Catholic consciences that put England before the pope. Many families were now divided in their religion, as individuals switched to the Church of England. Thomas Salusbury participated in a Catholic conspiracy, but his younger brother (later Sir John) was a Protestant;[1] John Weever wrote contemptuously of the 'spiritual fornication' of popery,[2] while his uncle, Henry Butler, was the husband and father of recusants; Sir Thomas Hesketh suffered imprisonment for the 'Old Faith', and his son and heir, Robert Hesketh, supported the government as J. P. and High Sheriff; the Hoghtons were firm Catholics until Richard became Sir Gilbert Gerard's ward, at the age of 19, whereupon he turned Protestant, and also served the government as J.P. and High Sheriff. The principal families dealt with in this book are probably representative of England's Catholic families as a whole: many individuals abandoned Rome – in the Armada years patriotism pulled strongly in the other direction – and young William Shakespeare, if he did so too, responded to the spirit of the times.

Shakespeare's religion has been much debated, partly because the surviving evidence lends itself to diametrically opposed interpretations. Richard Davies, Archdeacon of Coventry, recorded (probably late in the seventeenth century) that Shakespeare 'lays a heavy curse upon anyone who shall remove his bones. He died a papist'[3]; yet Davies also repeated the unlikely story that William was 'much given to all unluckiness in stealing venison and rabbits' from Sir [blank] Lucy, who had him 'oft whipped and sometimes imprisoned', and that William revenged himself by portraying Lucy as 'Justice Clodpate', who 'bore three louses rampant for his arms'. Davies confused Justice Clodpate (in Shadwell's *Epsom-Wells*, c. 1672) and Justice Shallow (*Merry Wives of Windsor*, I.1.16), and is therefore dismissed as an unreliable gossip.

Equally inconclusive, we are told, is the evidence as to Shakespeare's father's religion. That John Shakespeare ran into financial difficulties c. 1577 cannot be denied, but I am not convinced that his problems were merely financial. Let us be clear about the facts before we take sides – all the more necessary since some of the details have only recently come to light. Having flourished in the 1560s, and acquired considerable property in and around Stratford, John Shakespeare became in turn alderman, one of the town's two treasurers, and high bailiff (or mayor) in 1568. From 1577, however, he stopped attending the meetings of Stratford's council, except on rare occasions; in 1578 'he was excused from a levy for the relief of the poor, and rated at an exceptionally low amount for the expense of the musters, which still remained unpaid in 1579'.[4] Also in 1578, John and Mary Shakespeare borrowed £40 from Mary's cousin, Edmund Lambert; they later claimed that they offered repayment in 1580, but this was denied, and so they lost the security they had mortgaged, a house and land in Wilmcote.[5] Later in 1578 the Shakespeares conveyed more land to another relative for a period of years, in return for cash,[6] and in 1579 they sold their share of a Snitterfield property. In 1580 John was summoned to appear in court at Westminster, and was fined £20 for non-attendance, and another £20 for the non-attendance of John Audeley, for whom he acted as surety. At about the same time other worries multiplied: he had sold wool in 1568 to John Walford, a clothier, and was still trying to collect £21 for this sale in 1599.[7] He had leased a house in Stratford to William Burbage, which led to contention, until arbitrators decided that John should give back the lease to Burbage and pay him £7, on Michaelmas Day, 1582; by 1588–9 the £7 remained unpaid, and Burbage sued for the debt plus £10 damages.[8] In 1582, again, John craved 'sureties of the peace' against Ralph Cawdrey and other influential townsmen, 'for fear of death and mutilation of his limbs'[9] – legal phrasing that betokened a serious quarrel between two of the town's aldermen. Some months later John Shakespeare and Richard Court quarrelled and went to law,[10] and John's 18-year-old son William married Anne Hathaway, a wife eight years his senior (November 1582). Troublesome years!

Two explanations of John Shakespeare's difficulties have been proposed. Either he was genuinely in financial difficulties, as seems to be confirmed by his inclusion in 1592 in a list of Stratfordians 'presented for not coming monthly to church, according to her Majesty's laws', John being one of nine that 'come not to church for fear of process for debt'.[11] Or – he was a recusant, who excused himself for not attending church by pretending to fear legal action for debt. Chambers rejected this second possibility: 'Much ingenuity has been spent in interpreting what little is known of John's personal and official life on the theory that he was in fact a recusant. The theorists differ, however, as to whether he was a Catholic or a nonconforming Puritan, and I do not think that there is much to support either contention.'[12] Since Chambers expressed this view, however, new facts have emerged which lend some support to the theory that the Shakespeares were Catholics.

(1) The poet's elder daughter, Susanna, was cited in 1606 in a list of recusants at Stratford; the authorities were vigilant about 'persons popishly affected', and that seems to have been thought her crime. (She was later dismissed without fine, and had presumably received Communion. A year thereafter she married John Hall, a Protestant.)[13] (2) We now know more about John Shakespeare's Spiritual Testament, a Catholic profession of faith discovered in 1757 behind the rafters of his house in Henley Street. Malone first published the Testament in 1790, and it has since disappeared. Some biographers remain sceptical about it, because (a) it passed through the hands of John Jordan, a Stratford man who probably invented stories about Shakespeare to satisfy the curiosity of eighteenth-century bardolaters;[14] (b) Malone, having accepted the Testament's authenticity, later renounced it. As regards (a), I agree with Chambers that 'there is no reason to believe [Jordan] capable of any fabrication which required scholarly knowledge';[15] moreover, independent witnesses remembered in 1789 the finding of the Testament in 1757, so the fact that it passed through Jordan's hands between these two dates rules out the theory that it was Jordan's fabrication. As for (b), we can now explain Malone's later statement that 'I have since obtained documents that clearly prove it [the Testament] could not have been the composition of any one of our poet's family' – namely, that the indefatigable Malone must have

tracked down the testament's 'source'. James G. McManaway established in 1967 that the testament is an English version of Carlo Borromeo's *Testament of the Soul*, a standardised 'spiritual testament' signed by Catholics as a profession of faith; Borromeo died in 1585, and his formulary was translated and dispersed by the thousand. A Spanish version printed in 1661 in Mexico City and an English one dated 1638 have now resurfaced – and if Malone came across such a document without knowing that it reprinted a much earlier text, he would naturally assume that Jordan or another had forged the testament by copying from a booklet printed after John Shakespeare's death. But that inference can no longer stand, and the belated proof that the testament conformed with Catholic practice, instead of being an eccentric, self-incriminating gesture by John Shakespeare, suggests that it must have been genuine.[16]

John Shakespeare's Spiritual Testament, as printed by Malone, consists of fourteen sections, and very closely corresponds to the English version of Borromeo printed in 1638. Here is a specimen, the beginning of section X: 'Item, I John Shakspear do protest, that I am willing, yea, I do infinitely desire and humbly crave, that of this my last will and testament the glorious and ever Virgin Mary, mother of God, refuge and advocate of sinners, (whom I honour specially above all other saints,) may be the chief Executress, together with these other saints, my patrons, (saint Winefride) all whom I invoke and beseech to be present at the hour of my death ... ' Since the original has disappeared we do not know whether John Shakespeare wrote out the complete text or simply inserted his name and patron saint etc. wherever the document left blanks to be filled in.

The Testament remained in private hands and no one sought to profit by it from 1757 until 1784 (when Jordan borrowed and copied it, with a view to publication). Although it has disappeared, there is no good reason for impugning its authenticity, or for doubting that William Shakespeare was brought up by a father who, like so many of his generation, continued in the Old Faith. Returning now to the two explanations of John Shakespeare's puzzling career from *c.* 1577 (cf. p. 115), we may ask whether they are mutually exclusive, as is normally assumed. John must have had cash-flow problems, or else he would not have sold so much property; at the same time he would have found it convenient, if a Catholic, to plead fear of 'process for debt', and thus to avoid church-going. Let us remember that 'he never became poor. He was never forced to part with the three houses he owned in Stratford';[17] and the two fines of £20 that he had to pay in 1580 would not have been imposed on a beggar. His withdrawal from the 'halls' or meetings of Stratford's Corporation is best explained as connected with the Corporation's responsibility for church affairs: since the Corporation fined Stratfordians for profanity and for non-attendance at church, a Catholic John Shakespeare would have been most uncomfortable helping to persecute his co-religionists. His retiring from the 'halls' as the government's hostility to Catholics increased, even though he was still a substantial property-owner in 1577–80, taken together with his Spiritual Testament, drives us to the conclusion that the dramatist's father was a Catholic.[18]

A forthcoming paper on 'John Shakespeare in the Exchequer', by D. L. Thomas and N. E. Evans of the Public Record Office, significantly changes our picture of the dramatist's father, and supports the view that he is unlikely to have withdrawn from Corporation business for financial reasons. Thomas and Evans have discovered that John Shakespeare faced four prosecutions in the Exchequer, in the 1570s, for usury and illegal wool dealing. One alleged that John Shakespeare, of Stratford upon Avon, glover, had lent £100 at 20 per cent; another, that he lent £80 at 20 per cent. (Usury at 10 per cent was permitted at certain times in the sixteenth century.) John was also accused of buying 200 tods of wool (5,600 pounds) with another purchaser, and 100 tods on his own. Large sums of money were involved; and, even though John paid a £2 fine in one case, and probably similar fines in others, it now appears that he was a much wealthier man than has been assumed. The theory that he ran into serious financial difficulties in 1577 (when he stopped attending 'halls', while still possessed of many properties that were only disposed of later) becomes more implausible the more we learn about the full range of his business dealings. In fact, we now know so much more about John Shakespeare than did nineteenth-century biographers that it is high time to challenge the much-repeated statement that John Shakespeare could not have been worth £500 in 1596, as was claimed when he applied for a grant of arms,[19] unless William's assets were included with John's; on the contrary, William may well have got rich so quickly because he was given a helping hand by a wealthy father.

To return to our starting-point: William, we have reason to believe, was brought up as a Catholic. And if William also served Alexander Hoghton and Sir Thomas Hesketh, two very positively committed Catholics, how can we reconcile this with the anti-Catholic tone of some of his early plays? We may do so by examining the career of his patron from c. 1586 (as I have argued, p. 59 ff.), viz. of Ferdinando Stanley, Lord Strange, and of Ferdinando's father, the fourth Earl of Derby. The Earl officiated as President at the trial

of Mary, Queen of Scots, and as Lord High Steward at the trial of the
Earl of Arundel, eldest son of the Duke of Norfolk, who was
arraigned on a charge of high treason in 1589; his family, however,
included an embarrassing number of known or suspected Catholics:
'Lady Margaret Clifford [his wife] from whom he was separated was
a Catholic – as was also his brother, Thomas Stanley of Winwick.
His sisters, daughters of his devout stepmother, Margaret,
Countess of Derby, née Barlow, were Catholics also, as were his
brothers-in-law, Lords Stafford and Morley, Sir John Arundell and
Sir Nicholas Pointz.'[20] The Earl, we may suppose, persecuted
recusants partly because he felt he had to prove himself. As we have
recently learned, some Lancashire Protestants wanted the Earl to act
much more positively against Catholics. 'Resentment flared into
clashes between a Protestant ginger group and the earl of Derby and
his fellow members of the ecclesiastical commission. In 1587 the
most vociferous spokesman of the Protestant group, Edward
Fleetwood, indicted the earl for being too lax and he urged Burghley
to carry out a purge of the commission.'[21] Lord Strange, commended
by the Privy Coucil in 1587 for his diligence against recusants,[22] no
doubt felt equally incriminated by his family and by his Catholic
friends in Lancashire: when he was approached by the Jesuits in
1593 to claim the crown in succession to Queen Elizabeth (cf. p. 37)
he could hardly have been surprised to learn that government spies
were closely watching him. In such an atmosphere of general
suspicion the Earl and Lord Strange needed to demonstrate their
loyalty, and Lord Strange's Men could help by producing plays with
an unmistakable anti-Catholic bias.

Shakespeare's first flights in anti-Catholic propaganda are to be
found in Parts 1 and 2 of *Henry VI* (*c.* 1588–9). The feeling of these
plays irresistibly supports 'good Duke Humphry', the Lord Protec-
tor, against the arrogance of that 'scarlet hypocrite', Cardinal Beau-
fort, the Bishop of Winchester. 'Thou that giv'st whores indulgences
to sin', the Duke tells the Bishop –

> Under my feet I stamp thy cardinal's hat,
> In spite of Pope or dignities of church.
>
> (*I Henry VI*, I.3)

Here the feeling is largely directed against an individual, rather than
against Rome. In *King John*, however, Shakespeare's anti-papal
rhetoric fires on all cylinders, with astonishing ferocity; and, since
there are two entirely different explanations of this play's origins, it
is worth pausing, to ask how they reflect on the dramatist's religion.

King John used to be thought a revision of *The Troublesome Reign*

of John King of England, an anonymous, two-part play first published in 1591. When it was still fashionable to hold that Shakespeare began his writing career as a 'play-patcher' (cf. p. 60), or
reviser of other men's work, this explanation of the two puzzlingly
similar King John plays was inevitable. In more recent times, however, the play-patcher theory has been pretty well abandoned, the
relationship of the two plays has been re-examined, and J. S. Smart
and Peter Alexander proposed that *Troublesome Reign,* far from
being the 'source' of *King John*, should be seen as a reconstruction of
Shakespeare's play. (Copyright did not exist in Queen Elizabeth's
time; when a play proved to be popular, another play with more or
less the same story was not infrequently written for a rival company,
as in the case of *The Taming of the Shrew* and *The Taming of a
Shrew*.) The two King John plays present very much the same events
and characters, with some differences of emphasis – notably in their
anti-Catholic propaganda. In *King John*, the King sends Falconbridge back to England to 'shake the bags / Of hoarding abbots'
(III.3.6 ff.), and Falconbridge later reports that he collected large
sums from 'the clergymen' (IV.2.141 ff.). Instead of briefly alluding
to these exactions, *Troublesome Reign* contains a comic scene with
Falconbridge 'leading a Friar, charging him to show where the
Abbot's gold lay'; the Friar points out the Abbot's chest, it is broken
open and reveals the Abbot's 'treasure' – a beautiful nun.

> *Friar.* O, I am undone! Fair Alice the nun
> Hath took up her rest in the Abbot's chest.
> Sancte benedicite, pardon my simplicity!
> Fie, Alice, confession will not salve this trangression.

The author, with obvious relish, demonstrates that friars and nuns
are money-hoarders, fornicators and hypocrites. And towards the
end of the play, where *King John* merely reports that the King 'is
poisoned by a monk' (V.6.23 ff.), *Troublesome Reign* again inserts
additional material – a scene in which the monk discloses the
intended murder to his Abbot and is absolved in advance, and
another scene that dramatises the poisoning.

Formerly, when it was taken for granted that Shakespeare
'revised' *Troublesome Reign*, it seemed that he toned down its anti-
Catholic feeling by omitting these scenes of crude propaganda. Such
a view of gentle Shakespeare's good taste will have to be abandoned
by those who hold that *King John* preceded *Troublesome Reign*:
they can say that the writer of the second play vulgarised it by adding
the friar scenes, but they make Shakespeare directly responsible for
the anti-Catholic chauvinism, the appeal to the mob, which is the

life-blood of *King John*. He devised the plot, inventing the Bastard
Falconbridge, giving a central importance to Cardinal Pandulph as
universal manipulator, and omitting Magna Carta; that is, he re-
wrote history (as he found it in Holinshed) to emphasise the threat
from Rome, instead of merely translating another man's dramatised
account of John's reign into more effective dialogue. Comparing the
king's defiance of Rome in Holinshed and the two plays we can see
how Shakespeare does his utmost to arouse anti-papal fury.

(i) [King John wrote to the Pope in 1207] that he marvelled not a
little what the Pope meant, in that he did not consider how
necessary the friendship of the King of England was to the see of
Rome, sith there came more gains to the Roman church out of
that kingdom than out of any other realm on this side the
mountains. He added hereto, that for the liberties of his crown he
would stand to the death, if the matter so required. ...

(Holinshed, iii, 171)

(ii) K. *John.*   What earthy name to interrogatories
Can task the free breath of a sacred king?
Thou canst not, cardinal, devise a name
So slight, unworthy and ridiculous,
To charge me to an answer, as the pope.
Tell him this tale; and from the mouth of England
Add thus much more, that no Italian priest
Shall tithe or toll in our dominions;
But as we, under God, are supreme head,
So under Him that great supremacy,
Where we do reign, we will alone uphold
Without th'assistance of a mortal hand:
So tell the pope, all reverence set apart
To him and his usurp'd authority.

K. *Phi.*   Brother of England, you blaspheme in this.

K. *John.*   Though you and all the kings of Christendom
Are led so grossly by this meddling priest,
Dreading the curse that money may buy out;
And by the merit of vild gold, dross, dust,
Purchase corrupted pardon of a man,
Who in that sale sells pardon from himself;
Though you and all the rest so grossly led
This juggling witchcraft with revenue cherish,
Yet I alone, alone do me oppose
Against the pope, and count his friends my foes.

(iii) *King John.* And what hast thou or the Pope thy master to do to
demand of me how I employ mine own? Know, Sir Priest, as I
honour the Church and holy churchmen, so I scorn to be subject
to the greatest prelate in the world. Tell thy master so from me,
and say John of England said it, that never an Italian priest of

them all, shall have either tithe, toll or polling penny out of
England, but as I am King so will I reign next under God,
supreme head both over spiritual and temporal; and he that
contradicts me in this, I'll make him hop headless.[23]

Is it really conceivable that a dramatist brought up as a Catholic,
a former servant of Alexander Hoghton and Sir Thomas Hesketh,
would wish to write so venomously of Rome? Let us remember
that about ten years would have passed since William Shakeshafte
worked for Sir Thomas Hesketh (in 1581 or 1582) if *King John*
was composed, as I believe, in 1590 or 1591:[24] and that this
was a decade when the menace of Rome, as seen by English Protestants, increased alarmingly. Leaving aside the treason trials of
seminary priests, there was the Babington conspiracy to murder the
Queen (1585-6); the trial and execution of Mary, Queen of Scots,
who was accused of encouraging Babington (1586-7); the Spanish
Armada, expected for some years before 1588, and, it was
rumoured, soon to be followed by a second attempt; and the
murder of Henry III, King of France, after he joined forces with the
Huguenots against the Catholic League, by a fanatic monk (1589) –
this last almost certainly the immediate inspiration for the writing
of *King John*. It goes against the grain to think of 'gentle Shakespeare' as a turncoat, inflaming the mob against his former friends,
if that is how we interpret his play. Considering, though, that *King
John* chiefly attacks the pope's temporal claims, and that loyal
English Catholics felt free to defend the Queen against Catholic
invaders, we may take a more lenient view: in 1590–1 Shakespeare
detested Rome's intrigues and abuses, but nowhere stoops to
rabble-rousing against English Catholics, as *Troublesome Reign*
does in the friar scenes.

That having been said, it is still surprising – some will say shocking
– that a former Catholic would choose to write a play like *King John*.
The theory that Shakespeare began life as a Catholic, changed
religion, wrote *King John* (perhaps spurred on by Lord Strange, his
patron, or merely hoping to please Lord Strange), is disconcerting, I
admit; it gives a less flatteringly consistent picture of the dramatist
than the traditional one, that he was born a Protestant, wrote some
anti-Catholic plays and died a Protestant. But we must never lose
sight of the fact that the poet who described himself in the sonnets
was a most unusual man. His love-hate relationship with the Dark
Lady may even help us to understand how he felt about the Whore of
Babylon: not long after *King John* he wrote *Romeo and Juliet*
(?1591), where the 'holy friar' represents good sense and modera-

tion; and in *Hamlet* (?1600) he relapsed into a Catholic view of purgatory, in the Ghost's statement that it is doomed 'for a certain term' to fast in fires 'Till the foul crimes done in my days of nature / Are burnt and *purged* away' (I.5.12–13). I find it easier to imagine that a former Catholic might slip into this way of thinking than that a Protestant writer who had never been a Catholic would do so.

There is a similar 'lapsed Catholicism' in *Measure for Measure*. The Duke-as-friar, confessor to Angelo, takes advantage of his disguise to intrigue incessantly, trying to make rings round those who trust him – very much as Catholic priests played games with other men's lives according to Protestant propaganda (compare Marlowe's *Massacre at Paris* or Middleton's *Game at Chess*); and the play's Catholic ramifications, of course, were Shakespeare's additions to the story (Isabella's wish to be a nun; the 'friar', and his officious meddling). Critics of *Measure for Measure* have not paid as much attention as one might expect to its insistent Catholicism, which must have affected the audience-response in 1603–4. Would Protestants at the Globe have sympathised with a novice belonging to the sisterhood of Saint Clare when Angelo tells her to yield up 'thy body to my will', or when the Duke proposes marriage to her? Would she have worn her novice's habit right through the play, even when the Duke proposes? (Modern producers usually get Isabella to change her clothes as quickly as possible: they want a 'feminine' heroine, at all costs.) Would they have sympathised with a friar who takes it upon himself to play the role of 'power divine'? Isabella's willingness to go along with the friar's proposed bed-trick, after she had so roundly condemned the cohabitation of Claudio and Juliet – an inconsistency that has puzzled many commentators – might well be viewed, by a Protestant audience, as another example of Catholic authoritarianism: a novice *must* suppress her conscience when a 'good father' orders her to. The play is not overtly anti-Catholic, yet it activates latent anti-Catholic feeling – while at the same time it manages to present a Catholic point of view persuasively from the inside. This entirely Shakespearian complication of the story, which now centres on a nun and a friar who do *not* arouse the normal Protestant hysteria, is as revealing as the vision of purgatory in *Hamlet*.

Shakespeare's detailed knowledge of Samuel Harsnet's *A Declaration of Egregious Popish Impostures* (1603) has been demonstrated by Kenneth Muir and others. When he wrote *King Lear*, probably in 1605, Shakespeare echoed Harsnet's 284-page treatise in various ways (adopting the unusual names of devils such as Modo and Mahu, Frateretto, Fliberdigibbet, etc., and borrowing other unfamiliar words and phrases, such as 'hysterica passio'.[25]) Why did he read this long-winded exposure of 'popish impostures'? Clearly there was much general interest, witnessed by a stream of books all concerned with the same topic – John Darrell's *A Brief Narration of the Possession of W. Sommers* (1598) and *A Brief Apology proving the Possession of W. Sommers* (1599); Samuel Harsnet's *A Discovery of the fraudulent Practices of J. Darrell* (1599); Darrell's reply, *A Detection of that sinful and ridiculous Discourse of S. Harshnet (sic)* (1600), and *A True Narration of the Vexation by the Devil of 7. Persons in Lancashire* (1600); George More's *A True Discourse concerning the Possession of 7 Persons in one Family in Lancashire* (1600); John Deacon and John Walker, *A Summary Answer to Master Darrell his Books* (1601); *The Reply of J. Darrell* (1602) – and a number of other books that appeared at the same time. As is already evident from two of the titles, some of the 'fraudulent practices' involved Catholics, and their opponents, in Lancashire. Harsnet's *Declaration* of 1603 described the activities of Catholic priests and their supporters in the 1580s, and therefore mentioned names that would particularly interest William Shakespeare if, as I have argued, he worked for some years for Alexander Hoghton, Sir Thomas Hesketh and Lord Strange. For example, Harsnet printed 'the confession of Richard Mainy, gentleman', dated 1602, in which Mainy stated that about fourteen years ago (i.e. in 1588) the Privy Council 'did write their letters unto Ferdinando, then Lord Strange, to examine me' (p. 258 ff): 'it seemeth they had been informed that I should publish how I was possessed with certain wicked spirits, and of them dispossessed by some priests of the Catholic Roman Church, and that I should take upon me, in company where I came, to justify the same. So as being called before the said Lord Strange, he demanded of me whether I had given out such speeches. He examined me upon my oath.' Shakespeare, if one of Lord Strange's Men at this time, would be bound to have heard of the examination of suspected Catholics; and he would also be interested in Harsnet's references to 'Master Salisbury that was executed' (p. 244), one of many to the Babington conspiracy ('Salisbury' was the older brother of Sir John Salusbury of Lleweni: cf. Chapter IX, above); and in Harsnet's account of 'the three worthy champions sent from his Holiness and from hell, for firework[s] here in England, about *anno* 82, Cottam, Brian, and Campian' (pp. 118–19, 216, 249), Cottam being the brother of the former Stratford schoolmaster, John Cottom (cf. p. 40 above). One can see, therefore, that anyone with Lancashire connections who was aware of the Lancashire implications of the Darrell–Harsnet pamphlets would expect

Harsnet's *Declaration* of 1603 to name sensitive names – perhaps even Shakespeare's own.

To continue this very selective survey of Shakespeare's Catholic allusions: in *Macbeth* he dragged in Father Henry Garnet, the Jesuit who was tried for complicity in the Gunpowder Plot: 'Faith, here's an equivocator that could swear in both the scales against either scale; who committed treason enough for God's sake, yet could not equivocate to heaven' (II.3.10 ff.). Towards the end of his life he again echoed an uncompromisingly Protestant attitude in an aside given to Henry VIII, 'I abhor / This dilatory sloth and tricks of Rome' (II.4, a scene generally attributed to Shakespeare). Here, as in *Henry VI* and *King John*, there can be little doubt that the dramatist himself detested the tricks of Rome – after all, we must assume that he chose to write these plays. What is significant, however, is not that he normally wrote as one would expect from a committed Protestant, but that he sometimes reverted to a Catholic viewpoint – which was most unusual in the drama of his day.

The plays, we may therefore say, give some support to the theory that Shakespeare belonged to a Catholic family. It is in the nature of things that the external evidence should be meagre, since Catholics were persecuted and tried to keep their religion a secret; nevertheless, contemporary or near-contemporary witnesses suggest that Shakespeare and his father and his daughter were Catholics. In Shakespeare's own case we may rush to the wrong conclusion simply because he seems to have been a Protestant from the 1580s, during his active writing career, until the year of his death. His will (drawn up in January 1616, and revised in March)[26] is also Protestant in its phrasing. I would not rule out the possibility, however, that a priest was fetched when he lay dying, and that 'he died a papist' – a report that originated with an Anglican clergyman who lived near Stratford, in Gloucestershire and Coventry,[27] and who had no motive for untruthfulness. Former Catholics *have* been known to return to the fold on their death-bed; if it happened in 1616 one can only hope that there was less domestic pressure than in the case of Evelyn Waugh's Lord Marchmain.

XI

Conclusion

This book presents a very different picture of the young William Shakespeare from the traditional one. It will be useful to draw attention to some of the differences, and, bringing together the seemingly unrelated conclusions of separate chapters, to ask which are probable and which merely possible.

Aubrey's story that Shakespeare had been in his younger years 'a schoolmaster in the country' has never been seriously challenged, but those who accepted it have doubtless assumed that 'in his younger years' meant in the middle or later 1580s; and such an assumption would be natural at a time when traditionalists held that Shakespeare only started to write plays in 1590–1. The theory, which is steadily gaining ground, that Shakespeare wrote plays for some years before 1590, opens up the possibility that his schoolmastering must be pushed back as well. That he worked as an assistant teacher from the age of sixteen or so is not, in itself, as surprising as the suggestion that he started life as a Catholic and served for a while in the Catholic households of Alexander Hoghton and Sir Thomas Hesketh. Yet this idea, that Shakespeare could have been a Catholic, is not new either – and additional evidence has recently come to light which supports it in other ways. I anticipate that there will be strenuous opposition to Chapter X – though, considering how slowly Queen Elizabeth's government turned the screws and brought pressure to bear on English Catholics, in the 1560s and 1570s, and how many Catholics became Protestants in the 1580s, a Catholic upbringing cannot be thought improbable, especially when one also recalls that three Stratford schoolmasters in the 1570s were closely associated with the Jesuits.[1]

Let us brace ourselves, then, for howls of anguish about a Catholic Shakespeare, and proceed with our assessment. This book restates views that others have also advocated – the schoolmaster in the country, Shakespeare's 'early start' as a dramatist, his Catholicism. I have introduced a new element by focusing on John Cottom, the

Conclusion

Stratford schoolmaster who could have recommended Shakespeare to Alexander Hoghton in far-off Lancashire. This led to the new suggestion that, if 'Shakeshafte' was Shakespeare, he need not have served Alexander Hoghton as a full-time 'player', but could have taken up playing as a sideline, being initially engaged as a teacher. All this, I hear the reader mutter, is *possible* – but surely it cannot be said to be *proved*! At this point I would like to distinguish between two groups in the 'Lancashire connection', the second of which may seem to have weaker claims than the first. (1) Like E. K. Chambers and others, I consider it probable that Shakespeare worked for a while as one of Lord Strange's Men. My discussions of *The Phoenix and the Turtle* and of the Stanley epitaphs belong to the same group – let us call it the 'Stanley connection'. (2) On the face of it the other group – the 'Hoghton connection' – appears to be possible rather than probable. There are threads that link William Shakespeare and Alexander Hoghton (John Cottom), Hoghton and Hesketh (Fulk Gillam, the musical instruments), Shakespeare and Hesketh (Thomas Savage), Shakespeare and Hoghton again (John Weever); yet some of this intricate criss-crossing of individuals living far apart in Stratford, Lancashire and London could just be explained as a series of coincidences. Thomas Savage could have been a friend of John Heminges rather than of Shakespeare (in 1611 Heminges lived in one of Savage's houses), and Weever could have heard of Shakespeare from his Cambridge acquaintances rather than from the Hoghtons. For this reason I do not think of Savage and Weever as decisively establishing the 'Hoghton connection'; they are, let us say, supportive attachments. The 'Hoghton connection' seems to me a distinct possibility, supported as it is by the local traditions that link Shakespeare with the Hoghtons and with Rufford, by Alexander Hoghton's reference to William Shakeshafte in 1581, and by Beeston's statement that Shakespeare worked in his youth as 'a schoolmaster in the country.' And yet it would have to be relinquished as nothing more than a possibility, were it not for one other crucial factor. The discovery that John Cottom, the Stratford schoolmaster, was also linked with the Hoghton family makes a significant difference and, I think, converts a possibility into a probability.

While I do not claim that all the suggestions in this book are equally probable, I shall now set them out, for the reader's convenience, in chronological order. This will make it easier to relate one to another, and to compare my account of Shakespeare's earlier years with the traditional one. Some non-controversial dates and 'facts' are added, since new suggestions must tie in with what we already know – or think we know – about John and William

Shakespeare. The dates of Shakespeare's plays, I must emphasise, are highly controversial; I have not assigned a date to every play, but where a date is indicated I have given some reasons for it elsewhere.[2]

1564	William Shakespeare born.
1570	John Shakespeare accused of large-scale usury and illegal wool-dealing in the Exchequer.
1577	John Shakespeare stops attending 'halls' at Stratford.
1579	John Cottom begins to teach in Stratford (July).
1580–1	William Shakespeare employed as assistant teacher by Alexander Hoghton.
1580	Thomas Hoghton I dies abroad (June); Thomas Cottam captured and imprisoned in England.
1581	Alexander Hoghton dies (August); William Shakespeare perhaps works briefly for Thomas II, then for Sir Thomas Hesketh. Richard Hathaway dies (September: he was father of Shakespeare's later wife). Thomas Cottam arraigned (November). John Cottom leaves Stratford (December).
1582	Shakespeare back in Stratford (by August); William Shakespeare and Anne Hathaway marry (November).
1583	Susanna Shakespeare born (May). Shakespeare perhaps worked for his father at this time (1582–5?), and became a Protestant.
1585(?)–94	Shakespeare serves Lord Strange (Earl of Derby, 1593–4).
1586	John Salusbury marries Ursula Stanley (December), Shakespeare writes *The Phoenix and the Turtle*; also, a 'schoolmaster' play inspired by Ovid and Seneca: *Titus Andronicus*.
1587	*The Two Gentlemen of Verona*.
1588	*1 Henry VI, The Taming of the Shrew*.
1589	Robert Greene dedicates *Ciceronis Amor* to Shakespeare's patron, Lord Strange; Thomas Nashe attacks the author of a lost tragedy called *Hamlet*. Shakespeare writes *The Comedy of Errors, 2 Henry VI*. Thomas Hoghton II dies.
1590	*3 Henry VI, Richard III*; Shakespeare appears in plot of *Seven Deadly Sins*, Part II, as 'Will'.
1591	Spenser alludes to Shakespeare, 'our pleasant Willy'. Shakespeare writes *King John, Romeo and Juliet*.
1592	Lord Strange's Men perform Greene's plays (spring); Nashe praises Lord Strange and Shakespeare's

Conclusion

1 Henry VI in *Pierce Penilesse* (summer); Greene's *Groat's Worth of Wit* attacks Shakespeare and implies that he is active as a money-lender (September).[3] Greene dies (September). Shakespeare writes *Love's Labour's Lost* (winter).

1593   Theatres closed because of plague; Shakespeare not included in warrant for Strange's men to travel in country. Shakespeare writes additions (3 pages) for *Sir Thomas More*, and dedicates *Venus and Adonis* to Southampton (S. R. 18 April). Lord Strange succeeds father as 5th Earl of Derby (25 September). Richard Hesketh's conspiracy (tries to persuade 5th Earl to claim crown after Queen Elizabeth).

1594   *Titus Andronicus* published. Ferdinando, Earl of Derby, dies (16 April). *The Rape of Lucrece* dedicated to Southampton (S. R. 9 May). Shakespeare is now a leading member of the Lord Chamberlain's Men.

1595   *A Midsummer Night's Dream* performed at wedding of 6th Earl of Derby (26 January)? Spenser refers to Shakespeare as 'Aetion'.

1596   John Shakespeare applies for a grant of arms, and is said to be 'of good wealth', worth £500.

1597   William Shakespeare buys New Place for £60.

1598   R. Quiney asks William Shakespeare to lend £30. Weever's sonnet 'Ad Gulielmum Shakespeare' written (1597–9?). Francis Meres praises Shakespeare's plays and poems (*Palladis Tamia*, S. R. 7 September).

1599   Richard Hoghton serves as High Sheriff of Lancashire, and is knighted. Weever's *Epigrammes* published. Thomas Savage of Rufford involved in purchase of Globe theatre.

1600–3   Shakespeare writes epitaphs for Sir Thomas and Sir Edward Stanley.

1601   Robert Chester publishes *Love's Martyr*, with Shakespeare's *The Phoenix and the Turtle*. John Shakespeare dies (September).

Claiming that Shakespeare's 'Stanley' and 'Hoghton' connections are not merely possible but probable, I am aware that many questions remain unanswered. Let me attempt to grapple with some that may trouble the wakeful reader. (1) Why should Shakespeare have been sent so far from home when he was only 15 or 16? (Lea in Lancashire is about 130 miles from Stratford as the crow flies). I take it that John Shakespeare wanted his eldest son to join him 'in his own employment' (cf. p. 2), and that William wanted a different career. If a wealthy patron beckoned, the opportunity would seem too good to miss; many boys left home at 15 or earlier, either to serve as pages, or to learn a trade as apprentices, or to go to university. Perhaps, though, Anne Hathaway's interest in her future husband began a year or two before they were married, and John and Mary Shakespeare felt that a wife eight years older than their teenage son would be unsuitable, and therefore sent him away. In the very decade of Shakespeare's marriage the Privy Council intervened in a somewhat similar case, condemning the contrivers of a 'very lewd marriage between Richard Tylden, being a boy about xv years old, and Franklin's niece, being xxv years old', ordering that the young gentleman be sequestered to his guardians during his minority, and that those who persuaded 'the young parties' to marry be punished.[4] If Shakespeare left for Lancashire in 1579 or 1580 he would have been a boy of 15 or 16 and Anne Hathaway would have been 23 or 24: unequal marriages were by no means unheard of at this time, but a considerably older woman was evidently thought a mismatch for a boy 'during his minority'.

(2) Is it likely that Alexander Hoghton would leave an annuity of £2 a year to a youth aged 17 who had only served him one or two years? It would be unusual to reward a young servant so generously, but we should recall that Shakespeare struck those who knew him as an unusually attractive person, and that he received special gifts from other patrons and well-wishers.

> He had the honour [wrote Rowe in 1709] to meet with many great and uncommon marks of favour and friendship from the Earl of Southampton. .... There is one instance so singular in the magnificence of this patron of Shakespeare's that, if I had not been assured that the story was handed down by Sir William Davenant, who was probably very well acquainted with his affairs, I should not have ventured to have inserted that my Lord Southampton at one time gave him a thousand pounds, to enable him to go through with a puchase which he heard he had a mind to.[5]

The sum seems too enormous to be credible, yet we have no reason to doubt that he received 'great and uncommon marks of favour' from Southampton (the dedication of *The Rape of Lucrece* implies 'favour and friendship'); and Heminges and Condell, earlier and better witnesses than Rowe, must have meant something similar when they claimed that the earls of Pembroke and Montgomery 'prosecuted' Shakespeare's plays and their author 'with so much favour'[6] – one assumes that 'favour' again includes financial rewards. All the same, would a master reward a retainer who was little more than a boy? Sir Thomas Hesketh did: 'Also,' he ordained in his will, 'I give to Richard Stannynowght, my foot-boy, xls.' (forty shillings; but this was a single bequest, not an annuity).

(3) If Shakespeare lived for two years with the Hoghtons, and Weever's sonnet suggests that the Hoghton circle remained aware of this former 'servant', why are there no other documents that testify to this long-lasting connection? At the age of 16 or 17 Shakespeare, a minor, is not likely to have been called to witness legal documents, if older men were available: the absence of his name from Hoghton documents prior to Alexander's will is perfectly understandable. And if he was William Shakeshafte he must have changed his religion in the 1580s, whereas the Hoghtons and Heskeths remained Catholics; his earlier employers would therefore see him as a potential informer, which must have cooled their relationship. When Richard Hoghton became a Protestant, after his father's death in 1589, this obstacle would be removed, and perhaps Richard (who was knighted at court in 1599, and no doubt visited London at other times) renewed his acquaintance with Shakespeare. Richard must have been aware of Shakespeare, for presumably he transmitted the family tradition that the dramatist served the Hoghtons in his youth.

(4) Would it not be reasonable to expect John Cottom, the former Stratford schoolmaster, to be a book-lover? Why then did he bequeath no books in his will? One might equally ask why did William Shakespeare bequeath no books in his will? Were there no copies of Holinshed's *Chronicles* or Plutarch's *Lives* at New Place? And why did the meticulous John Weever, a book-lover if ever there was one, likewise pass silently over the books that he surely must have owned? The answer is, quite simply, that books were rarely mentioned in wills at this time; the fact that John Cottom did not refer to books in his will, and that none are listed in the inventory of his goods, is regrettable – but it tells us nothing about his attitude to books or to the greatest writer of his day, and should not be taken as evidence that he owned no books.

(5) If Shakespeare worked for the Hoghtons and Heskeths in Lancashire, is John Cottom the only possible link with Stratford? By no means: it is remarkable that four out of five consecutive Stratford schoolmasters were Lancashire men: Walter Roche (1569–71), Simon Hunt (1571–5), John Cottom (1579–81) and Alexander Aspinall (1582–1624); the only exception was Thomas Jenkins (1575–9), a Londoner. This suggests that there might have been other 'connections' between Stratford and the Hoghtons; it

could be, for instance, that Simon Hunt was a Hoghton tenant, since he went from Stratford to Douay College, where Thomas Hoghton I was an important benefactor. At present, however, we are ignorant of Roche's, Hunt's and Aspinall's territorial roots in Lancashire. Taking Shakespeare's age into account, it seems likely that he left school when either Jenkins or Cottom reigned at the Grammar School: Jenkins was not from Lancashire, whereas Cottom and his family seem to have known the Hoghtons well. Other Stratford–Lancashire contacts may still emerge, but John Cottom remains the obvious link between the two places.

Some questions have, I hope, been disposed of – but by no means all. Much more work needs to be done before we shall discover all we want to know about the schoolmaster in the country. I thought it right to present an interim report since local historians, and others more expert in Elizabethan archives than I am, may be able to pick up the scent where I have lost it. To return once more to John Cottom: if Shakespeare was really recommended to Alexander Hoghton by the Stratford schoolmaster, one would like to see Cottom's books and papers. Every gentleman had his books and papers – might there not be letters from a former pupil, or quartos from a famous dramatist, hidden away in a family collection that no one has thought of prying into for centuries? Cottom's papers would have gone to the only one of his three daughters to survive him, Priscilla; and she, as bad luck would have it, married a man with a common surname, Thomas Walton of Walton le Dale. I was able to trace their descendants to the later seventeenth century and no further. Then, remembering that John Cottom's pedigree was recorded by the Norroy King of Arms in 1613, I wrote to the College of Arms for help. Mr J. P. Brooke-Little (Norroy and Ulster) replied as follows:

> The only recorded pedigree of Walton of Walton le Dale, co. Lancaster, is that entered on 8th April 1665 at the Heralds' Visitation of co. Lancaster made in that year (c37, folio 144r).
>
> The marriage of Thomas Walton to Priscilla Cottam (or Cotham) is entered. Their children were William, John and James. William married Dorothy, daughter of Christopher Anderton of Hurwich, co. Lancaster. Their son Thomas, of Walton le Dale, married Anne, daughter of Roger Hesketh of Turneaker, co. Lancaster, and their sons were Wiliam, Thomas and Roger.
>
> There are no other pedigrees of this family, nor could I find any references to printed pedigrees, save that in the Victoria County History of Lancashire mentioned by you.
>
> I also checked all records for later Cottam pedigrees, just in case Priscilla were not an heiress but, as expected, there were none.

Even if one contacted all the Waltons in Preston, or in Lancashire, that would not necessarily lead one to the right family, for John Cottom's papers could have passed again to a female descendant. That such papers once existed cannot be proved; that they still survive, if they ever existed, is doubtful – but the present writer, undeterred, adjures all readers possessed of mouldering family papers to sally forth instantly into lofts, cellars, outhouses etc. and to search for the dusty remains of the Stratford schoolmaster.

It is hard to believe that the Hoghton archives will yield other major surprises, apart from Alexander Hoghton's references to William Shakeshafte. This is because J. H Lumby, preparing *A Calendar of the Deeds and Papers in the Possession of Sir James de Hoghton, Bart.* (1936) over a period of thirty years, has already sifted the material with exemplary care. When Sir Bernard de Hoghton invited me to look through a dozen large strong-boxes crammed with family documents which had not been deposited in the Lancashire Record Office, I was naturally hopeful – yet soon found that Lumby had examined these boxes as well, and had indexed some of their (mostly eighteenth and nineteenth-century) contents. And there are two other reasons for being pessimistic about further Hoghton discoveries.

> Concerning many of the heirlooms of the Hoghtons, including furniture, pictures, plate and other relics of former days, which to-day would have been priceless, a dismal story must be told. The complete disappearance of Sir Charles the fourth baronet's valuable library has already been mentioned. Much else, in the nature of furniture, family portraits, etc., doubtless went the same way during the long years between 1710 and 1870 when the place stood empty and deserted, completely at the mercy of the casual visitor.
>
> ... But the tale of disaster is not yet complete. About the year 1870 a notable misfortune fell upon the family in the complete destruction of all the pictures, including many family portraits, and much of the family plate, all of which had been stored away for safety in London. These treasures, preparatory to being moved from London to Hoghton, had been placed in a pantechnicon. By some means the conveyance caught fire and its entire contents were destroyed, including a number of valuable papers.[7]

John Weever must have presented a copy of his *Epigrammes* (1599) to Sir Richard Hoghton, the dedicatee, but, like so much else, the volume has disappeared.

John Weever himself is the member of the 'Lancashire connection' most likely to lead us to other discoveries. He was an admirer of Shakespeare, and he had the true magpie habits of a collector, as *Ancient Funeral Monuments* amply illustrates. 'And here let me tell you that amongst many letters of important affairs, which I found in certain chandlers' shops of our parish, allotted to light tobacco pipes and wrap up pennyworths of their commodities, all which I gave to Sir Robert Cotton, Knight and Baronet, the only repairer of ruined antiquity. . . .' (pp. 80–1). Weever differed from other antiquarians of his day in being interested in poetry, including very recent poetry, and therefore I believe that his papers, if they are ever located, will be rewarding. My guess is that they may turn up not in the Cottonian Library, which has been known to generations of scholars, but amongst the Vincent manuscripts in the College of Arms. In *Ancient Funeral Monuments* Weever referred several times to 'my dear deceased friend, Augustine Vincent' (To the Reader', and pp. 419, 604, 734), and leaves us in no doubt that Vincent, the Windsor Herald and keeper of the Records in the Tower, shared his interests and greatly helped him. Vincent, in fact, wrote a treatise of roughly the same length as Weever's eighteen introductory chapters on funeral customs, entitled *Parentalia, or Funeral Rites, Ceremonies and Solemnities* (Vincent MS. 87), which shows how closely the two friends worked in tandem; and Vincent, we know, owned a presentation copy of the Shakespeare First Folio, for he recorded that he received it from William Jaggard, the printer, 'anno 1623'. Vincent, in short, appears to have been a Shakespeare enthusiast, like his friend John Weever, and he was definitely a collector. The cataloguing of the many Vincent Manuscripts in the College of Arms goes along steadily, though the end is not yet in sight. There are papers in unidentified hands, and it is probable that in the course of cataloguing unexpected treasures will come to light. Weever's notes on the contemporary poets he knew personally and quoted so freely? or some scraps of Shakespeare? Only time will tell.

Appendix A. Extracts from wills

(In these extracts I have modernised the spelling and expanded contractions. The punctuation in the wills is minimal, and sometimes confusing; I have changed it here and there, without attempting to modernise it completely.)

1. Alexander Hoghton of Lea, Esq. (3 August 1581; proved 12 September 1581). Extracts printed by G. J. Piccope in *Lancashire and Cheshire Wills* (Second Portion, CS, vol. li, 1860). Facsimile of 'Shakeshafte' passage in Oliver Baker, *In Shakespeare's Warwickshire* (1937), p. 298.

In the name of God Amen. The third day of August . . . after the Incarnation of Jesus Christ one thousand five hundred eighty-one. I Alexander Hoghton of the Lea in the county of Lancaster, Esquire, being sick in body yet of good & perfect ‹. . .› memory, thanks be to almighty God, and considering with myself that nothing is more certain than death, nor nothing more incertain & doubtful than the hour of death, and also what great troubles & inconveniences do for the most part grow after the death of those that are possessed of lands or goods for lack of good ordering & disposing of the same in their life-time; therefore & to th'intent no cause of contention or trouble should arise after my decease among my kinsfolks & friends for or concerning any of my possessions goods or chattels; and to th'intent also that my wife & children, if it shall please almighty God to bless me with any, might not be left desolate or unprovided; and that my true and diligent servants which hath taken pains with me in my life-time might be recompensed, the poor people according to my ability relieved, & other deeds of charity performed, and my debts truly paid & discharged. I have already, by sufficient conveyance in the law executed in my life-time, disposed all my manors, messuages, lands & tenements to such uses, intents & purposes as I doubt not but do stand with the pleasure of almighty God, the comfort of all my friends, & the contentation of all good men, and are as I trust to the upholding & maintenance of that house, whereof myself and all my ancestors have lineally descended. And now for the ordering & disposing of my goods & chattels, concerning the which I have heretofore done nothing, and for the making perfect in some points of such conveyances as is aforesaid & for the cases aforesaid, I do make my last will & testament in manner & form following. First I do bequeath my soul into the hands of almighty God, desiring most instantly in my daily prayers that the same may be dissolved from this mortal & w[r]etched body & be with Him in the communion of saints & fellowship of all the company of heaven, when and as soon as it shall please his divine majesty, not doubting but to be saved by the merits & passion of Jesus Christ my only saviour & redeemer, in whom only I do repose my trust & confidence. And my body to be buried in the parish church of Preston, so near that place where my father Sir Richard Hoghton Knight & Dorothy my wife do lie buried as convenient may be. The which I would have done if so be that it shall fortune that God do call me from this transitory life within forty miles of the same church. And I do constitute ordain & make my sole executrix of this my last will & testament Elizabeth my well beloved wife; and if she do refuse to take upon her the charge & administration of the same or shall fortune to die in my life-time, then I will that my loving brother-in-law Thomas Hesketh of Gray's Inn in the county of Middlesex, gentleman, and my trusty & well-beloved servants George Beseley & James Helme shall be my executors, desiring my said wife if she take upon her the same charge & administration, & if she do not then the same Thomas Hesketh, George Beseley & James Helme, that they & ‹...› of them, as they will answer before the tribunal seat of Jesus Christ at the dreadful day of judgement, to execute this my last will in every part & parcel thereof according to the purport & effect thereof, all advantages shifts & escapes which may be found out by curious searching heads out of the common law of England or any other law to the contrary notwithstanding. Item, I will that all my debts shall be paid & discharged at such days & times as they shall be due & payable, as well those & such ... debts as are due & owing by matter in writing, as also all my simple contracts & bargains without writing which can be so sufficient proved to be due, as shall be thought meet & convenient by the supervisors of this my last will & testament or any ‹...› of them. Item, I give & bequeath to Elizabeth my wife all my plate, that is to say as well all my bowls, tuns, spoons & salts as also all her apparel, rings & jewels whatsoever which she hath been accustomed to wear and have during my life-time. Item, it is my will that if the residue of my goods & chattels, my debts & funerals being discharged, and the said several sums of money bestowed in such sort as is aforesaid, do amount unto the sum of two hundred marks, then I give & bequeath to Margaret my bastard daughter, wife to Roger Crichelawe of Charnock Richard in the said county & to all her children the sum of one hundred marks equally to be divided amongst them. And if the residue of my goods & chattels ... do not extend to the sum of two hundred marks, then I give & bequeath to the said Margaret my bastard daughter & to all her children the third part of all my goods & chattels, whatsoever value or sum the same shall then be, extend, amount or come unto, in three parts to be divided, the said third part to be equally divided amongst the said Margaret & her children. The said sum or sums as shall happen to be as aforesaid to be delivered unto the said Roger her husband within six months after my decease. So that he do enter into such sufficient bond as shall be thought convenient by my said supervisors or any two of them for the leaving of the same with the increase thereof after his decease unto the said Margaret & her children or to the survivor or survivors of them. Item, I give & bequeath unto the wife of John Tomlinson th'elder the sum of forty shillings. Item, it is my mind & will that the said Thomas Hoghton of 'brynescoules' my brother shall have all my instruments belonging to musics, & all manner of play clothes if he be minded to keep & do keep players. And if he will not keep & maintain players, then it is my mind & will that Sir Thomas Hesketh knight shall have the same instruments & play clothes. And I most heartily require the said Sir Thomas to be friendly unto Fulk Gillom & William Shakeshafte now dwelling with me & either to take them unto his service or else to help them to some good master, as my trust is he will. Item, I give and bequeath to William Wall, clerk, five pounds. Item, I give and bequeath to Thomas Gryffyne, servant to the said Sir William Wall, twenty shillings. Item, I give unto every one of my servants that shall fortune to be in my service at the time of my decease & is or shall be hired with me for yearly wages, be they men or woman, to every one of them one whole year's wages. And whereas I the said Alexander & the said Thomas Hoghton my younger brother, in consideration of an agreement between the said Thomas & me for the establishing of all my manors lands & tenements after divers remainders upon the said Thomas & the heirs male of his body lawfully begotten, by our deed bearing date the twentieth day of July in the year of our lord God one thousand five hundred & four score ... have granted unto Thomas Fleetwood, son & heir apparent of John Fleetwood of Penwortham in the said county of Lancaster, Esquire, & unto Robert Talbot bastard son of the said John Talbot the annual rent of sixteen pounds thirteen shillings four pence issuing and going out of certain my lands & tenements in Withnell, in the said county of Lancaster, to have ... the said yearly rent to the said Thomas & Robert & their heirs from the day of the decease of me the said Alexander for & during the term of the natural lives & of such person & persons & of the longest liver of them, as I the said Alexander shall declare & appoint in & by my last will & testament in writing, yearly payable at the feast of Pentecost & St Martin the bishop in winter by even portions. And further as by the said deed more at large it doth & may appear, and for so much as the said rent was granted in such sort as is aforesaid unto the said Thomas & Robert only upon trust & confidence reposed by me in them that they & their heirs should suffer such persons as should be nominated & appointed by me to have & enjoy the same in such order & manner as should be by me directed, and not intended nor meant that any profit or commodity should grow thereby unto the said Thomas & Robert or their heirs. The which my intention & meaning I trust that whosoever shall fortune to be the judge for matters in the Chancery from time to time will see duly executed according to equity & good conscience. Therefore for the plain declaration how & in what sort the said rent shall be disposed & how long the same shall continue, it is my will, first, that the said rent shall have continuance unto the said Thomas & Robert & their heirs for & during the natural life & lives & of the longest liver of these my servants, that is to wit, Thomas Barton, William Rigby, Roger Livesey, John Hoghton, Henry Bounde, William Clough, Thomas Coston, John Kitchen, James Pemberton, Robert Tomlinson, Richard Fishwick, John Cotham, Thomas Barker, Henry Browne, Miles Turner, Richard Snape, James Greaves, Thomas Sharp, George Bannister, John Beseley, Thomas Ward, Robert Bolton, John Snape, Roger Dickinson, Fulk Gillom, William Shakeshafte, Thomas Gyllom, William Ascroft, Roger Dugdale & Margery Gerrard. And it is my will that the said rent shall be divided amongst my said servants in manner & form following, so that there shall be yearly due & payable, unto the said Thomas Sharp the sum of three pounds six shillings eight pence, unto the said Thomas Coston twenty shillings, unto the said Thomas Barker twenty shillings, unto the said Roger Dickinson thirteen shillings four pence, unto the said William Ormesheye alias Ascroft thirteen shillings four pence, unto the said Robert Bolton twenty shillings, unto the said Thomas Ward twenty shillings, unto the said Fulk Gyllom forty shillings, unto the said William Shakeshafte forty shillings, unto the said Thomas Gyllom forty shillings & unto the said Roger Dugdale forty shillings. To every of them according to several portions, to have & perceive unto every one of them the said several sums for & during their natural lives. And if it fortune any of them to die living ['Lyvinge', ?leaving] the rest, then it is my will that the portion of that party that shall so die shall be equally divided amongst them that shall survive & so from one to one as long as any of them shall be living, so that the survivor of them all shall have for and during his natural life the said whole and entire rent of sixteen pounds thirteen shillings four pence. And it is my especial desire & I straitly charge the said Thomas Fleetwood & Robert Talbot & their heirs as they will answer me before God that they see my will in this point duly & truly executed. And lastly I give unto my said wife all the residue of my goods & chattels being not before by me bequeathed or given. And I shall most earnestly desire my trusty and loving friends John Talbot of Salebury, Edward Standish of Standish, Esquire, Thomas Fleetwood son & heir apparent of the said John Fleetwood & my brother-in-law Bartholomew Hesketh to be supervisors of this my last will & testament. Witness hereof I have put my hand & seal the day & year first above written, these being witness Thomas Fleetwood, Bartholomew

Hesketh, Robert Park, Adam Boulton, William Wall, clerk, John Houghton & Peter Melling. Debts owing unto me Imprimis Richard Bannister gent of Darwin Hall alias Bannister in Walton xv*l.* for which he hath pledged to me all his wheat now growing more of the said Richard in lent money xl*s.*

Provided alway and further it is the will & pleasure & the true intent & meaning of me the ‹ . . . › named Alexander Hoghton that all such obligation & bonds wherein any my tenants of Ashton under Lyne are indebted and stand bound unto me the said Alexander my executors or assigns shall be void & no advantage taken thereof either of principal debt or forfeiture by any my executrix or executors, but that my said executrix or executors shall the same release & make void unto my said tenants so bounden, and shall not take any advantage of benefit thereby any ways but the said tenants shall be clearly acquitted exonerated and discharged in every respect by & unto my said executrix or executors to & for the same, for & in consideration & so that the said tenants that so my will is shall be acquitted of their bonds shall not hereafter claim ask or demand of my said executrix or executors or their assigns any debt or duty owing or due by me the said Alexander unto any of the said tenants so acquitted by any means, except such money as Edmund Duckenfylde my servant did last borrow of the said tenants to & for my use. The which it is my will to be discharged as parcel of my debts, desiring the said tenants that they will deal friendly with my said executrix or executors in giving reasonable days for payment of the said money excepted. In witness whereof I the said Alexander have put to my seal to this schedule & the same annexed to my said last will & testament as parcel thereof with my seal in presence of Thomas Fleetwood, Thomas Whittingham, Thomas Barton, Richard Whittingham & Robert Parke.

Memorandum that the said Alexander Hoghton after the writing of his will did, lying upon his death-bed, videlicet, within two days before his death being of good and perfect memory, revocate & call back by express words a certain legacy which before in his written will he had given & bequeathed to one Margaret bastard daughter of the said Alexander wife unto Roger Crichelowe of Charnock Richard and to all her children, & did will & command that the said legacy should be stricken out of the said will and this did he divers times or at the least once in the presence of sundry witness.

Item, he did also lying upon his death-bed that is to say whilst he lay sick after [?alter] a certain schedule made & annexed to his will concerning the making void of certain obligations & bonds wherein his tenants of Ashton under Lyne were bound, being informed that his debts being paid & funerals discharged & the said obligations & all such money as he had appointed to be given again unto his tenants were discharged, that then his wife would have no part of his goods left unto her for her maintenance. He then perceiving the same likely to be true, did will appoint & declare that his intention & meaning was that if so be that his wife should have sufficient furniture for her house meet for her calling, her plate & jewels, which were bequeathed by him unto her and twelve oxen twenty kine & a bull & horses convenient for her & also necessary stuff of husbandry or to the like effect & purpose, that then his will & schedule annexed to the said will concerning the same should therein be performed or else every of them to be answered penny pound like of the residue of his goods and not otherwise.

The last three paragraphs were written out separately and attached to the will. Piccope printed the first of the three ('Provided alway . . . Robert Parke') last. It should be noted that Piccope omitted many words and longer passages without warning the reader.

Appendix A

Many of those named in Alexander Hoghton's will appear in other contemporary records. I subjoin a list, in alphabetical order, with basic information about Hoghton's friends and servants; more information is of course available. Lumby's *Calender* is cited below as *Cal.*, and the numbers after *Cal.* refer to document numbers. A. H. is Alexander Hoghton.

Bannister, Richard (gent.). See Livesey, Roger, and *Cal.* 50.

Barton, Thomas (gent.). A. H.'s steward (see p. 17);*Cal.* 50.

Beseley, George (gent.). Bracketed frequently with James Helme in Hoghton documents; both were trusted Hoghton 'servants'. Mentioned 1560 (*Cal.*, 738), etc. An indenture of 1580 names Beseley as 'of Goosnargh gent' (*Cal.* 1403). A George and Ellen Beesley of Goosnargh were the parents of the priests George and Richard Beesley (Godfrey Anstruther, *The Seminary Priests*, 1969).

Bound, Henry. Cf. p. 17, above. A witness, with Thomas I, in 1566 (*Cal.*, 418).

Clough, William. Witness for Thomas I, 1567 (*Cal.*, 353).

Coston, Thomas. Cf. p. 17, above and *Cal.*, 654 (Sir Richard Hoghton is 'to hold Thos. Cosson' to fulfil a covenant, 1615); 671.

Cotham, John. See Chapter IV, 'John Cottom of Tarnacre'. Described as 'gentleman' in his will.

Crichelawe, Roger and Margaret. Perhaps A. H.'s daughter was the Margaret 'Critchlowe', widow, defendant (with William Duddell, James Helme, etc) *v.* Thomas Hoghton, Esq., in 1584 (*Cal.*, 211). But a Roger 'Crechley' served as cook in 1592 (*The House and Farm Accounts of the Shuttleworths*, ed. J. Harland, CS, 1856, Part I, pp. 75, 79). Thomas, bastard son of Margery 'Croichlawe', appears in Blackburn in 1602 (Tait, *Quarter Sessions*, p. 148).

Fishwick, Richard. Married to Margaret, daughter of Richard Snape (*q.v.*) of Goosnargh (BL, Add. MS. 32,115 [S140]).

Fleetwood, John (Esq.). High Sheriff of Lancashire, 1578. See Hasler. There are copies of his will (1590) in the LRO (damaged), and in PCC (6 Sainberbe).

Fleetwood, Thomas (gent.) Son of above; married Mary, daughter of Sir Richard Sherburne of Stonyhurst. See *Cal.*, 1212, for the grant by A. H. and Thomas II to Thomas Fleetwood and Robert Talbot, 20 July, 1580 (i.e. for the annuities mentioned in A. H.'s will) and below, p. 141.

Gillam, Fulk. See Chapter III (p. 31).

Gillam, Thomas. See p. 32.

Helme, James (cf. Beseley, George). Appears as Hoghton witness in 1561 (*Cal.*, 206), etc. Described as 'of Chipping yeoman' in 1580 (*Cal.*, 1403.) Janet Helme of Chipping, widow, named her son James as one of her two executors (1599), and a James Helme of Chipping, husbandman, made his will in 1633 (BL, Add. MS. 32, 115, fos. 276b, 295b). James Helme, constable of Chipping, was committed in 1605 for allowing an arrested man to escape, and a 'James Helme of Lea' was licensed to buy corn in 1601 (Tait, *Quarter Sessions*, pp. 242, 73). There were several James Helmes in the Preston area (cf. also p. 48).

Hesketh, Bartholomew (Esq.). A.H.'s brother-in-law. Deponent in DL4 29 (39): he was about 42 in 1587, i.e. was born *c.* 1545. Included in a list of Lancashire gentlemen 'not seeming to be recusants but discovered to be dangerous persons' in 1592. Accused of keeping a Catholic schoolmaster (cf. p. 20); examined by Privy Council, 1581, suspected of being Campion's friend, and 1593 (on bond of £500) in connection with Hesketh conspiracy (cf. above, p. 37, and *APC*, XIII, 256–7; HMC, Hatfield House, IV, 241, 402).

Hesketh, Sir Thomas. See Chapter III: 'Sir Thomas Hesketh of Rufford'.

Hesketh, Thomas (of Gray's Inn, gent.). A. H.'s brother-in-law. Bencher and

Reader of Gray's Inn, 1588; Recorder of Lancaster; M.P., 1597; Attorney
of the Court of Wards; knighted 1603 (see *The Stanley Papers*, Part 2,
p. 205). Sir Thomas Heneague wrote to Cecil in 1595 that no one in
Lancashire has done more to further 'her Majesty's service' against recusants than Mr Hesketh (HMC, Hatfield House, V, 359–60); if, as seems
likely, he meant A.H.'s brother-in-law, Thomas may have been the kinsman who denounced Sir Thomas Hesketh's laxness against recusants
(cf. p. 35). See Hasler.

Hoghton, Elizabeth. A.H.'s second wife and widow (*Cal.*, 1406). Daughter of
Gabriel Hesketh of Aughton, to whom an unknown poet dedicated his
poetry (Harleian MS. 7578, no. 5). Shortly after A.H.'s death she married
George Warburton, gent., and sued her brothers, Bartholomew and
Thomas Hesketh, for properties left to them by A.H. in trust for her. Dead
by June, 1599 (cf. above, pp. 12, 28).

Hoghton, Thomas (Esq.). Thomas II, A.H.'s brother: cf. p. 146.

Livesey, Roger. A.H.'s 'bailiff of Hoghton, Wheelton and other places'; died
not long after A.H. His widow, Mary Livesey, took Thomas II to law, and
many Hoghton friends and retainers deposed or were named as witnesses,
including Richard Bannister, Thomas Barton, Bartholomew Hesketh,
Richard Hoghton of Park Hall, Richard Whittingham, and Robert
Swansey of Brindle, gent., A.H.'s attorney (DL4 29 (39)).

Melling, Peter. A Hoghton tenant in Lea (*Cal.*, 206); made his will in 1583
(BL, Add. MSS. 32,106 fo. 317b; 32,115 (M18)).

Pemberton, James. Catholic recusants brought before the ecclesiastical
commissioners in 1584 included James Pemberton of Whiston the younger
and the wife of James Pemberton the elder (*CRS*, V, 69 ff.). James
Pemberton witnessed Sir Richard Hoghton's 'settlement' of 1607
(DDCl 916).

Snape, Richard. Richard Snape of Goosnargh made his will in 1627 (Add.
MS. 32,115 (S140)). See Fishwick, Richard.

Standish, Edward (Esq.). One of A.H.'s supervisors. J.P.; died 1603. Married
Ellen, daughter of Sir William Radcliffe of Ordsall (Gillow, *Map*, p. 30);
when A.H. married his first wife, Dorothy Ashton, her stepfather was Sir
W. Radcliffe of Ordsall (*Cal.* 1396).

Talbot, John (Esq.). There are extracts from his will, dated 23 Jan., 24 Eliz.,
in the Bodleian (MS. Top. Lancs. C6, fo. 2b): he leaves all goods and
chattels, real and personal, 'unto Robert Talbot my base begotten son'.
Addressed as 'the Right Worshipful Mr John Talbot Esq.' by the priest
John Amias, 8 June 1580, and clearly a Catholic (*CRS*, V, 319).

Talbot, Robert. Natural son of above. Married Elizabeth, natural daughter of
Sir Richard de Hoghton, a half-sister of A.H. (Miller, *Hoghton Tower*,
p. 149). See Fleetwood, Thomas.

Wall, William. Thomas Wall, clerk, vicar of Preston, named William Wall as
his second son in 1599 (Add. MS. 32,115 (W26)).

Ward, Thomas. Helped to defend Thomas Hoghton at Lea in 1589. See also
Cal., 356.

Whittingham, Richard (gent.). A deponent in DL4 29 (39): see Livesey,
Roger. Bracketed with George Beseley in 1560 (*Cal.*, 738).

Whittingham, Thomas (gent.). See *Cal.*, 909.

N.B. Most of A.H.'s closer friends are shown to have been known or
suspected Catholics in *Lord Burghley's Map of Lancashire in 1590*, ed.
Joseph Gillow (1907). See Fleetwood, John and Thomas; Hesketh, Gabriel;

Appendix A

Hesketh, Sir Thomas; Hoghton family; Standish, Edward; Talbot family, etc. Miller (*Hoghton Tower*, p. 156) mentions that in 1575 the Bishop of Chester wrote to the Privy Council about recusancy in his diocese, and named Alexander Hoghton as one of those 'of longest obstinacy against religion'.

As already stated (p. 24), Alexander Hoghton's will refers back to a deed or grant of 20 July 1580, in which he made preliminary arrangements for the annuities to be paid to his 'servants'. This deed is printed from DDHo GG1090 (Lumby, *Calendar*, no. 1212).

To all Christian people to whom this present writing shall come ... Alexander Hoghton of the Lea in the county of Lancaster, Esquire, & Thomas Hoghton the younger brother of the said Alexander, send greeting in our lord God everlasting. Know you that we the said Alexander Hoghton & Thomas Hoghton for divers good & reasonable causes & considerations ... have given granted & confirmed, & by these presents for us & our heirs do give grant & confirm unto Thomas Fleetwood, gentleman, son & heir apparent of John Fleetwood of Penwortham in the said county, Esquire, & Robert Talbot, gentleman, bastard son of John Talbot of Salesbury in the said county, Esquire, one yearly rent of sixteen pounds thirteen shillings & four pence of good & lawful money of England, to be issuing & going out of all & every those messuages, cottages, lands, tenements and hereditaments with th'appurtenances mentioned & expressed hereafter in these presents, situate lying & being in Withnell in the said county of Lancaster & in the several tenures of those whose names hereafter severally be named & mentioned, that is to wit one messuage or tenement now or late in the holding or occupation of John Benson, of the yearly rent of xvjs vijd ... [To save space I cite the remaining tenures as a list of names and rents.] The late wife of Edmond Woodd [i.e. the wife of the late E. Wood], 25s 8d; Richard Gar‹sting›, 14s; Thomas Watson, 12s 10d; James Haydocke, 25s 8d; Thomas Catterall, 17s 1d; John Haworthe, 16s 11d; the late wife of George B‹..›ye, 21s 5d; Richard Livesey, 8s 8d; Christopher Marsden, 14s; Christopher Wilkinson, 16s 6d; Adam Blacklatch, 2s 4d; Thomas Clayton, 11s 9d; John Lucas, 8s 6d; Geoffrey Marley, 11s; John Hoghton de land, 6s 6d; Oliver Lucas 6s 4d; John Abbot, 16s 4d; Thomas Osboldston, 7s; Thomas Bolton, 23s 11d; the late wife of Richard Woodcock, 22s 2d; Nicholas Darwin, 15s 2d; the late wife of John Aspeden, 2s 4d; Alexander Hoghton, 3s; the tenants of 'bremecroffte' [cf. Lumby, index: *Brimmicroft*], 6s 8d. To have perceive levy & take the said yearly rent of sixteen pounds thirteen shillings four pence unto the said Thomas Fleetwood & Robert Talbot & their heirs from the day of the decease of me the said Alexander Hoghton for & during the term of the natural life of such person & persons & of the longest liver of them as I the said Alexander Hoghton shall declare & appoint in or by my last will & testament in writing, yearly payable & to be paid at the feast of Pentecost & St Martin the bishop in winter by even portions, & the first payment thereof to commence & begin at the first feast of the said feasts that shall next ensue & follow after the death of me the said Alexander Hoghton. And if it fortune that the said yearly rent of sixteen pounds thirteen shillings four pence to be behind & unpaid in part or in all at any of the said feasts in which it ought to be paid, being lawfully demanded, that then & so often it shall & may be lawful unto the said Thomas Fleetwood & Robert Talbot & their heirs during the term & time aforesaid, into the said messuages lands tenements & other the premises to enter & distrain, and the distress & distressor then & there ‹...› take away, impound & with them to detain & keep until such time as they shall be of the said yearly rent of sixteen pounds thirteen shillings four pence together with the arrearages thereof, if any such ‹be›, well & truly contented satisfied & paid. Provided always that if I the said Alexander Hoghton do not declare & appoint in & by my last will & testament in writing some person or persons during whose life or lives the said yearly rent ... may have continuance according to the grant aforesaid, that then this present grant & every matter & thing therein contained shall be merely frustrate void & of none effect force or strength in the law [*interlined*: any‹thing afore› said to the contrary notwithstanding]. In witness whereof we the said Alexander Hoghton & Thomas Hoghton to this our present writing have set our seals. Given the xxth day of July in the two & twentieth year of the reign of our sovereign lady Elizabeth, by the grace of God Queen of England, France & Ireland, defender of the faith, &c. [*Signed*:] Alexander Hoghton, Thomas Hoghton. [Sealed and delivered in the presence of eight witnesses, whose signatures are partly illegible. They include: ‹ ... › Fleetwood, Thomas Southworth,Thomas Morte, John Talbot, Alexander Rigby, William Hulton.]

2. Sir Thomas Hesketh of Rufford (20 June 1588). Extracts printed in (*a*) *The Stanley Papers*, Part 2, p. 124 ff.; (*b*) W. G. Procter, 'The Manor of Rufford and the Ancient Family of the Heskeths' (*HSLC*, 1908, LIX, 104 ff.); manuscript copies are found in (*c*) Add. MS. 32,104 (inaccurate: cf. above, p. 35), and (*d*), the Cheshire Record Office (EDA 2/2, fo. 142b). The following extracts are taken chiefly from (*a*) and (*d*).

'I resign my soul into the hands and to the mercy of the most mighty and everlasting God my only maker and redeemer and sanctifier, trusting by the death and passion of our Lord Jesus Christ and by the shedding of his most precious blood I shall rest with him for ever as one of his elect, and my body I will shall be buried by God his grace and sufferance in the new work and chancel of the chapel of Rufforth in such place, manner and sort as I shall hereafter appoint.' (See p. 36, above). He bequeathes property in Mawdesley and Croston to 'Thomas Hesketh my second son'; to Richard Hesketh, 'my third son ... my capital messuage called Beconsall'; other bequests to 'Thomas Hesketh my bastard son' and 'Hugh Hesketh my bastard son', to 'Henry Squire and Dorothy his wife, my daughter', to 'Richard Hesketh and Christopher Hesketh my bastard brethren'.

Annuities to 'servants' include one to 'Hugh Haughton my servant': 'during all his natural life one annuity or annual rent charge' of £20; one to Diggory Rishton (£6 13s 4d p.a.); one to John Spencer (5 marks, i.e. £1 13s 4d p.a.). 'Item I give to Tristram Knowles, Thomas Backhouse, Thomas Farbeck, Richard Baker, Nicholas Conse, Thomas Werden, Henry Squire, James Tomson, Richard Davie, every one of them xls. [forty shillings] yearly during their natural lives. ... Also I give to Richard Stannynowght my foot-boy xls.'

'To Dame Alice Hesketh, my wife, the third part of all my goods.' To Robert Hesketh, his son and heir, Sir Thomas bequeathes his chain of gold, two silver cans, his best silver basin and ewer, the newest hangings, the cup and cover whereon was engraved the spread eagle, all beds, bed coverings, carpets, cushions whereupon his arms or crest were either carved or wrought with needle, and all armour, munitions and weapons wherewith to serve her Majesty.

Appendix A

As executors he named Sir Richard Sherburne, Henry Stanley of the Cross, Esq., Thomas Hesketh of Gray's Inn, gent., and Hugh Hesketh, his bastard son. The supervisors to be John Towneley, Esq., and Robert Hesketh, his son and heir.

3. Thomas Savage of Rufford and London (3 October 1611). PCC (78 Wood), contemporary copy.
'In the name of God the Father, God the Son and God the Holy Ghost, in whose name I was baptised and in whom only I believe to be saved. Amen. I, Thomas Savage, citizen and goldsmith of London, being sick in body but of perfect mind and memory.... First I bequeath my soul into thy hands O God – Father, Son and Holy Ghost. Thou hast first made me, and Thou hast given thy Son to become man, who died for my sins and for the sins of the people. O Father, for this thy Son's sake, have mercy upon me. O Lord Jesus Christ, thou Son of God which hast bought me with thy precious blood by one oblation sufficient for all, I believe in Thee. . .'
Savage's goods to be divided into three parts: one third for his wife Alice; one third for his children (excluding Richard, his eldest son, already provided for); one third for the executor, to pay for legacies etc. to be specified.
To Richard, eldest son, the house in Silver St, parish of St. Olave's, which 'Mr William Peirson, goldsmith, now inhabiteth'.
To Alice, his wife, the house he now dwells in, in Great Wood St, in the parish of St. Alban.
To John Savage, youngest son, the house in Addle St, parish of St Mary in Aldermanbury, 'wherein Mr John Heminges, grocer, now dwelleth'. (This is John Heminges the actor, a member of Shakespeare's company, who belonged to the Grocers' Company.) It should be noted that Richard Savage also had two sons to whom he did not leave houses: Thomas and George.
To Elizabeth Savage, daughter, the house in Addle St in which Mr John Wotton, gent., now dwelleth.
Thomas Chappell, John Rowden, Wm. Adderley and Wm. Tribecke, on 30 May last, sold to Thomas Savage a 'messuage or tenement called The George, with all shops, cellars ... gardens', in St Sepulchre's, London, occupied by Arthur Strangwayes, together with four shops. These are bequeathed 'unto the parson and churchwardens of the parish church of St Alban in Great Wood St in London and to their successors'. To the poor people of the above parish, forty shillings.
'Item, I give and bequeath unto the poor people of the town of Rufforth in the parish of Croston in the County of Lancaster, where I was born, the sum of forty shillings to be distributed amongst them at the discretion of my brother-in-law John Palmer, Thomas Spencer, Thomas Awly and Hugh Watkinson or so many of them as shall be then living at the time of my decease.'
To 'the worshipful Company of Goldsmiths in London, whereof I myself am a free member, one spout pot of silver white to weigh thirty ounces', and £8 'to make them a supper'.
To 'my mother Janet Savage the sum of ten pounds, to be paid within two months next after my decease if she be then living'.
'Item, I give unto my two sisters Cicely Peacock and Katherine Palmer to

[143]

each of them the sum of five pounds, to be paid to them within six months next after my decease ... Item, I give unto my brothers-in-law John Palmer and Ambrose Peacock to each of them twenty shillings to make each of them a ring of gold, if their wives be then living.' To Thomas Peacock, son of sister Cicely, £3; to each of his brothers and sisters, twenty shillings.

'Unto my cousin Francis Savage of Rufforth the sum of forty shillings. .... And to each of his children twenty shillings.'

'Unto my cousin Hesketh, widow, late wife of Thomas Hesketh of Rufforth, the sum of twenty shillings.'

'Unto my mother-in-law Mrs Wootton, widow, three pounds to make her a ring of gold. ... Unto my sister Sara Flint three pounds.'

'Item, I give unto my fellows the sea-coal m‹. ›ters of the city of London', £3 for a dinner.

'Unto my cousin Anne Leland the sum of three pounds and a mourning gown.' Savage appoints 'my trusty friend Robert Hill, citizen and merchant tailor of London, the full and sole executor', and gives him £10. He appoints 'my very loving friends Mr Doctor Lister and Mr John Jackson to be my overseers', and gives each of them £3.

4. John Cottom of Tarnacre (17 July 1616). Lancashire Record Office.

> In the name of God Amen. I, John Cottom of Tarnacre in the parish of St Michael upon Wyre in the county of Lancaster, gentleman, being now of good and perfect remembrance, do ordain and make this my last will and testament in manner and form following. First, I give and bequeath my soul unto almighty God my maker and redeemer, by whose death and passion I trust to be saved and my body to be buried at the discretion of my executors. Item, I give and bequeath all my lands, leases, goods and chattels to my daughter Priscilla and her assigns during her natural life, my debts funeral charges and legacies discharged. Item, I give unto William Walton, son to Thomas Walton and Priscilla, and to his heirs for ever, all my lands, leases lying within Tarnacre and Sowerby within the aforesaid parish of St Michael, yielding and paying out of the same to John Walton his brother one hundred pounds, to James Walton his other brother one hundred pounds, and to Ann Walton his sister £200, to be paid in 4 years after his entrance unto the whole. And for default of payment of the aforesaid sums yearly for four years after to the aforesaid John, James and Anne to charge my lands therewithal for those years. Item, I ordain and make Thomas Walton my son-in-law my sole and lawful executor of this my last will and testament, in witness whereof I have hereunto set my hand and seal the day and year above
> written in the presence of   John Cottom
> per me Thomas Walmesley
> curate de Walton in le Dale
>   [the marks of two witnesses]

Attached, two statements, one by Thomas Walmesley, curate of Walton le Dale: on or about 17 July he was sent for to the decedent to be a witness unto his will; he found the will ready drawn, and then the decedent signed, sealed and delivered the writing to Mr Thomas Walton, sole executor; Cottom asked Walmesley to read the will aloud, which he did three several times; Cottom then took the will into his own hands, lying in his bed, and perused the same, and acknowledged it. The second statement confirms.

Inventory of John Cottom's goods at Tarnacre, made by George Brown and others, 27 July 1616.

Imprimis, 4 pair of breeches 50s; 4 doublets 30s; 4 jerkins 25s; 4 cloaks £3 6s 8d; 3 pair of stockings 10s; 2 hats 10s; 3 pair of shoes, 2 pair of boots, one pair of spurs 10s; 5 horses £14; one saddle, one bridle 5s; one brass pot 10s; in pewter 3s 4d; one chest 10s; 3 standing beds 30s; one feather bed, one bolster, one blanket, one covering, for a board, one coverlet 30s; one beef tub 6s 8d; 2 chairs 2s; one long table in the hall & forms 40s; one caliver, one head-piece, one flax and touchbox 10s; milk boards and shelves 3s 4d; one 'Rakentyth' [?chain] 8d; one table in the kitchen, one dishboard, one cheese-press and one other board 10s; one old chest 3s; 12 sapling boards & other woods in the chamber over the kitchen 13s 4d; one other 'Rackenteth' & bulk, 18d; one board clog [?] 20d; one corn wain chest & one muckwain chest 13s 4d; in wheels 7s 8d; one great ark in the barn 40s; one turf wain 6s 8d; 8 pieces of wood in the barn 5s; one tugwithy 10d; one plough & coulter 2s; two staples & two rings, two oxen yokes & one wimble 20d; two swine troughs 20d. [Total] £37.

5. John Weever, gent. (16 February, 1632; proved 29 March 1632). PCC.

In Dei nomine Amen. I, John Weever of the parish of St James Clerkenwell in the county of Middlesex, gent., being in sound mind and perfect health of body, thanks be to almighty God, do make and ordain this my last will and testament in manner and form following. Imprimis, I commit my soul into the hands of the almighty, omnipotent and everliving God, in full assurance of everlasting salvation through the merits, death and passion of his only begotten Son, Jesus Christ, my alone saviour and redeemer. As for my body, I commit the same to Christian burial expecting a joyful resurrection. And for and concerning such worldly estate as God hath blessed me withal, I bequeath the same in manner and form following. Item, I give and bequeath unto my brother William Weever my black cloak with many laces. Item, I give to my sister Alice Cawthorne twenty shillings. Item, I give to my sister Anne Caton twenty shillings. Item, to my sister Isabel Holt twenty shillings. All which said several legacies to be given and paid to my brother and three sisters as aforesaid, my will is shall be given and paid by Anne my dearly beloved wife within one year next after my decease. And I do make and ordain my said wife Anne Weever the sole executrix of this my last will and testament. And I do make and appoint my nephew William Cawthorne overseer of this my will, to whom I give twenty shillings to buy him a ring. Item, I give and bequeath my lease of my house in Gray's Inn Lane, now in the tenure of George Dawson, and the lease of my house in Clerkenwell wherein I now dwell, together with all goods, chattels, moneys, plate, household stuff and all the rest of my personal estate whatsoever, not before bequeathed, to my said executrix Anne Weever, my beloved wife. And lastly I do hereby revoke and make void all former wills and testaments by me made. In witness whereof I have hereto set my hand and seal the sixteenth day of February in the seventh year of the reign of our sovereign lord Charles, by the grace of God King of England, Scotland, France and Ireland, defender of the faith &c Annoque Domini one thousand six hundred thirty one John Weever. Signed and sealed in the presence of John Witt and Wm. Gardner.

Appendix B. *Genealogical tables*

(1) *Hoghton of Hoghton Tower*

(Based on a pedigree at Hoghton Tower; *A Short Guide to Hoghton Tower*; *The History of Preston* (1900), by Henry Fishwick.)

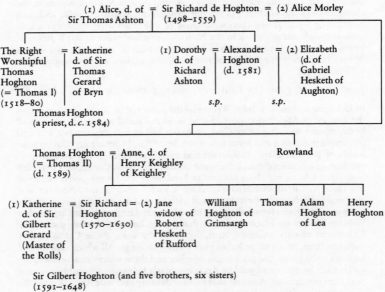

(1) Alice, d. of Sir Thomas Ashton = Sir Richard de Hoghton (1498–1559) = (2) Alice Morley

The Right Worshipful Thomas Hoghton (= Thomas I) (1518–80) = Katherine d. of Sir Thomas Gerard of Bryn

Thomas Hoghton (a priest, d. *c.* 1584)

(1) Dorothy d. of Richard Ashton *s.p.* = Alexander Hoghton (d. 1581) *s.p.* = (2) Elizabeth (d. of Gabriel Hesketh of Aughton)

Thomas Hoghton (= Thomas II) (d. 1589) = Anne, d. of Henry Keighley of Keighley

Rowland

(1) Katherine d. of Sir Gilbert Gerard (Master of the Rolls) = Sir Richard Hoghton (1570–1630) = (2) Jane widow of Robert Hesketh of Rufford

William Hoghton of Grimsargh

Thomas

Adam Hoghton of Lea

Henry Hoghton

Sir Gilbert Hoghton (and five brothers, six sisters) (1591–1648)

N.B. (1) In this and the following tables I have simplified by omitting some younger brothers and sisters, and childless wives.

(2) Sir Richard de Hoghton, who married four times, also had many illegitimate children. These included Leonard, Richard, Richard the younger (later known as Richard of Park Hall: cf. p. 10 above), Gilbert, Arthur, George, and at least two daughters (Elizabeth, wife of Robert Talbot (cf. p. 140, above), and another Elizabeth). See Lumby, *Calendar*, no. 1410 and Index, and Miller, *Hoghton Tower*, p. 149.

(3) Thomas, the son of Thomas I, has caused some confusion. John Talbot, Thomas Barton, Bartholomew Hesketh and other Hoghton friends testified on 30 July 1580 that Thomas I died without 'heirs male of his body', and that Alexander Hoghton 'is living at Lea' and is his brother (Lumby, *Calendar*, no. 50). But Thomas I is thought to have had a son, Thomas, a priest (who was therefore an outlaw, so could not be an heir), who died in Salford gaol *c.* 1584: that may explain why Thomas II sought an exemplification that he was the lawful heir in Feb. 1584 (Lumby, *Cal.*, no. 1407).

Appendix B

(2) *Butler of Middle Rawcliffe*

(Based on Henry Fishwick, *The History of the Parish of St Michaels-on-Wyre*, CS, 1891, XXV, p. 159.)

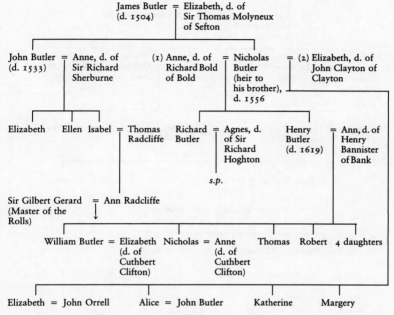

N.B. (1) Either Katherine or Margery, daughters of Nicholas Butler and Elizabeth Clayton, could have been the mother of *John Weever* (the nephew of Henry Butler); but Weever could also have been the son of an unrecorded daughter or illegitimate daughter of Nicholas Butler.

(2) Sir Gilbert Gerard and Ann Radcliffe were the parents of Sir Thomas Gerard, dedicatee of Weever's *Epigrammes*, and of the three sisters who married three other dedicatees (Sir Richard Hoghton, Sir Richard Molyneux, Sir Peter Leigh): cf. p. 51.

Shakespeare: the 'lost years'

(3) *Cottam (Cottom) of Tarnacre*

(Based on *Visitation 1613*, and on Chapter IV, above.)

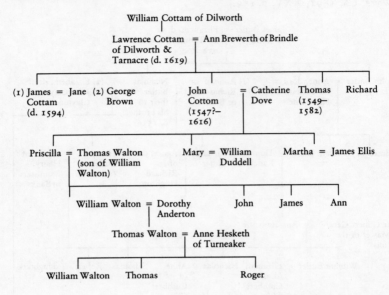

William Cottam of Dilworth

Lawrence Cottam = Ann Brewerth of Brindle
of Dilworth &
Tarnacre (d. 1619)

(1) James = Jane (2) George   John   = Catherine Thomas Richard
Cottam   Brown   Cottom   Dove   (1549–
(d. 1594)   (1547?–   1582)
                         1616)

Priscilla = Thomas Walton   Mary = William   Martha = James Ellis
(son of William   Duddell
Walton)

William Walton = Dorothy   John   James   Ann
               Anderton

Thomas Walton = Anne Hesketh
              of Turneaker

William Walton   Thomas   Roger

Appendix B

(4) Salusbury of Lleweni and Rug

(Based on *Calendar of Salusbury Correspondence 1553 – circa 1700*, ed. W. J. Smith (Cardiff, 1954); and Brown, *Salusbury and Chester*.)

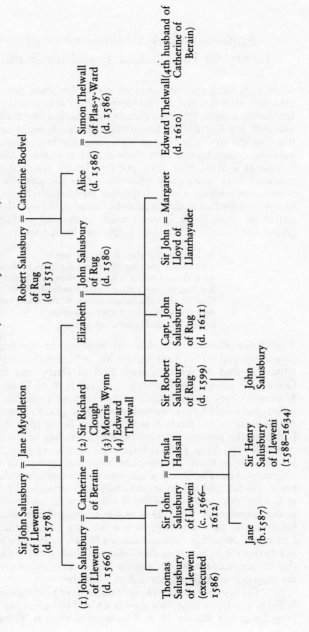

Appendix C. *A Midsummer Night's Dream*, *Henry VI* Parts 2 and 3, and the Stanley Family

After suggesting that Shakespeare served for some years as one of Lord Strange's Men, I noted that he seems to have rearranged history in *Richard III*, giving a more flattering picture than did the chronicles of his patrons' ancestor, the first Earl of Derby; and that he brought Lord Strange more prominently into *Love's Labour's Lost*, his most topical comedy, than previous commentators have suspected (cf. p. 63ff.). *A Midsummer Night's Dream* is a third play with possible Derby connections. Editors have repeated, with remarkable unanimity, that this comedy must have been written – or adapted – for an important wedding, preferably one attended by Queen Elizabeth. The elaborate compliment in II.1.157 ff. would have had a particular relish if the Queen herself, 'in maiden meditation, fancy-free', graced the bridal celebrations. Cupid, we hear, took aim

> At a fair vestal throned by the west,
> And loosed his love-shaft smartly from his bow
> As it should pierce a hundred thousand hearts;
> But I might see young Cupid's fiery shaft
> Quenched in the chaste beams of the watery moon;
> And the imperial votaress passed on
> In maiden meditation, fancy-free.

The Queen attended a number of weddings in the 1590s but, as E.K. Chambers and others have shown, the effective choice lies between two: either (1) that of William, sixth Earl of Derby and Elizabeth Vere at Greenwich on 26 January 1595; or (2) that of Thomas Berkeley and Elizabeth Carey at Blackfriars on 19 February 1596. Shakespeare and his colleagues would have a reason for making a special effort on each occasion: (1) the sixth Earl of Derby was a brother of Ferdinando, Lord Strange, who had been the patron of several leading members of the company from c. 1586 till 1594 (cf. p. 59); (2) Elizabeth Carey was a granddaughter of Lord Hunsdon, the Lord Chamberlain who was patron of the company in February 1596. The Queen was present at the Derby wedding, and, since the bride was her god-daughter, may well have attended Elizabeth Carey's as well. Chambers and Harold Brooks, the New Arden editor, both favour (2) as the occasion for which *Dream* was composed but admit that the choice between the two weddings is not an easy one. 'Either wedding', said Chambers, 'would fit such indications of date as the play yields'.[1] Believing as I do that Chambers post-dated many of Shakespeare's early plays,[2] I think that more can and should be said for the earlier of the two most likely dates – the marriage of William, sixth Earl of Derby.

(1) 'The much-travelled Theseus might have been thought appropriate to William Stanley, whose own travels are said to have taken him as far as the Holy Land and Russia' (E.K. Chambers[3]). Even if William Stanley never

reached the Holy Land and Russia, as sceptics have alleged, he certainly travelled abroad for some years.[4] (2) William Stanley was keenly interested in poetry and drama; he kept his own company of players, and, a few years after his marriage, in 1599, was said to be 'busy penning comedies for the common players'.[5] Shakespeare's Theseus similarly takes a special interest in poetry and drama. These two possible allusions have been pointed out before, but there are additional reasons for connecting Theseus and Earl William. (3) The Earl married late, compared with his contemporaries: he was born between 1560 and 1562,[6] and would be in his thirties when he married in 1595. (His brother, Ferdinando, was born c. 1559 and married in 1579.) This, again, connects him with Theseus, a 'mature' bridegroom in the play. (4) It is a curious coincidence that, of the three marriages that are the strongest contenders as the 'occasion' of A Midsummer Night's Dream, one and only one fits in with what appears to be a topical allusion in the play's opening speeches.

> Now, fair Hippolyta, our nuptial hour
> Draws on apace; four happy days bring in
> Another moon; but, O, methinks, how slow
> This old moon wanes! ...
> Four days will quickly steep themselves in night;
> Four nights will quickly dream away the time;
> And then the moon, like to a silver bow
> New bent in heaven, shall behold the night
> Of our solemnities.

Could the four days be a clue to the play's date? Find out moonshine, find out moonshine! According to H. H. Goldstine's tables of new and full moons,[7] there was a new moon on 30 January 1595, exactly four days after Earl William's wedding; and Goldstine also tells us that new moons appeared on 18 February 1596 (one day before the Berkeley–Carey marriage) and on 10 May 1594 (eight days after the Heneage–Southampton marriage, to which I shall return in a moment). It is true that the play proclaims that the marriage itself will coincide with a new moon; as I suggested in dealing with 'Ferdinand' in Love's Labour's Lost, however, dramatists had to be careful not to mirror contemporary great ones too obviously (cf. p. 69). If Dream was performed on a wedding-day, as is usually assumed, the emphatic statement that a new moon is due in precisely four days, which happened to be true on 26 January 1595, would alert spectators to expect other topical allusions, and that would be as far as it would be prudent to go. For the play is not a roman à clef, and Theseus is not Earl William, though there are teasing similarities. It would, of course, have been a simple matter to add the play's nineteen opening lines as it neared completion, when the exact date of this long-awaited marriage was at last decided.

The date of the Derby wedding, by the way, is given by Stowe. 'The 26 of January William Earl of Derby married the Earl of Oxford's daughter at the court then at Greenwich, which marriage feast was there most royally kept.' Chambers pointed out that a different date seems to be indicated by the churchwardens' accounts of St Martin's Westminster, for 1595: 'Item, paid the 30th of January for ringing at her Majesty's coming to the Lord Treasurer's to the Earl of Derby's wedding, and at her departure from thence the first of February, 2s'. Chambers added that such bell-ringings 'are often entered with only approximate accuracy',[8] but his argument for preferring Stowe's date seems to me not proven, especially since he concedes that Stowe was wrong as to the place of the wedding. The later date would fit in pleasingly with the play's emphasis that the Theseus wedding will coincide with a new moon; whichever date turns out to be the correct one, however – 26 or 30 January 1595 – it looks as if the 'new moon' lines contain a topical allusion. And this is confirmed by (5), the description of Theseus' impatience –

> but, O, methinks how slow
> This old moon wanes! She lingers my desires
> Like to a step-dame or a dowager
> Long withering out a young man's revenue.

Earl William's wedding had to be deferred for some months, Ferdinando's widow being pregnant when he died. Had the dowager Countess of Derby given birth to a son, Earl William would have been 'unearled', and his long-expected marriage would have been stopped. Earl William wrote impatiently about these delays in September 1594,[9] and might well have thought that a *dowager* lingered his desires and 'withered out' his revenue. The lawsuits of Ferdinando's widow and daughters against Earl William dragged on for years, and it must have become obvious in the months preceding the earl's wedding that they would. (Ferdinando's widow married Thomas Egerton, the Lord Keeper and later Lord Chancellor, in 1600. We know from Egerton's private papers that she was a strong-willed and difficult woman: he complained of her greed, extravagance and ill-temper, her 'cursed railing and bitter tongue'.[10] If Shakespeare alluded unkindly to his former master's widow, as I suggest, there are good reasons for believing that she deserved it.)

(6) Once we are alerted to the possibility that Theseus may be an idealised portrait of Earl William, other passages in the play, that have not been seen as 'topical' by previous commentators, need to be scanned afresh. For example, Theseus' pride in his hunting-dogs:

> My hounds are bred out of the Spartan kind,
> So flewed, so sanded; and their heads are hung
> With ears that sweep away the morning dew;
> Crook-kneed and dew-lapped like Thessalian bulls;
> Slow in pursuit, but matched in mouth like bells. (IV.1.106 ff.)

It has long been a belief, wrote F. A. Bailey, 'in which so great an authority as J. H. Round concurred [*Peerage and Pedigree* (1910), II, 32–5], that the original Stanley coat ... may have owed its three stags' heads to a fortunate marriage with an heiress, Joan, daughter of Philipe de Bamvile, in the late thirteenth century; this was, in Round's estimation, 'the turning point in the history of the family', for Joan brought to the Stanleys (hitherto of Stafford-shire) the lordship of Storeton and the hereditary office of Master Forester of Wirral in Cheshire'.[11] The Earls of Derby kept the three stags' heads in their coat of arms. Theseus, to be sure, was a famous huntsman – yet his speech about his marvellous dogs has an air of being there for its own sake. And what would be more natural than that the Master Forester kept his own hounds, and was proud of them? We know that the Leighs of Lyme, who were Deputy Stewards of the forest of Macclesfield under the Earls of Derby, maintained a celebrated breed of Lyme mastiffs, and perhaps Shakespeare referred to these (the Earls of Derby addressed the Leighs of Lyme as their 'servants'), or to others like them – hounds that may well have been present at the Derby wedding.

I now return to two other topical allusions that have been discussed before. (7) The play seems to refer to an episode at the Scottish court in August 1594, described in *A True Reportarie* (S.R., 24 October 1594). While King James was at dinner, a chariot was drawn in by a Moor. 'This chariot should have been drawn in by a lion, but because his presence might have brought some fear to the nearest ... it was thought meet that the Moor should supply that room.' 'Bottom and his fellows', said Harold Brooks, 'likewise planning a performance before their sovereign, anticipate the fear that bringing in "a lion among ladies" may produce, and likewise modify their plan in order to avoid it.'[12] Though Shakespeare might still refer back to this episode in 1596, a joke about something that happened four hundred miles from London would lose its savour more quickly than one concerned with local events; Earl William's marriage in January 1595, would come at the right time for such an allusion, the 1596 marriage less so. (8) 'The bad weather described in II.1.81–117 is probably that which began in March, 1594, prevailed during the greater part of that year, and ushered in a long period of corn shortage' (E. K. Chambers). It is noteworthy that the bad weather extended over four seasons –

> The spring, the summer,
> The childing autumn, angry winter, change
> Their wonted liveries

– not only because four seasons bring us precisely to the period of Earl William's marriage in January 1595, but also because this allusion rules out another possible marriage, that of Sir Thomas Heneage and Mary, Countess of Southampton, on 2 May 1594. The Countess's son, the Earl of Southampton, was another patron whom Shakespeare might wish to please at this time, and Sir Thomas was a 'mature' bridegroom (aged sixty-two or so in 1594), but, as we have seen, quite apart from the weather the 'new moon' eliminates this marriage, and no one now presses its claims.

While I am primarily concerned with Shakespeare and Lord Strange (the fifth Earl), the possibility that he also wrote *A Midsummer Night's Dream* for the sixth Earl's wedding, when he was no longer officially attached to the Stanleys, deserves a place in our story. For if Theseus gives us an idealised portrait of Earl William it follows that Shakespeare's two most obviously topical plays, *Love's Labour's Lost* and *A Midsummer Night's Dream*, were written for the same family, and this would be additional proof – if more is needed – of the dramatist's very special relationship with the brilliant Ferdinando, Lord Strange.

Let us now turn to *Henry VI*, Parts 2 and 3, where the dramatist tampered with history as in *Richard III*, though not quite so transparently. It has long been recognised that in his account of the Wars of the Roses Shakespeare leaned towards Lancaster (and the 'Lancashire connection' that I have outlined may help to explain this bias). Why, we may ask, did he magnify the achievements or sufferings of some individuals, while he left others more or less as he found them? Was it because of a general prejudice in favour of Lancaster, or could there have been a more particular reason? The emphasis given to the deaths of Lord Clifford and of his son (2 *Henry VI*, V.1.122–216, V.2.1–65; 3 *Henry VI*, II.6.1–86) is a case in point. Geoffrey Bullough said of the second that 'the prolonged ill-treatment of [young Clifford's] corpse was intended to illustrate the growing cruelty of the civil war';[13] and Kenneth Muir has suggested that young Clifford's speech on discovering his father's body (2 *Henry VI*, V.2.31–56) is stylistically more mature than the rest of the play, and has left no trace in the reported text or 'bad quarto' – that is, was an afterthought.[14] We may think that the highlighting of the Clifford scenes, and Shakespeare's retouching of some of the material, needs no justification other than that it adds to dramatic balance. It is worth bearing in mind, however, that Ferdinando, Lord Strange, was the son of Margaret Clifford, and was therefore a direct descendant of the Cliffords represented in *Henry VI*; also, that Ferdinando's 'Stanley' ancestors had not yet risen to prominence in the reign of Henry VI – if Lord Strange was to have the pleasure of identifying himself with any of the principal figures in Shakespeare's version of history it had to be through his mother's family. That could explain why Shakespeare inserted what is in effect a 'Clifford sequence' in *Henry VI*, exalting young Clifford as one of the most resolute champions of the house of Lancaster, and attempting to account for the killing of Rutland and York by showing that these brutalities all resulted from young Clifford's devotion to his elderly father, and horror on discovering his father's mangled body.

> Wast thou ordained, dear father,
> To lose thy youth in peace, and to achieve
> The silver livery of advised age,
> And, in thy reverence and thy chair-days, thus
> To die in ruffian battle?
> (2 *Henry VI*, V.2.45–9)

The chronicles are silent about old Clifford's age, merely mentioning him as one of the many who fell at the battle of St Albans. We know that 'old' Clifford was 41 when he died, but Shakespeare made him a much older man, 'in thy reverence and thy chair-days', and thus increased young Clifford's outrage and thirst for revenge.

Whether Shakespeare saw from the outset that young Clifford's killing of Rutland and York had to be prepared for, or added young Clifford's speech over his father's body as an 'afterthought', is not easy to prove. I think, though, that the absence of this speech from the reported text must be related to the text's origins. The purpose of the speech is to prepare for the sequel, 3 *Henry VI*. If 2 *Henry VI* and 3 *Henry VI* were performed consecutively, the speech is needed; if, however, 2 *Henry VI* was performed on its own when the reported text came into being, such a long preparatory speech would be less functional and might well be dropped, since it obstructs the 'closure' of 2 *Henry VI* in its dying moments.

Notes

Preface

1 See Baker, *In Shakespeare's Warwickshire*, and Chambers, *Gleanings* ('William Shakeshafte'). Chambers had noted the existence of William Shakeshafte in 1923 (*Stage*, I, 280, n.) but, as Harold Jenkins points out to me, did not connect Shakeshafte and Shakespeare before Baker did so in 1937.

I. Introduction

1 T. W. Baldwin points out (*Small Latine*, I, 487) that, while some theorists said that a boy ought to be ready to go to university at fifteen, the available statistics show that some went earlier and many later. Between 1567 and 1579, 40 went to Oxford at 12 years of age, 56 at 13, 115 at 14, 135 at 15, 193 at 16, 247 at 17, 306 at 18, 198 at 19, 144 at 20. This suggests that 16 or 17 would be a more usual age to leave school than 15.
2 Chambers, *Shakespeare*, II, 252. As Chambers explains (I, 17), '"killing a calf" seems to have been an item in the repertory of wandering entertainers'; it could be that Aubrey and others misunderstood this phrase when they said that Shakespeare worked as a butcher's apprentice.
3 Schoenbaum, *Documentary Life*, 27.
4 See Leslie Hotson, *Shakespeare's Sonnets Dated*, p. 231, and below, p. 118.
5 See Baldwin, *op. cit.*, I, 464: 'the King's free Grammar School at Stratford.'
6 I, 480 ff.

II. Hoghton of Hoghton Tower

1 J. H. Lumby indexed the most important documents in *A Calendar of the Deeds and Papers in the possession of Sir James de Hoghton, Bart.* (1936). The DDHo Index at the LRO 'relates to documents deposited by Sir Cuthbert de Hoghton, Bart., in addition to those in the Calendar published by [Lumby]. Presented to the County Council, 1953.' Sir Bernard de Hoghton still has many strong-boxes filled with undeposited (mainly eighteenth- and nineteenth-century) deeds and papers, which were recently moved from the estate office to Hoghton Tower.
2 BL, Harleian MS. 7386, fo. 290b; see also Miller, *Hoghton Tower*, p. 101. Miller's book contains many illustrations of Hoghton Tower, pedigrees, etc., and is most useful, though sometimes unreliable.
3 Miller, *op. cit.*, p. 168; cf. J. Gillow, *English Catholics*, III, 328.
4 Lumby, *Calendar*, no. 1393; BL, Add. MS. 32,106 fo. 131.
5 Add. MS. 32,106 fo. 132b.
6 Add. MS. 32,106; PRO, DL4 48 (49).
7 Quoted from J. Gillow, *The Haydock Papers: a Glimpse into English Catholic Life* (1888), p. 10 ff.; Miller (*Hoghton Tower*, p. 74) calls the author of the ballad Roger Anderson.
8 Gillow, *op. cit.*, p. 15.
9 *APC*, XIII, 149.
10 *APC*, XIII, 290.

11 W. D. Selby, *Lancashire and Cheshire Records Preserved in the Public Record Office, London* (RSLC, 1882, vol. VII), II, 342.
12 Gillow, *Haydock Papers*, 9, 17.
13 *APC*, XII, 346.
14 See Lumby, *Calendar*, no. 1406; Miller (*Hoghton Tower*, p. 158) calls it Ashton Hall.
15 DL1 125 (H3); Selby, *op. cit.*, II, 279; DL4 25 (27).
16 *SPD*, 229.25; BL, Add. MS. 32,106, p. 206.
17 *SPD*, 241.52.
18 *Lancashire Funeral Certificates*, ed. T. W. King (*CS*, vol. 75), 1869, p. 66.
19 See Lumby, *Calendar*, no. 52.
20 J. Gillow, 'The Catholic Registers of Salwick and Lea in the Fylde' (*CRS*, XV, 155).
21 *The Letters of John Chamberlain*, ed. N. E. McClure (2 vols., Philadelphia, 1939), I, 75.
22 *SPD*, 226.18; HMC, Hatfield House, X, 30.
23 HMC, Hatfield House, X, 343–4.
24 DDIn 47 (2).
25 Miller, *Hoghton Tower*, 87–8; cf. Lumby, *Calendar*, no. 54.
26 See Douglas Hamer, 'Was William Shakespeare William Shakeshafte?' (*RES*, 1970, XXI, 41–8).
27 E. K. Chambers, *Sources for a Biography of Shakespeare* (Oxford, 1946), p. 11.
28 Privately communicated.
29 Cf. p. 13.
30 Chambers, *Shakespeare*, II, 372.
31 See Mark Eccles, *Shakespeare in Warwickshire* (Madison, Wis., 1961), p. 7.
32 Eccles, p. 11.
33 *Henslowe's Diary*, p. 273.
34 *APC*, XIII, 269 (3 Dec. 1581).
35 The entries in the *Household Book* (DDF 2429) are written in a difficult hand, which is sometimes a form of shorthand. The last letters of many words are simply squiggles.
36 *SPD*, 240.138.
37 See William Beamont, *Winwick* (Warrington, 1878), p. 75, for Mather; A. L. Rowse, *Sex and Society in Shakespeare's Age Simon Forman the Astrologer* (1974), p. 276 ff.; E. C. Gaskell, *The Life of Charlotte Bronte* (ed. 1858), p. 30 ff.
38 *SPD*, 243.52.
39 See Add. MS. 32,106, no. 379; Henry Fishwick, *The History of the Parish of Preston* (1900), p. 260 ff.
40 PRO, *Calendarium Inquis. post Mortem*.
41 See *The Stanley Papers*, Part II, p. lxxiii.
42 Cf. Leatherbarrow, *Elizabethan Recusants*, p. 55 etc.
43 Joseph Gillow, *Lord Burghley's Map of Lancashire in 1590*, 1907, p. 1; cf. Christopher Haigh, *Reformation and Resistance in Tudor Lancashire* (Cambridge, 1975).
44 A typescript owned by Sir Bernard de Hoghton, Bt.
45 G. C. Miller, *Hoghton Tower*, pp. 154–5.
46 Gillow, *English Catholics*, III, 327. Not all of the Hoghtons supported Catholic education, of course. Sir Gilbert (son of Sir Richard) became a Governor of Blackburn Grammar School, at the early age of twenty (Miller, *Hoghton Tower*, pp. 174–5).
47 William Beamont, *A History of the House of Lyme* (Warrington, 1876), p. 93; *The House of Lyme* by Lady Newton (1917), p. 43.
48 Cf. Lumby, *Calendar*, no. 1409: 'the manors of English Lea and French Lea commonly known as the Lea'.

49 Baker, *In Shakespeare's Warwickshire*, p. 303.
50 Lumby, *Calendar*, no. 1396.
51 Ed. 1882, 3 vols, I, 574.
52 Cf. Baker, *op. cit.*, and Chambers, *Gleanings*.
53 Miller, p. 158.

III. Sir Thomas Hesketh of Rufford

1 In this paragraph I am indebted to *Rufford Old Hall* (The National Trust, 1979), p. 32.
2 Alan Keen and Roger Lubbock, *The Annotator*, p. 46.
3 L. Hotson, *Shakespeare's Sonnets Dated* (1949), pp. 128–9.
4 *HSLC*(1908), LIX, 93 ff.
5 *Mary Lyvesey v. Thomas Houghton* (DL4, 25 Eliz.); DDHe 6.19; DDHe 18.26; Add. MS.32,104 fo. 32b.
6 See Add. MS. 32,104 fo. 352.
7 Procter, p. 107.
8 Dame Alice Hesketh's will, in the LRO, is dated 20 November 1604.
9 *Rufford Old Hall* (The National Trust, 1979), pp. 14–15.

IV. John Cottom of Tarnacre

1 T. W. Baldwin, *Small Latine*, I, chap. xxii.
2 DL1 227 (62); DL4 52 (30).
3 BL, Add. MS. 32,115 (C 162).
4 DL4 52 (30).
5 This may be the Edward Gregson who made his will on 8 May 1607, and bequeathed 'to his master Henry Butler, Esq., and his wife, either of them, £5. He gives to Nicholas Butler [their son] £5' (abstract in Add. MS. 32,115 (G63)). If so, this helps to show that John Weever's uncle, Henry Butler, and the Cottom family must have known each other.
6 See also *Quarter Sessions*, ed. James Tait, pp. 128, 147, 157.
7 DDH 710; cf. DDCl 916.
8 BL, Add. MS. 32,115 (H 149).
9 DL4 48 (49).
10 Cf. the long list of 'Debts owing to me George Duddell ... 1589', endorsed 'This is a true copy of the debitory' (DDF 1241).
11 DDIn 64 (74 and 75).
12 BL, Add. MS. 32,115 (D89).
13 DL1 153.
14 DL1 168.
15 DDCl 142, 208.
16 PCC; cf. also *The Stanley Papers*, Part II, pp. 24, 84: William Doddill served the Earl of Derby as Yeoman of the Pantries (1587) and Groom of the Chamber (1590).
17 BL, Add. MS. 32,115 (D52).
18 York wills (Borthwick Institute), vol. 28, fo. 708.
19 *SPD*, 275.64.

V. John Weever and the Hoghtons

1 For Henry Bannister of Bank and Sir Thomas Hesketh see DL4 26 (29); DL4 26 (83); DL1 125 (H 14); DDHe 19 (5). In DDHe 6 (11) Henry Bannister is a witness for Sir Thomas (1584).

2 I assume that Robert Dalton of Pilling, Esq., was also Robert Dalton of
Thurnham, Esq., just as Alexander Hoghton was 'of Lea' and also of 'Hoghton
Tower', and Sir Thomas Hesketh was 'of Rufford' and also 'of Holmswood'.
Weever included a verse epistle 'to the author's most honoured friend, *Richard*
Dalton of Pilling' in his *Mirror of Martyrs* (1601); Richard here may be a misprint
for Robert.

3 McKerrow, in his edition of Weever's *Epigrammes*, almost certainly misidentified
Sir Thomas Gerard as 'of Bryn, in Lancashire' (who was also related to the
Hoghtons). Sir Gilbert Gerard's son, Sir Thomas, was the Knight Marshal; see
HMC, Hatfield House, XI, 109; 'the letters which Sir Thomas Garrat,
K. Marshall, wrote to his brother in law, Sir R. Mull.' (=Mullineux); XI, 160 (Sir
R. Molyneux to Cecil, 1601: 'Not long ago you delivered to my brother [i.e.
brother-in-law] Sir Tho. Gerrard, to be sent to me, a letter'). According to Hasler,
Sir Thomas Gerard became knight marshal of the Household in 1597.

4 'Honey-tongued Shakespeare' was also Meres's phrase (quoted above, p. 54).
Did Weever simply repeat Meres? That would help us to date Weever's sonnet
(*Palladis Tamia* was entered in the S.R. on 7 Sept. 1598); *OED*, however, first
records 'honey-tongued' in *Love's Labour's Lost*, V.2.334, and by 1598 this word
may have been in common use. For *tainted* (l. 3) read *tinted*. Weever's 'rose-
cheek'd Adonis' (l. 5) quotes *Venus and Adonis*, l. 3. And, as A. Davenport
noted, Weever re-used l. 10 in *Faunus and Melliflora* (1600): 'And thus fair words
and power attractive beauty / Bring men to women in subjective duty' (ed.
Davenport, 1948, p. 17). Presumably Weever meant 'power-attractive'. According to McKerrow 'the word "het" in l. 13 means "heated".' I would paraphrase
lines 13–14 as follows: 'They [i.e. the thousands entranced by Shakespeare's
characters] burn in love; thy children [characters] heated them. Go, woo thy muse,
and beget more beautiful children [brood, *OED*, 1c] for them!'

5 Eleven leaves survive from a lost edition of *Passionate Pilgrim*, which is tentatively
dated 1599 (cf. *A Short-Title Catalogue...1475–1640*, revised edition (ed. W. A.
Jackson, F. S. Ferguson, K. Pantzer), *before* the first complete edition of 1599.

6 I assume that Weever's text of *Epigrammes* was not properly 'finalised', and that,
being an inexperienced author, he expected the printer to tidy it as instructed; the
printer, however, was more anxious to finish quickly (hence the large quota of
misprints). Another sign that Weever did not check through his text before it was
printed occurs in the heading of vi.1, 'Ad Richardum Houghton Militem':
dedication i, to 'Sir Richard Houghton', shows that the book came out after
Hoghton was knighted in June 1599.

7 The date of Weever's sonnet depends on 'honey-tongued Shakespeare' (cf. note 4,
above). If Weever echoed Meres, he probably wrote his sonnet in the autumn or
winter of 1598; if not, in 1597 or 1598. Interestingly, Weever only names works
already printed (*Venus and Adonis*, *Lucrece*, *Romeo*, and either *Richard III* or
Richard II: all printed by 1597); he could have written his sonnet while a student
at Cambridge, before he had seen one of the plays in the theatre.

8 See A. Davenport, ed. *The Whipping of the Satyre* (Liverpool, 1951).

9 *Ben Jonson* (ed. C. H. Herford, P. and E. Simpson, 11 vols, Oxford, 1925–52),
VIII, 32. The quotation from *Every Man In His Humour* differs in the Quarto and
Folio texts.

10 *Op. cit.*, p. 27.

11 Weever, p. 279. Halle's *Chronicle* says that the heads were fixed on poles, and that
Cade 'caused them in every street [to] kiss together' (2 *Henry VI*, New Arden ed.,
p. 170).

12 *Ancient Funeral Monuments*, p. 234. Weever refers to the son of Sir Richard
Hoghton's brother-in-law.

13 Henry Butler's will was printed by G. J. Piccope (*Lancashire and Cheshire Wills
and Inventories*, Third Portion, CS, 1861, p. 182). Ann Butler, Henry's widow,

Notes

died in 1622, and a 'note' of her bequests survives in the LRO, made out by her son Thomas.

VI. Shakespeare and Lord Strange's Men

1 Cf. p. 4.
2 Cf. Chambers, *Stage*, II, 123, 197–8.
3 W. W. Greg thought Strange's Men alone acted *Seven Deadly Sins*, Part 2 (*Henslowe Papers*, ed. Greg, 1907, p. 129); Chambers (*Stage*, II, 120) thought that Strange's men could have combined with Admiral's Men.
4 Cf. Andrew Gurr, *The Shakespearean Stage* (Cambridge, 1970), p. 69.
5 Chambers, *Stage*, II, 128.
6 Honigmann, *Shakespeare's Impact on his Contemporaries* (1982), p. 53 ff.
7 P. Alexander, *Shakespeare's 'Henry VI' and 'Richard III'* (Cambridge, 1929).
8 II, 130.
9 Chambers, *Stage*, IV, 347–8.
10 *Stage*, II, 129.
11 *Stage*, II, 130.
12 I am aware that it has also been suggested that Shakespeare began his career with the Queen's Men. See G. M. Pinciss, *Shakespeare Survey* (1974), XXVII, 129–36; S. McMillin, *RES* (1976), XXVII, 174–7.
13 *Stage*, II, 128.
14 Abel Lefranc and Alan Keen both argued that Shakespeare remodelled events in *Richard III* because of his connection with the Stanley family, anticipating some of my points in this paragraph (*Sous le Masque*, I, 244 ff.; *The Annotator*, pp. 84–5).
15 Barry Coward states that '*Sans Changer*' was adopted 'by the fourth and fifth earls of Derby in the sixteenth century along with the motto '*Dieu et ma Foy*' (*The Stanleys*, p. 15, n. 3). Ferdinando, however, had the motto '*Sans changer ma vérité*' inscribed in his portrait: cf. *The Stanley Papers*, Part 2, p. lxv; *The Annotator*, Plate V.
16 Cf. Honigmann, *Shakespeare's Impact*, p. 139, n. 37.
17 See F. P. Wilson's Supplement to McKerrow's *Nashe*, V, 15–16.
18 Chapman, letter to M. Roydon prefixed to *The Shadow of Night*.
19 Lord Strange was descended (through his mother, Margaret Clifford) from Mary, the younger sister of Henry VIII, and was therefore seen as a possible successor to Queen Elizabeth.
20 *The Stanley Papers*, Part 2, p. v.
21 *Love's Labour's Lost*, ed. R. David, p. xxxi.
22 Greene's *Groat's Worth of Wit* (1592).
23 See my articles in *MLR* (1954), XLIX, 293–307; *The Library* (1982), IV, 142–73; and in *The New York Review of Books* (1984), XXXI, 16–18.
24 See *Henslowe's Diary*, p. 16 ff.
25 Chambers, *Shakespeare*, II, 188.
26 Chambers, *loc. cit.*
27 Chambers, *Shakespeare*, II, 219.
28 Chambers, *Shakespeare*, II, 186.
29 *Shakespeare's Impact*, p. 135.
30 Chambers, *Shakespeare*, II, 189.
31 *Shakespeare's Impact*, p. 74.
32 Cf. Chambers, *Stage*, IV, 229–33; Honigmann, '*John a Kent* and Marprelate' (*Yearbook of English Studies*, 1983, XIII, 288–93). It should be noted that, while there is a good deal of support for 1589–90 as the date of *Tears of the Muses*, the poem is sometimes dated earlier.

33 Honigmann, *Shakespeare's Impact*, chap. I.
34 Chambers, *Shakespeare*, II, 214. My italics.
35 Cf. A. C. Judson, *The Life of Edmund Spenser* (Baltimore, 1945), p. 160.
36 Chambers, *Shakespeare*, II, 245.
37 Judson, *op. cit.*, p. 146.
38 Alfred Harbage also thought that 'pleasant Willy' and 'Aetion' referred to Shakespeare (*Shakespeare Without Words and other Essays*, Cambridge, Mass., 1972, pp. 139–41).

VII. The Shakespeare epitaphs and the Stanleys

1 See Chambers, *Shakespeare*, II, 268–9; I, 551 ff.; and Schoenbaum, 'Shakespeare's Epitaphs' (in *Lives*, 1970, pp. 75–82).
2 See Chambers, *Shakespeare*, I, 550; II, 140; I, 554.
3 Hotson, *Shakespeare's Sonnets Dated* (1949), pp. 111 ff., 134.
4 *Shakespeare Encyclopaedia*, p. 821; so Schoenbaum (as in n. 1, above), p. 78.
5 PPC (110 Wingfield).
6 D. N. Durant, *Bess of Hardwick* (1977), p. 200.
7 *Ancient Funeral Monuments*, p. 18.
8 According to the Victoria County History, there is a Leigh chapel in Winwick church, and Sir Peter Leigh re-founded Winwick Grammar School in 1619 (*Lancashire*, IV, 124, 130).
9 Chambers, *Shakespeare*, I, 553.
10 DL4 26 (18).
11 PCC (39 Carew). Sir Thomas was 'in trouble' in 1571 when he tried to rescue Mary Queen of Scots, and was imprisoned in the Tower for his pains.
12 PCC (92 Drake).
13 See Chambers, *Shakespeare*, II, 246–7, 181.
14 Chambers, *op. cit.*, II, 259.
15 Cf. Chambers, *op. cit.*, II, 181.
16 Chambers, *op. cit.*, II, 153.

VIII. Thomas Savage of Rufford

1 *Shakespeare Encyclopaedia*, p. 736.
2 *Lives*, p. 746.
3 Her will is in the Lancashire Record Office.
4 *The Registers of the Parish Church of Croston in the County of Lancaster*, ed. Henry Fishwick (Wigan: Lancashire Parish Register Society, 1900), I, 124.
5 Minute Book, I, 47.
6 See Savage's will, Appendix A, p. 143, and above, p. 37, for Jane Spencer.
7 PCC (82 Hayes).
8 L. Hotson, *I, William Shakespeare* (1937), pp. 160, 244.
9 PRO, Req 2 111–16.
10 PCC (55 Dale).
11 *APC*, XIV, 97.
12 HMC, Hatfield House, VI, 19, 29, etc.
13 HMC, Hatfield House, XI, 404.

IX. *The Phoenix and the Turtle*

1 Carleton Brown has shown, I think convincingly, that Sir John Salusbury, the

dedicatee, must be the turtle, and his wife the phoenix (*Poems of Sir John Salusbury and Robert Chester*, Early English Text Society, Extra Series, no. 113, 1914 (for 1913)). But there are other interpretations: A. B. Grosart, the editor of *Robert Chester's 'Loves Martyr'* (New Shakspere Society, 1878), argued that the phoenix and turtle represent Queen Elizabeth and the Earl of Essex, and William H. Matchett agreed (*The Phoenix and the Turtle*, 1965). Matchett, however, could not explain why Shakespeare should refer to Queen Elizabeth in the past tense in 1601; and Matchett seems not to have known J. E. Neale's studies of the Denbighshire elections (cf. p. 93), which contradict his theory that Salusbury could have been an Essex supporter. Roy T. Eriksen has suggested (*Spenser Studies*, 1981, II, 193–215) that Bruno's *De gli eroici furori* (1585) influenced Shakespeare's poem, which is possible; if he is right, 'the theory that Essex was the poem's turtle becomes highly improbable' (p. 210). But Eriksen's idea that the poem also alludes to 'the death of the Italian philosopher-poet at the stake in Rome' is surely far-fetched.

2 See *The Derby Household Books* (*The Stanley Papers*, Part II), ed. F. R. Raines (*CS*, 1853, vol. xxxi).

3 See 'Robert Parry's Diary' (*Archaeologia Cambrensis*, 1915, XV) p. 121. Matchett (*op. cit.*, p. 140) also prints a letter from the 6th Earl of Derby 'To my loving brother John Salusbury, Esq.', dated 1598.

4 Cf. Carleton Brown, p. lxxiii; Chambers, *Shakespeare*, I, 550.

5 See note 1.

6 Carleton Brown, p. 8.

7 HMC, Hatfield House, XI, 445 (24 Oct. 1601).

8 A. H. Dodd, 'North Wales in the Essex Revolt of 1601' (*EHR*, 1944, LIX, 368).

9 Lewys Dwnn, *Heraldic Visitations of Wales* (2 vols, Welsh Manuscripts Society, 1846), II, 331.

10 HMC, Hatfield House, IX, 180.

11 *Op. cit.*, IX, 181.

12 *DNB*; cf. J. Y. W. Lloyd, *The History of the Princes, The Lords Marcher, and the Ancient Nobility of Powys Fadog* (6 vols, 1881), IV, 307 ff.

13 PCC (41 Wallop).

14 Huntington Library, Ellesmere MSS., 669. According to Hasler (entry for Sir Robert Salesbury), Sir Robert asked Lord Keeper Egerton to be the guardian of his son.

15 Ellesmere MSS., 1782g.

16 Carleton Brown, p. lxix. Matchett disagrees with Brown's dating (p. 117, n.), but at this point ignores the piecemeal composition of *Love's Martyr*, about which he writes illuminatingly elsewhere.

17 For 'the Strong' see Lewys Dwnn (as in note 9). For Salusbury's formidable enemies see also the *Calendar of Salusbury Correspondence 1553 – circa 1700*, ed. W. J. Smith (Cardiff, 1954), pp. 30 ff.

18 Ellesmere MSS., no. 60.

19 Quoted by Carleton Brown, p. xxiv, n.

20 *SPD*, 270.48.

21 Carleton Brown, p. lxxi.

22 P. lxxiii.

23 P. lxix.

24 P. 125. My page references are to the 1601 edition of *Love's Martyr*.

25 Pp. 127–8.

26 P. lxiii.

27 For the rival theories about Shakespeare's commencement as a dramatist, 'early start' *v.* 'late start', see Honigmann, *Shakespeare's Impact on his Contemporaries*, pp. 53 ff.

28 First Folio, epistle.

29 There are good reasons for dating *Love's Labour's Lost* in 1592 or early 1593 (Honigmann, *op. cit.*, pp. 68–9).
30 Ed. 1635, p. 308.
31 *Op. cit.*, p. 112.
32 Cf. p. 119.
33 Camden, *Annals* (ed. 1635), p. 307.
34 Carleton Brown, p. 22; *DNB* (Thomas Stanley, first Earl of Derby).
35 Christ Church MS. 184, fo. 179b.
36 Carleton Brown, pp. 36, 37.
37 See the wills of Simon and Margaret Thelwall (PCC, 55 Windsor).
38 *The Autobiography of Edward Lord Herbert of Cherbury* (ed. S. Lee, 1888), p. 20.
39 P. xxv.
40 See also Penry Williams, *The Council in the Marches of Wales Under Elizabeth I* (Cardiff, 1958), pp. 124, 240, 285, etc.
41 *The Letters of John Chamberlain*, I, 61; *SPD*, James I, 2.2.
42 DDCl 915; papers deposited 24 Nov. 1954, DDCl 1108.
43 See the *Lleweni Estate Muniments* in the National Library of Wales, no. 516; Brown, p. xxv; also, the *Calendar of Salusbury Correspondence*, ed. W. J. Smith, pp. 9–10.
44 J. Y. W. Lloyd, *op. cit.*, VI, 432 ff. See PCC (126 Law) for Parry's will, and the *Lleweni Estate Muniments* (as in n. 43), nos. 807 and 808, for *Parry v. Salusbury*.
45 See *Archaeologia Cambrensis*, Sixth Series, 1905, V, 103–4.
46 J. P. Earwaker, ed., *Lancashire and Cheshire Wills and Inventories at Chester* (CS, New Series, 1884, III, 240).
47 See Chambers, *Shakespeare*, II, 234. The poem is in NLW MS. 5390. Mr G. C. G. Thomas of the National Library of Wales has kindly examined the MS. and writes (privately) that 'a number of hands belonging to the first half of the 17th century have contributed poems to the manuscript. Many of these were either composed by Sir Thomas Salusbury and Sir Henry Salusbury or addressed to them, and the majority of these are clearly holographs. The poem addressed to Heminges and Condell is anonymous in the manuscript but I believe it to be in the same hand as other poems in the manuscript to which the name "Henry Salusbury" or the initials "H.S." have been added.'
48 See *DNB*.

X. Shakespeare's religion

1 Cf. p. 91
2 *Ancient Funeral Monuments*, p. 288.
3 Chambers, *Shakespeare*, II, 255–7.
4 Chambers, *Shakespeare*, I, 14.
5 See *Shakespeare Encyclopaedia*, p. 445.
6 Schoenbaum, *Documentary Life*, p. 37.
7 Cf. p. 2.
8 L. Hotson, *Shakespeare's Sonnets Dated*, p. 237.
9 Hotson, p. 227.
10 Hotson, *loc. cit.*
11 Chambers, *Shakespeare*, I, 15.
12 Chambers, *loc. cit.*
13 Schoenbaum, *op. cit.*, p. 41.
14 *Shakespeare Encyclopaedia*, p. 409.
15 *Shakespeare*, II, 380.
16 Cf. Schoenbaum, *Documentary Life*, pp. 41–7, and Chambers, *Shakespeare*, II, 381.

Notes

17 *Shakespeare Encyclopaedia*, p. 753.
18 E. I. Fripp argued that John Shakespeare withdrew from the Stratford 'halls' in 1577 because of The Grand Commission Ecclesiastical (1575) and its hunting out of recusants; Fripp, however, thought that John Shakespeare was a Puritan (*Minutes and Accounts of the Corporation of Stratford-upon-Avon and other Records 1553–1620*, 3 vols, Dugdale Society, 1921–6; II, xlv ff.). See also J. H. de Groot's careful survey of the evidence in *The Shakespeares and 'The Old Faith'* (New York, 1946).
19 Chambers, *Shakespeare*, II, 20.
20 Leatherbarrow, *Elizabethan Recusants*, p. 43.
21 Coward, *The Stanleys*, p. 167.
22 *APC*, XV, 361.
23 See *King John*, New Arden ed., pp. 155, 63–4; and G. Bullough, *Narrative and Dramatic Sources of Shakespeare* (8 vols, 1957 etc.), IV, 98.
24 Honigmann, *Shakespeare's Impact*, pp. 53–90.
25 See Kenneth Muir's New Arden edition of *King Lear*.
26 Chambers, *Shakespeare*, II, 175.
27 Chambers, II, 256.

XI. Conclusion

1 Cf. Baldwin, *Small Latine*, I, 464 ff. Simon Hunt, the Stratford schoolmaster from 1571 to 1575, later became a Jesuit; Thomas Jenkins (1575–9) had been a Fellow of Campion's college (St John's, Oxford), a college that had treated Catholics with tolerance (Baldwin, I, 486); John Cottom (1579–81) was brother of the Jesuit Thomas Cottam.
2 *Shakespeare's Impact* (1982).
3 Honigmann, *op. cit.*, pp. 1–14.
4 *APC*, XVII, 95.
5 Chambers, *Shakespeare*, II, 266–7.
6 Shakespeare's First Folio, dedication.
7 Miller, *Hoghton Tower*, p. 222.

Appendix C. *A Midsummer Night's Dream, Henry VI, Parts 2 and 3*, and the Stanley family

1 See Chambers, *Shakespeare*, I, 359, and 'The Occasion of *A Midsummer Night's Dream*' (in *Gleanings*).
2 See Honigmann, *Shakespeare's Impact on his Contemporaries* (1982), p. 77.
3 Chambers, *Gleanings*, p. 63.
4 See Coward, *The Stanleys*, and Lefranc, *Sous le Masque*.
5 *SPD*, 271.35.
6 This is the accepted date, confirmed by Mr J. J. Bagley, the author of a forthcoming book about the Earls of Derby.
7 H. H. Goldstine, *New and Full Moons 1001 B.C. to A.D. 1651* (Memoirs of the American Philosophical Society, vol. 94. Philadelphia, 1973).
8 Chambers, *Gleanings*, p. 61.
9 B. M. Ward, *The Seventeenth Earl of Oxford 1550–1604* (1928), pp. 317 ff.
10 Huntington Library, Ellesmere MSS., no. 213.
11 F. A. Bailey, 'Some Stanley Heraldic Glass from Worden Hall, Lancashire' (*HSLC*, 1950 (for 1949), CI, 69).
12 Harold Brooks, ed. *A Midsummer Night's Dream* (New Arden, 1979), pp. xxxiv–xxxv.

13 G. Bullough, *Narrative and Dramatic Sources of Shakespeare*, vol. 3 (1960), p. 161.
14 K. Muir, *The Sources of Shakespeare's Plays* (1977), p. 27.

Index

Index

Butler, Richard, 51
Butler, Thomas, 159

Cade, Jack, 57, 158
Camden, William, 102, 162
Campion, Edmund, 5, 11, 22, 40, 124, 139, 163
Cannon, J. A., 48
Carey, Elizabeth, 150
Carmarthen, Richard, 88
Caton, Anne, 145
Catterall, Thomas, 141
Cawdrey, Ralph, 115
Cawthorne, Alice, 145
Cawthorne, William, 145
Cecil, Sir Robert, ix, 14, 88, 93, 95, 110, 140, 158
Cecil, Thomas, 50
Cecil, William: see Burghley, Lord
Chamberlain, John, 14, 98, 156, 162
Chamberlain's Men, Lord, 3, 59 ff., 71, 129
Chambers, E. K., 1–7, 16, 21, 29, 31, 34, 37, 41, 59 ff., 78–9, 100, 116, 127, 150 ff., 155 ff.
Chapman, George, 66–7, 92, 98, 101, 159
Chapman, William, 88
Chappell, Thomas, 143
Chester, Robert, 85, 91 ff., 129
Chettle, Henry, 73
Clayton, Thomas, 141
Clinch, Justice, 13
Clough, Sir Richard, 92
Clough, William, 137, 139
Combe, John, 77, 79
Combe, Thomas, 79
Condell, Henry, 59, 74, 87, 101, 112, 130, 162
Conse, Nicholas, 142
Coston, Thomas, 17, 137, 139
Cottam (Cottom) pedigree, 148
Cottam, Ann, 41, 48
Cottam, James, 42 ff.
Cottam, Lawrence, 41–2, 48
Cottam, Lawrence ii, 48
Cottam, Richard, 42
Cottam, Thomas, 5, 22, 40 ff., 124, 128, 163
Cottam, William, 41
Cottom, Catherine, 41
Cottom, John, 5–7, 15, 19–22, 40 ff., 51, 126 ff., 131–2, 137, 139, 144 ff., 157, 163
Cottom, John ii, 48–9
Cottom, Priscilla, 42 ff.

Cotton, Sir Robert, 134
Court, Richard, 116
Coward, Barry, 159, 163
Cowley, R., 18
Crichelawe, Margaret, 136, 138–9
Crichelawe, Roger, 136, 138–9
Crichelawe, Thomas, 139
Cross, Gabriel, 47

Dalton, Richard, 158
Dalton, Robert, 6, 52, 158
Darrell, John, 124
Darwin, Nicholas, 141
Davenant, Sir William, 130
Davenport, A., 158
David, Richard, 159
Davie, Richard, 142
Davies, Richard, 115
Dawson, George, 145
Deacon, John, 124
Debdale, Robert, 41
Derby's Men, Lord, 60 ff.
Dickinson, Roger, 137
Digges, L., 87
Dodd, A. H., 95, 161
Donne, John, 9, 103
Dove, Catherine: see Cottom, Catherine
Dowdall, Mr, 81
Drayton, Michael, 75
Duckenfylde, E., 138
Duddell, Cuthbert, 47
Duddell, George, 47, 157
Duddell, Jane, 47
Duddell, John, 47
Duddell, Mary, 43, 46
Duddell, Richard, 47
Duddell, William, 7, 43, 46 ff., 139, 157
Dugdale, Roger, 137
Dugdale, Sir William, 6, 9, 78
Duke, John, 59
Durant, D. N., 160
Dwnn, Lewys, 161

Earwaker, J. P., 162
Easton Neston, 33–4
Eccles, Mark, 32, 156
Egerton, Thomas (Lord Ellesmere), 55, 152, 161
Egerton, Thomas ii, 55
Eliot, George, 26
Elizabeth, Queen, 6, 11–13, 18, 22, 26, 29, 31, 64, 67, 87, 92, 96, 114, 119, 122, 126, 150, 159
Elliott, D. W., 16–7
Ellis, James, 43, 47
Ellis, Martha, 43

Index

Index

Index

Index

Salusbury, Capt. John, 93, 113, 149
Salusbury, Margaret, 95
Salusbury, Oriana, 111
Salusbury, Piers, 96
Salusbury, Sir Robert, ix, 95, 106, 113, 161
Salusbury, Roger, 111
Salusbury, Thomas, 91, 99, 102, 106, 114, 124
Salusbury, Sir Thomas, 162
Salwick Old Hall, 47
Savage, Alice, 86 ff., 143
Savage, Elizabeth, 143
Savage, Francis, 86, 144
Savage, George, 143
Savage, Jeffry, 85
Savage, Jennette, 85, 143
Savage, John, 143
Savage, Peter, 85
Savage, Richard, 85, 143
Savage, Thomas, 34, 36, 84 ff., 102, 127, 129, 143 ff., 160
Savage, Thomas ii, 143
Say, Lord, 57
Schoenbaum, S., 84, 155, 160, 162
Scholes, 20
Selby, W. D., 156
Seven Deadly Sins, The, 59, 128, 159
Shadwell, Thomas, 115
Shakeshafte, John, 15
Shakeshafte, William, 3–6, 8, 15 ff., 22 ff., 31 ff., 41, 51, 59, 84, 91, 114, 122, 127, 131, 136
Shakespeare, Anne (wife), 15, 39, 82, 116, 128, 130
Shakespeare, Hamnet (son), 1
Shakespeare, John (father), 1–5, 9, 20, 24, 115 ff., 127 ff., 130
Shakespeare, Judith (daughter), 1, 82
Shakespeare, Mary (mother), 115, 130
Shakespeare, Richard (grandfather), 4, 18
Shakespeare, Susanna (daughter), 1, 9, 39, 82, 116
Shakespeare, Thomas, 18
Shakespeare, William, *passim*
  Plays:
  Comedy of Errors, The, 72, 128
  Hamlet, 10, 58, 70, 83, 123, 128
  Henry IV, 57
  Henry VI, 60–3, 69, 76, 119, 125, 128, 153–4
  Henry VIII, 125
  Julius Caesar, 57
  King John, 10, 76, 119, 125, 128
  King Lear, 70, 123
  Love's Labour's Lost, 57, 62, 64 ff., 69, 71, 102, 129, 150, 153, 158–9, 162
  Macbeth, 125
  Measure for Measure, 123
  Merry Wives of Windsor, The, 115
  Midsummer Night's Dream, A, 62, 69, 129, 150 ff.
  Othello, 70
  Richard II, 158
  Richard III, 62–3, 69, 76, 128, 150, 153, 158
  Romeo and Juliet, 122, 128, 158
  Sir Thomas More, 129
  Taming of the Shrew, The, 60, 63, 72, 128
  Timon of Athens, 82
  Titus Andronicus, 59 ff., 62–3, 109, 128
  Troilus and Cressida, 74
  Two Gentlemen of Verona, The, 72, 109, 128

  Poems:
  Passionate Pilgrim, The, 54, 158
  Phoenix and the Turtle, The, 71, 85, 90 ff., 127–8
  Rape of Lucrece, The, 129–30, 158
  Sonnets, The, 54, 69, 72, 74, 89, 93, 122
  Venus and Adonis, 57, 62, 129, 158

Sharp, Thomas, 137
Shaw, Gabriel, 20
Sherburne, Richard, 14, 139, 143
Short-Title Catalogue, 158
Shute, Robert, 58
Simmes, Valentine, 50
Sly, William, 59
Smart, J. S., 120
Smith, T. C., 42
Smith, W. J., 149, 161
Snape, John, 137
Snape, Richard, 137, 140
Sommers, W., 124
Southampton, Countess of, 151, 153
Southampton, Earl of, 63, 129–30
Southworth, Thomas, 142
Sowerbutts, R., 48
Spencer, Jane, 37, 86, 160
Spencer, Thomas, 37, 86, 143

Index

Spenser, Edmund, 55, 71 ff., 97, 129
Squire, Dorothy, 142
Squire, Henry, 142
Stafford, Lord, 119
Standish, Edward, 137, 140–1
Stanley pedigree, 79
Stanley, Alice (wife of 5th Earl of
    Derby), 71 ff., 75, 152
Stanley, Edward (3rd Earl of Derby),
    79
Stanley, Sir Edward, 77 ff., 102, 129
Stanley, Ferdinando (5th Earl), 4, 13,
    37–9, 59 ff., 64 ff., 75, 118 ff., 122,
    124, 128, 150–1
Stanley, Sir George, 37
Stanley, Henry (4th Earl), 4, 7, 13, 17,
    36–9, 47, 67, 91, 106–7, 111,
    118–19, 157
Stanley, Henry, 143
Stanley, Margaret (wife of 4th Earl), 70,
    119, 154, 159
Stanley, Mary, 37
Stanley, Thomas (1st Earl), 63–4, 162
Stanley, Sir Thomas, 77 ff., 119, 129,
    160
Stanley, Ursula, 7, 91 ff.
Stanley, Sir William, 64
Stanley, William (6th Earl), 91, 150 ff.,
    161
Stannynowght, Richard, 131, 142
Starkie, George, 85
Starkie, Roger, 85
Stopford, William, 37
Stowe, John, 151–2
Strange's Men, Lord, 29, 59 ff., 62–3,
    98, 101–2, 119, 150, 159
Strangwayes, Arthur, 143
Stratford Grammar School, 1, 5, 40 ff.
Sussex's Men, Lord, 60, 62
Swansey, Robert, 140

Tait, James, 139, 157
Talbot, John, 136–7, 140–1
Talbot, Robert, 25–6, 136 ff., 140–1
Taming of a Shrew, The, 63, 120
Terence, 21
Thelwall, Cecily, 95
Thelwall, Edward, 92 ff., 109, 111,
    149
Thelwall, Simon, ix, 109, 149, 162
Thomas, D. L., 118
Thomas, G. C. G., 162
Tilney, Edmund, 80
Titus and Vespasian, 61, 63
Tomlinson, John, 136
Tomlinson, Robert, 137

Tomson, James, 142
Tong Church, 78
Towneley, John, 143
Trafford, Sir Edmund, ix, 35
Trafford, Thomas, 93
Trevor, Sir John, ix, 110
Trevor, Magdalen, 112
Trevor, Sir Richard, ix, 93, 96, 110,
    112
Tribecke, William, 143
Troublesome Reign of John, The,
    119 ff.
Turner, Miles, 137
Twiford, Blanche, 37
Twiford, Henry, 37
Tylden, Richard, 130

Velville, Sir Roland, 91
Vere, Elizabeth, 150
Vincent, Augustine, 134

Waad, William, ix, 88
Walford, John, 2, 115
Walker, John, 124
Wall, Thomas, 140
Wall, William, 136, 138, 140
Walmesley, Thomas, 144
Walmisley, Katherine, 45
Walmsley, Justice, 13
Walton pedigree, 132
Walton, Ann, 144
Walton, James, 144
Walton, John, 144
Walton, Thomas, 43 ff., 46, 132, 144–5
Walton, William, 42 ff., 46
Walton, William ii, 44, 132, 144
Warburton, George, 23, 28
Ward, B. M., 163
Ward, Thomas, 137
Warren, Sir Edward, ix, 6, 47, 53
Warren, Frances, 47
Watkinson, Hugh, 86, 143
Watson, John, 47
Watson, Thomas, 141
Waugh, Evelyn, 125
Weelkes, Thomas, 54
Weever, Anne, 145
Weever, John, 6–7, 14, 50 ff., 80, 85,
    102, 114, 127, 129, 131, 133–4, 145,
    147, 157–8
Weever, William, 145
Werden, Thomas, 142
Westminster Abbey, 57
Whittingham, Richard, 138, 140
Whittingham, Thomas, 138, 140
Wilkinson, Christopher, 141

Index

THE PREZELL R. ROBINSON LIBRARY
ST. AUGUSTINE'S COLLEGE
RALEIGH, N. C. 27611